MAPPING THE TOTAL VALUE STREAM

MAPPING THE TOTAL VALUE STREAM

A Comprehensive Guide for
Production and Transactional Processes

MARK A. NASH AND SHEILA R. POLING

CRC Press
Taylor & Francis Group
Boca Raton   London   New York

CRC Press is an imprint of the
Taylor & Francis Group, an **informa** business
A PRODUCTIVITY PRESS BOOK

CRC Press
Taylor & Francis Group
6000 Broken Sound Parkway NW, Suite 300
Boca Raton, FL 33487-2742

© 2008 by Mark A. Nash and Sheila R. Poling
CRC Press is an imprint of Taylor & Francis Group

No claim to original U.S. Government works
Printed in the United States of America on acid-free paper
10 9 8 7 6 5 4 3 2

International Standard Book Number-13: 978-1-56327-359-9 (Softcover)

Library of Congress Cataloging-in-Publication Data

Nash, Mark A., 1959-
    Mapping the total value stream : a comprehenisve guide for production and transactional processes / Mark A. Nash and Sheila R. Poling.
    p. cm.
    Includes bibliographical references and index
    ISBN 978-1-56327-359-9 (alk. paper)
    1. Production engineering. 2. Production management. 3. Process control. I. Poling, Sheila R. II. Title.
    TS176.N365   2008
    658.5—dc22   2007048326

**Visit the Taylor & Francis Web site at
http://www.taylorandfrancis.com**

**and the CRC Press Web site at
http://www.crcpress.com**

Dedication

This book is dedicated to the three most important women in my life—Staci, Ally, and Delaney—who continually put up with my time alone to work on projects like this. And a special thank you to Roxie Craycraft who years ago reminded me of the importance of documenting the current state before looking at the future.

Mark A. Nash

I would like to dedicate this book to all of the people I have worked with in the past, those I work with in the present, and those with whom I will work in the future. By collaborating with a variety of industry experts, I have been able to learn, share, and develop new concepts beyond any I would have created as an individual contributor. This is what continual improvement is truly about.

My involvement in this book is a direct result of my friendship with a person I consider to be a Lean Master—Mark Nash. I cannot express the pleasure I have had working on this and other projects with him. Due to our professional alliance, I have learned more about Lean and been given a new perspective and additional insights on quality improvement in general. I hope our successful partnership continues for many years to come.

Sheila R. Poling

Contents

SECTION II: FUTURE STATE: DESIGNING AND MAPPING YOUR NEW (OR DESIRED) PROCESS

SECTION III: IMPROVEMENT STATE: CREATING THE STRUCTURE FOR USING YOUR INSIGHTS AND KNOWLEDGE TO IMPROVE THE PROCESS

Acknowledgments

The authors would like to thank all the organizations and individuals who have shared their stories and experiences with us and to acknowledge all of their hard work as we observed and challenged them in seeking to use Value Stream Mapping in their industries. The challenges were great, but they were all certainly up to the task. Without their stories, we could not show you how to apply these techniques in real-world settings.

We would also like to specifically acknowledge Pelco Products, Inc., American Fidelity Assurance Company, Path Links Pathology Services, and Harris Methodist H.E.B. Hospital. In addition, this book would not have been possible without Chris Evans and Bobby Taylor. Chris's insights and the hard work he provided to prove many of these new concepts helped make this book possible. Bobby's new ideas, concepts, and relentless pursuit of perfection challenged all of us on this journey.

Special thanks to Billie Miller, executive assistant, Pinnacle Partners, Inc., for her work on this book and to the editors and staff at Productivity Press. The authors are especially indebted to a specific editor of this book, Lara Zoble. In addition, we would also like to recognize Michael Sinnochi, senior acquisitions editor of Productivity Press, without whose interest and support this and other books would not have been written.

Introduction

None so blind as those that will not see.

Matthew Henry

Waste is everywhere. Waste is defined as "to use, consume, spend, or expend thoughtlessly or carelessly." Every organization agrees that there is a need to eliminate waste from their processes. As we identify this waste and the associated cost of these activities, it becomes evident that there is substantial financial opportunity. But how can this waste not only be identified, but also presented to the employees of our organization in such a way that everyone understands what the waste is, where it exists in the process, what its sources are, and at what cost to the bottom line—forming the basis for an implementation plan for improvement?

In 1998, Mike Rother and John Shook introduced the concept of Value Stream Mapping (VSM) to the continuous-improvement world with their book, *Learning to See*. In the beginning of their book, they state, "Wherever there is a product for a customer, there is a value stream. The challenge lies in seeing it." They describe Value Stream Maps as a way of "seeing" these value streams. They become "the blueprints for Lean transformations," a foundation for an implementation plan for improvement. Whether or not Rother or Shook realized it at the time, they were taking what had once been an informal approach to understanding process flow and *creating a new discipline*—one that would open the eyes of not just engineers and logic-minded managers, but of all employees within an organization.

Since the publication of *Learning to See*, numerous other Value Stream Mapping books have been published that offer up new ideas and demonstrate how to use the technique in a variety of ways. For example, *Value Stream Management for the Lean Office*, by Don Tapping and Tom Shuker, introduced the concept of using VSM to map nonproduction processes in an office setting. Their book introduced the concept of the "customer as the supplier," as well as introducing how to depict a work queue: that pile of paperwork in an office setting that is worked on a regular basis.

Another book, *The Complete Lean Enterprise* (by Beau Kyte and Drew Lochor), gave us a macro-level method for showing labels on communication lines as process steps. For manufacturers whose primary focus early in the Lean transformation is on the production floor, this technique allows teams to "see" these transactional process steps as potential targets for Lean kaizen. This is a large step forward for many manufacturers implementing Lean, because it acknowledges that transactional processes wrapped around the manufacturing floor may slow down the total process lead time for a value stream.

The idea for this book evolved from a single concept: availability of personnel. Mark Nash and a coworker, Chris Evans from Argent Global Services, presented this concept to the Lean and industrial engineering world at the 2004 Institute of Industrial Engineers' Lean Management Solutions conference in Los Angeles, California. Struggling with how to convince employees working within a transactional value stream that it is possible to accurately map processes, Nash and Evans, relying on more than 40 years of combined process improvement experience, found a simple and yet powerful tool hidden within the existing Value Stream Mapping technique. A new concept was brought to the table—a new and much-needed tool to use when mapping transactional value streams.

As we (Mark Nash and Sheila Poling) were working on our first book together—*Using Lean for Faster Six Sigma Results*, along with Frony Ward—we kept coming back to the idea of how to synchronize Lean and Six Sigma concepts and tools earlier in the project life cycle. Out of these discussions, which were peppered with challenges from Sheila's perspective (over 25 years of quality industry experience, including time working with Dr. W. Edwards Deming) and Frony's view of quality (over 25 years of industry experience using her Ph.D. in statistics with some of the most prestigious organizations and companies in the United States), it became obvious that Mark's earlier presentation with Chris Evans needed to be transformed into a book of its own. And then the fun began. Our thoughts quickly expanded, and we decided to document all that we knew about Value Stream Mapping by creating a comprehensive resource.

What we envisioned, and hopefully have accomplished, is a single source of both learning and reference for those employees in any organization, within any sector or industry, who want to use Value Stream Mapping to document their processes. We wanted to give serious process-improvement change agents a consolidated source of Value Stream Mapping information for both production and transactional processes, because both types of processes exist within almost all organizations.

This book teaches the reader how to create Value Stream Maps for both production and transactional environments. The basics of capturing process flow, communication (or information) flow, employees or operators working within the value stream, any and all desired data about the process, and both cycle time and process lead time are covered in a systematic manner. Numerous examples and figures are included to demonstrate what the mapper (you) needs to do, as well as how to do it. Additionally, implementation tips and tricks are included.

The book is divided into three distinct sections: Current State, Future State, and Improvement State (action planning and implementation). These three sections will enable readers to understand their existing processes, design the needed processes, and determine an action plan for implementing the necessary changes for improvement.

Manufacturing value streams do not operate without support from transactional processes. From the sales order process to the purchasing of raw materials to the shipping of finished goods, transactional processes are intertwined with the production floor. This same issue holds true in many other sectors. For example, healthcare organizations and service organizations generally face similar situations. The healthcare laboratory can be described as a manufacturing center, with the specimen being the "raw material" and the test report being the "finished good." Although this may offend many healthcare practitioners, there is a growing population within healthcare that readily acknowledges this analogy.

Most service organizations can make similar comparisons. The core mission of the organization—whether it is repairing broken appliances, answering questions in call centers, or enrolling students in a university—can often be mapped in the same manner as a production process. There are many similarities in how these core processes are mapped. There are just as many differences. And some value streams truly do exist that require a significant difference in technique to paint the picture for an audience. The key to unlocking the technique lies in knowing what to look for, and how to draw it in a manner that the audience can interpret.

Current publications focus on VSM as a tool for manufacturing or transactional settings, but not both. The problem VSM mappers face is that there is no book that brings all the value stream concepts introduced since *Learning to See* together in a single text. The problem with any new process-improvement discipline is that new ideas and concepts will be discovered and introduced for years to come. However, this does not discount the need today for a complete guide for mappers to use. Both new mappers wishing to learn the basics of VSM and advanced mappers seeking new and improved tools should be able to look to a single source of knowledge.

The purpose of this book is not to be an all-inclusive Lean training solution. Its purpose is not to teach you the concepts and principles of Lean behind the mapping-icons methodology. Instead, the purpose of this book is to bring together fundamental and cutting-edge VSM concepts into a single text. Although many focused and highly specialized organizations claim their world is unique, the reality is that there are very few differences in the way VSM is used across industries and sectors. This book should help you understand the similarities and differences. Additionally, we provide detailed examples of real value streams from both the manufacturing/production world and the transactional/service world.

As this book came together, we repeatedly saw what Rother and Shook saw as they researched and documented the techniques they presented in *Learning to See*: Value Stream Mapping is not about managers and engineers; it's about the employee working within a process day in and day out. The power is behind the acceptance of everyone in an organization to have input into the maps and accept the story being presented through each map set. It's about everyday people having a way to explain and understand the world they live in and how it can be improved to make their lives easier.

What we didn't fully realize when we started on this project was that we had started out on this incredible journey—a journey that had no end, one that was moving at an incredible pace. Almost every time we finished a chapter, we saw or heard something new about how Value Stream Mapping was being used. Often, what we saw or heard forced us to revise a chapter.

When Rother and Shook first introduced us to *Learning to See*, they brought us a simple vision of an incredibly powerful tool. As the use of VSM grows, mappers need to remain true to the fundamentals presented in *Learning to See*. Although not every map can be as simple as what we saw in *Learning to See*, we can still stick to the rules that divide the map into logical sections presenting clear and concise pictures of a process that anyone can understand. We hope that the concepts discussed in this book assist you in your journey.

As we completed the last chapter, what we recognized was that this mapping tool we call Value Stream Mapping is in its infancy. What Mike Rother and John Shook presented to us in their book, *Learning to See*, was the start of something new and profound. Each day there seems to be a "mapper" somewhere in the world thinking of a new way to use this extremely powerful process mapping tool.

The changes are coming fast. Even as we prepared for submitting this book to the publisher, we encountered a new way to break down inventory on the timeline into raw material, work-in-process, and finished goods—a brilliant concept. When necessary, you can show multiple boxes at the end of the timeline, showing how many days' worth of process lead time are tied up in each category of inventory.

Although we had originally hoped to bring to the mapping community a single and complete source for reference and learning, what we accomplished was something different. It is just the start. The journey—not only for us but for all mappers—has just begun. In the years ahead, new ideas will emerge. New ways to use Value Stream Mapping will continue to appear on a regular basis.

So as you read and use the information in this book, we hope that you, too, will find a new way to use this fantastic tool. Join us on this journey. Where it will end, we aren't sure. But we plan on following it for a long time to come. Value Stream Mapping: what started as a simple act of documentation has become an incredible journey.

About the Authors

Mark A. Nash is operations manager for Pelco Products, Inc., and serves as a director for Argent Global Services. He has over 25 years of process improvement experience, both as an internal and external consultant/engineer, in manufacturing, distribution, and healthcare. Having spent 10 years working for the State of Oklahoma as a legislative auditor, as a fiscal analyst for the Oklahoma State Senate, and as director of finance for the Department of Public Safety, he also has considerable experience with financial and management analysis. This diversified background allows Mark to work outside the box, looking for process solutions many people cannot visualize.

Since joining the Argent team in 1994, Mark has completed numerous transactional reviews for Philips Consumer Electronics Co. and Abbott Laboratories. Over one 15-month period, these transactional reviews produced recommendations that led to more than $18 million in annual savings. These reviews focused on purchasing, central support staff, transportation, order entry, supply management, and product engineering. Mark has also completed extensive process improvement work for Iomega Corporation, helping to eliminate a 12-week receiving backlog and a 10-week shipping backlog in the Return Merchandise Authorization department in less than 40 days. His other endeavors include conducting operational audits and process improvement tool development for the Oklahoma Military Department and the Fleming Companies.

Now focusing his efforts on transforming Pelco Products into the "epicenter of efficiency," Mark has the opportunity to continue Lean improvements in a manufacturing facility known throughout the United States as one of the cleanest and best-organized machining and assembly operations. Having partnered with Pelco over the past several years as a Lean consultant, this new position allows Mark to add additional experience to his continuous improvement toolbox.

A multiskilled Six Sigma Black Belt, Mark has also been a certified NIST/MEP master trainer, partnering with the Oklahoma Alliance for Manufacturing Excellence to provide Lean manufacturing training throughout the State of Oklahoma. Over the past six years, Mark has facilitated more than 400 Lean classes and workshops dealing with principles of Lean manufacturing, Value Stream Mapping, the 5S system, pull/kanban systems, setup reduction, and Total Productive

Maintenance (TPM). Mark has personally facilitated kaizen events for more than 50 organizations worldwide.

Mark was a member of Iomega Corporation's process improvement team that was named a finalist in the large-manufacturer category of the 2000 RIT/USA Today Quality Cup Competition. He has presented at numerous quality and process improvement conferences around the world, including ASQ Six Sigma, IIE Lean Management Solutions, Frontiers in Laboratory Medicine, and Lab Quality Confab. Additionally, Mark serves as an advisor to the University of Central Oklahoma's Center for Strategic Improvement and has presented on the topic of Lean in higher education for the National Association of College and University Business Officers. Mark is a contributing columnist to *Quality Magazine* and is coauthor of the 2006 Productivity Press release, *Using Lean for Faster Six Sigma Results: A Synchronized Approach.*

Sheila R. Poling is a managing partner of Pinnacle Partners, Inc. With more than 20 years of experience in the quality and productivity industry, she previously served as vice president of two nationally recognized consulting/training firms and a book publishing firm. Her management responsibilities have included managing 25 consultants and administrative staff. Sheila's broad professional experience includes work in operations management, product development, training materials and seminar development, marketing and sales, client interface, and customer satisfaction initiatives focused on business excellence with an emphasis on leadership and quality.

A prolific writer, Sheila has coauthored several books, including the internationally recognized *Customer Focused Quality*, a book on customer satisfaction and service, and *Building Continual Improvement: SPC for the Service Industry and Administrative Areas*. She has served as a primary editor for a featured monthly column in *Quality Magazine* and is coauthor of *Brain Teasers: Real-World Challenges to Build Your Manufacturing Skills*, published by *Quality Magazine*. McGraw-Hill's *The Manufacturing Engineering Handbook*, released in 2004, features her chapter on "Six Sigma and Lean Implementation." She is a contributing columnist to *Quality Magazine* and is coauthor of the 2006 Productivity Press release, *Using Lean for Faster Six Sigma Results: A Synchronized Approach.*

Sheila has also coauthored several work manuals, including "Perfecting Continual Improvement Skills" and "Strategy-Driven Six Sigma: A Champion Overview." In addition, she has helped design multiple course offerings focused on leadership training, organizational and operations excellence, Six Sigma, and statistical process control.

Sheila holds a degree in Business Administration from the University of Tennessee and is a Fellow of the American Society for Quality as well as a member of the American Marketing Association and the American Management Association. She has also had the privilege to study and work closely with many distinguished industry leaders, including Dr. W. Edwards Deming.

Chapter 1

The Big Picture … Literally
Understanding the Purpose and Power of Value Stream Mapping

One picture is worth ten thousand words.

Chinese proverb

Introduction

Lean Enterprise has challenged all of us to look at our processes, or value streams, through a new set of eyes. A *value stream* is the process flow from the "point of requested need" to "closure of all activity" after the product or service has been provided. In a manufacturing setting, the overall value stream is often defined as from the point an order is received to the point the product is delivered and payment is received from the customer. On the manufacturing *floor*, however, the focus is typically on the point when *raw material* arrives to the point when *finished product* is shipped. This change in focus has allowed Lean practitioners, as well as many other quality and continuous improvement practitioners utilizing the technique, to break down departmental and other barriers to focus on systemic causes and solutions. Value Stream Mapping, as a process mapping tool, is a way to "see" both the process flow and communication within the process, or value stream. This technique has gained rapid acceptance in the continuous improvement world because of its ability to gather, analyze, and present information in a very condensed time period.

Most important, however, Value Stream Mapping has brought us a process mapping technique that enables all stakeholders of an organization to visualize and understand a process. These maps can enable everyone—i.e., management, the workforce, suppliers, and customers—to see value, to differentiate value from waste, and to create the plan of action for waste elimination. *Process mapping* was

1

once a process analysis tool coveted by engineers, analysts, and some managers. But now everyone from the CEO to the newest entry-level employee can understand process maps created with this powerful tool in a relatively short time.

Value Stream Maps are drawn as pictures of the process. Simple, yet logical and powerful representations of the process (i.e., the value stream) are used to document both the *current state* (i.e., reality) and the *future state* (i.e., the goal):

- The *Current State Map* is the baseline view of the existing process from which all improvements are measured.
- The *Future State Map* represents the vision of how the project team sees the value stream at a point in the future after improvements have been made.

Perhaps the most important, and powerful, part of the technique is the recognition that Current State Maps are like pictures: they are a snapshot in time of how the value stream was actually operating at a given point in time. When working with transactional processes that do not operate continuously, or that have extremely long cycle times, this picture is often more like a painting. It is the vision as interpreted by the operators within their value stream, showing how the current state looks when it is operating. Either way, this is an extremely powerful tool used not only to depict what the current state is, but also to gain acceptance by the employees working within it. Figure 1.1 shows an example of a typical Current State Map.

Dissecting a Basic Value Stream Map

A Value Stream Map is divided into three sections, as shown in Figure 1.2:

Process or production flow
Communication or information flow
Timelines and travel distances

It is important for the creator of the Value Stream Map to not only draw the map, but to be able to explain each of these sections in detail to any audience. So let's take a closer look at each of these three sections of a Value Stream Map.

The Process or Production Flow in a Value Stream Map

The *process or production flow* is the portion of the map that is most often associated with traditional flowcharting. Process flow is drawn showing the flow (or the lack of flow, as is often the case) from left to right on your page as shown in Figure 1.3. This production/process flow should always be drawn left to right; never doubling or angling back on itself. *Subtasks*, or *parallel tasks*, are drawn in similar fashion beneath the main flow. By drawing the value stream's process flow in this manner, it is possible to separate the major tasks conducted repetitively over time from the minor steps in the process. This allows a project team, as well as the employees working within the value stream, to see where optional paths occur, as well as where tasks are worked in parallel. In turn, the struggles, problems,

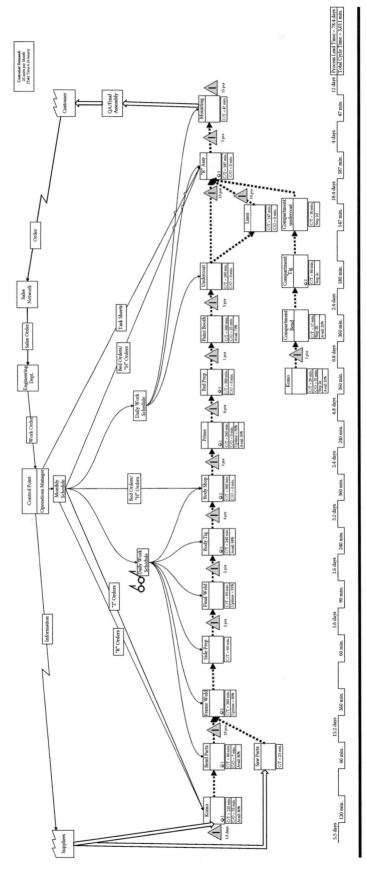

Figure 1.1 A typical Current State Map in a manufacturing setting shows how a value stream actually functions when it is mapped.

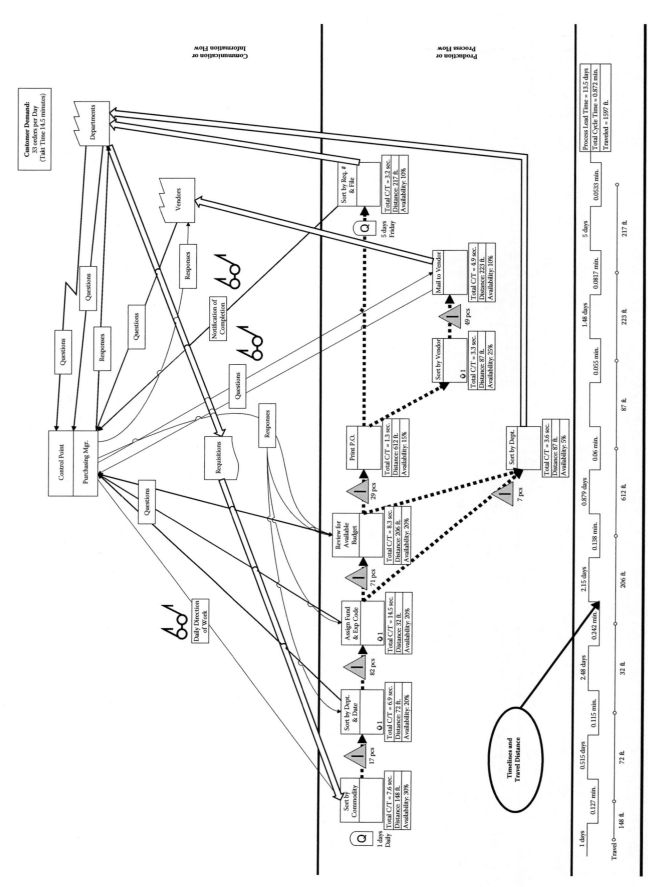

Figure 1.2 Value Stream Maps are divided into three basic parts.

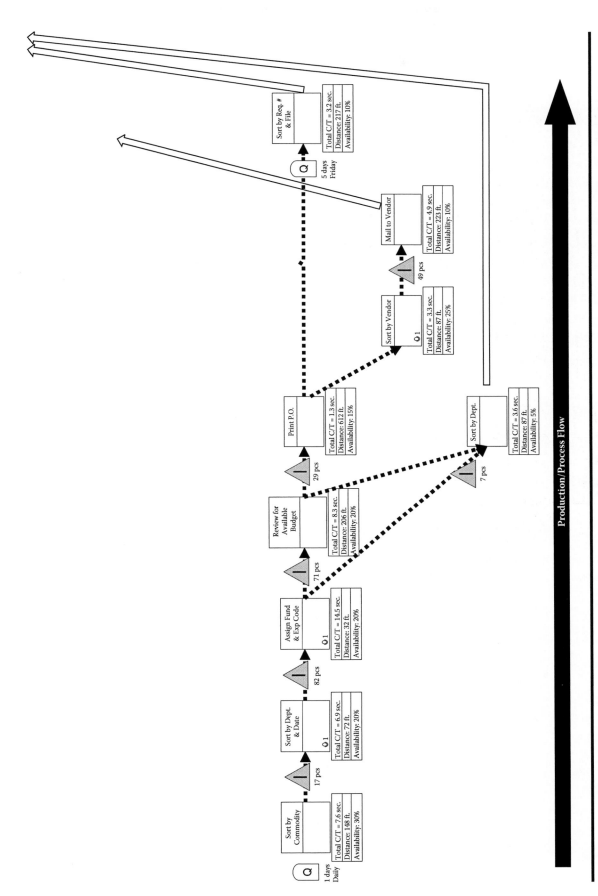

Figure 1.3 **The production/process flow of a Value Stream Map should always flow from left to right on the page, never doubling back or going straight up or down.**

and opportunities that exist in the current state can be discussed and analyzed by systematically looking for solutions, elimination of waste, and improvement of the process as a whole.

The Communication or Information Flow in a Value Stream Map

The *communication or information* section of the map is where Value Stream Mapping begins to expand from traditional process-mapping techniques such as flowcharting. By adding communication to the map, as shown in the top portion of Figure 1.2, it is possible to see all of the communication—both formal and informal—that exists within a value stream. Much of the chaos and confusion that often appears within a value stream can be traced directly to non-value-added (NVA) communication. NVA activities are those activities that add no value to the process or that the customer is not willing to pay for.

Although the base flow of communication goes from the customer back to the supplier, or right to left on the page, there is no standardized flow that exists throughout the process. In a Current State Map, it is not unusual to find that communication can flow in any direction. This includes flowing in one direction and then the other as communication and overcommunication occurs.

The Timelines and Travel Distances Shown in a Value Stream Map

At the bottom of a Value Stream Map is a series of lines that provide some of the most compelling information to the viewer. The set of lines that appears on almost every map are the *timelines*. These two lines are used to communicate to the audience the primary pieces of time data measured in process improvement. As shown in Figure 1.4, the top line measures the *process lead time*, sometimes called the *lead time* or *production lead time* in manufacturing settings. This line—which is based on the amount of product or work in the value stream and the level of customer demand—demonstrates how long it will take on average to move all the existing material or work through to completion.

The amount of work found between each process step is documented on the timeline, typically as the number of days' worth of work. When totaled up at the end of this timeline, you get the process lead time. The bottom line represents *total cycle time*. The cycle time observed at each process step and documented beneath each process box on the map is brought to the lower line. All cycle times are totaled up at the end of the process as the total cycle time. Some maps contain the labor content (or work content, as it is often referred to) instead of the cycle time. When work content is used, this line is referred to as *total work content*.

Another line placed at the bottom of many maps represents *travel distance* through the process. This line can be used to document the travel distance of the product or work, or it can represent the travel distance of the people moving within the process. It should be used for physical travel only, and not for distance that is moved electronically, such as when electronic forms are moved from one place to another over a computer network or the Internet. Figure 1.5 shows how a

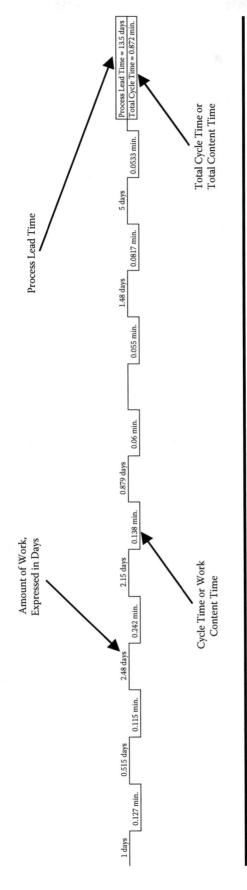

Figure 1.4   Timelines convey both process lead times and cycle times of process steps in the value stream.

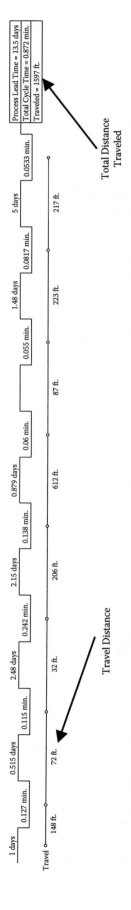

Figure 1.5   The travel distance line shown in relation to the timelines on a Value Stream Map.

typical travel distance line is displayed, with the total distance summed up underneath the calculations for process lead time and total cycle time.

Understanding the Icons Used in Value Stream Mapping

The basic icons used in Value Stream Mapping are a combination of flowcharting icons and unique shapes used to visually represent the various tasks and functions within a map. Icons are broken out into several groups:

■ Process, entities, inventory, and associated data
■ Flow, communication, signals, and labels
■ People and transportation

Figure 1.6 shows each of these basic icons. However, because the power in Value Stream Mapping lies within the ability of the person drawing the map (i.e., the mapper) to visually represent the value stream, it is common practice to create your own icons—but only when necessary. The most important part of creating your icons is to thoroughly explain the icon to the audience and consistently use this icon from the point of creation forward. Providing an overall map key or legend may also be useful for the audience (as well as for the mappers themselves).

These icons will be explained in detail later in this book. Although some are common sense and require little or no explanation, there are some icons and concepts that require in-depth discussion to clarify the various ways the interpretation of your map can be affected by the use of these more complex symbols. In Figure 1.6, the icons have been categorized by symbol type. As the book advances, they will also be shown grouped by their most common usage in Current State Maps and Future State Maps. Keep in mind that it is possible to see and use any of these symbols at any time in the mapping process. There is no rule that says a certain icon can only be used in a Current State Map versus a Future State Map, or vice versa.

Production versus Transactional Mapping: Understanding the Similarities and Differences

As the concepts of Value Stream Mapping (VSM) have evolved over the past several years, there has been an interesting line drawn between production process mapping and transactional process mapping. This is interesting because many continuous improvement practitioners who use this methodology to map a process seem to "see" a difference between production floor processes and office, service, and other transactional processes. Although there certainly are some differences in how you use some tools and concepts within VSM, the most powerful thing a mapper can do is to map the current state without any preconceived ideas of flow.

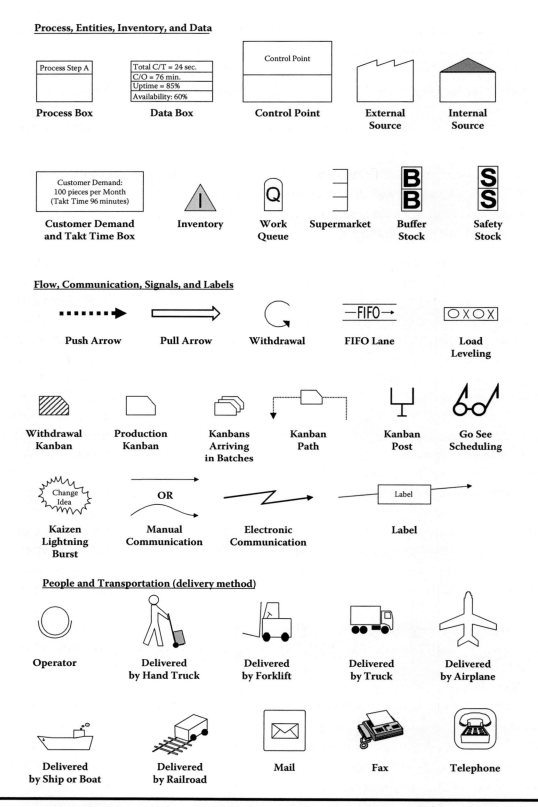

Figure 1.6   Basic Value Stream Mapping icons.

People working within every value stream tell mappers daily that "this is different. You can't use VSM to map what I do. You just don't understand." But the experienced mapper moves forward with a goal of persuading the audience that the map produced is a fair representation of the value stream, and convincing the workforce to work with the process improvement team to make positive change. In this respect, all maps are alike. The basic construction of the map is the same:

- Communication appears on top.
- Process or product flow appears in the middle (always flowing left to right).
- Timelines and travel distance are shown on the bottom.
- Process boxes, push and pull arrows, and communication lines are also all used in a similar fashion.

For the manufacturing world, *The Complete Lean Enterprise* by Beau Keyte and Drew Locher presented a way to show transactional data and their association with and impact on a production-focused value stream. This technique replaces *labels* on the communication/information lines of a production Current State Map with *process boxes* showing the transactional process that occurs, such as purchasing or invoicing. All pertinent data, such as cycle time, is captured in data boxes. On a macro level, this allows a continuous improvement team to quite effectively show the impact and interaction of these transactional support processes as the main focus of the company: producing a product or delivering a service. This is an excellent methodology for extending a Lean initiative beyond the Lean core, i.e., the production floor, into the rest of the organization. Figure 1.7 shows an example of this technique.

Using this "complete Lean enterprise" approach, it is possible to show everyone involved throughout the entire process how the complete value stream is impacted, based on activity on the shop floor and/or at any given support process step. Both operators and support staff alike respond to this type of map quickly. However, trying to provide the appropriate details of the transactional steps within this Value Stream Map is difficult at best. Once again, the similarities are apparent in that, to make substantial positive change, you must be able to map the value stream at the appropriate level to identify the wastes in the process. Because of this, when you attack support processes, you must map each support process or value stream at a level of detail similar to mapping the production floor.

Many support processes will be mapped in an identical manner to the shop floor. For example, printing services within an organization, as well as development of products or services through R&D departments and marketing departments, quite often will look and function exactly as a manufacturing production process. In these cases, there is no difference. However, you may just as often find yourself dealing with unique situations that act very differently from production processes. The flow may be indeterminate in nature, running on an as-needed basis very infrequently but needing immediate attention when it is operating. Persons involved in this value stream may multitask throughout the

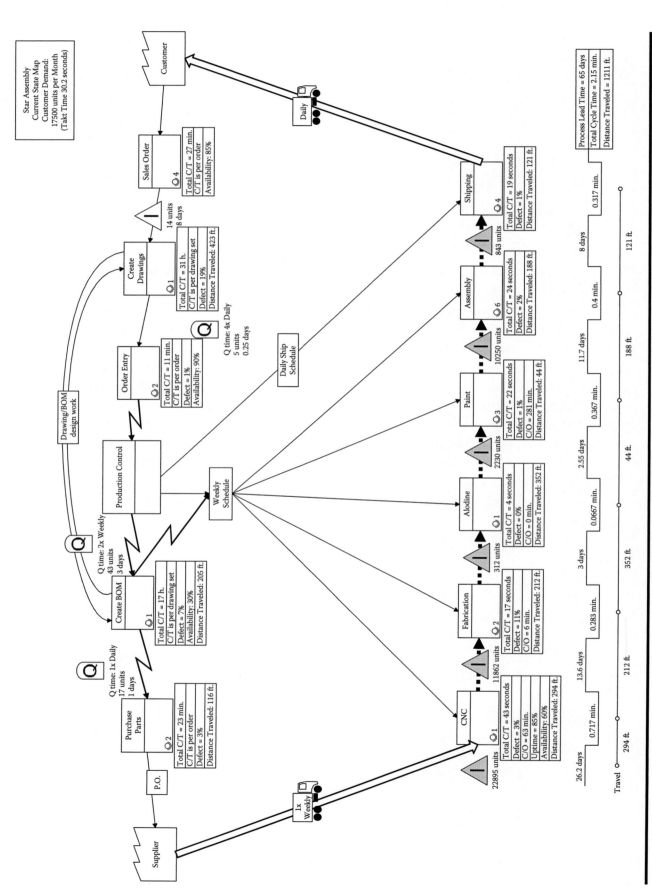

Figure 1.7   A Current State Map using process boxes with associated data boxes in place of labels on the communication portion of the map.

day, actually working within multiple value streams at a moment's notice. Calculating *Takt time* (i.e., the speed at which the value stream must operate to meet customer demand, as explained in Chapter 3) may appear to have no value whatsoever in some of these situations. These are where most of the differences between manufacturing and transactional processes become apparent.

The Current State Map depicted in Figure 1.8 demonstrates another scenario where transactional value streams may differentiate from the production-process-mapping concept. As you can see in Figure 1.8, there is no supplier, or external source, feeding the process. In this transactional setting, the customer also functions as the supplier. It is possible that the customer may also be the control point (see Chapters 3, 13, and especially 14). Unfortunately, there is no set rule, so you must go into the mapping exercise with your eyes and mind open.

To an experienced mapper, the challenge is to not subscribe to a preconceived notion of what the map should look like or how to go about mapping the current state. The challenge is being able to truly see the flow. Mike Rother and John Shook set the stage in *Learning to See*, when they stated, "Whenever there is a product (or service) for a customer, there is a value stream. The challenge lies in seeing it." When Rother and Shook wrote this statement, their focus was on *production* value streams. However, this is also true with *transactional* processes. You may be mapping a service instead of a product, but ultimately your goals and objectives are the same. The challenge is in keeping an open mind and letting yourself see the value stream. Then and only then can you map the current state (i.e., paint the picture) for your audience in a way such that everyone can see the actual flow.

Next in Chapter 2, you will learn how to create a map of the current state of your process—what your process looks like today.

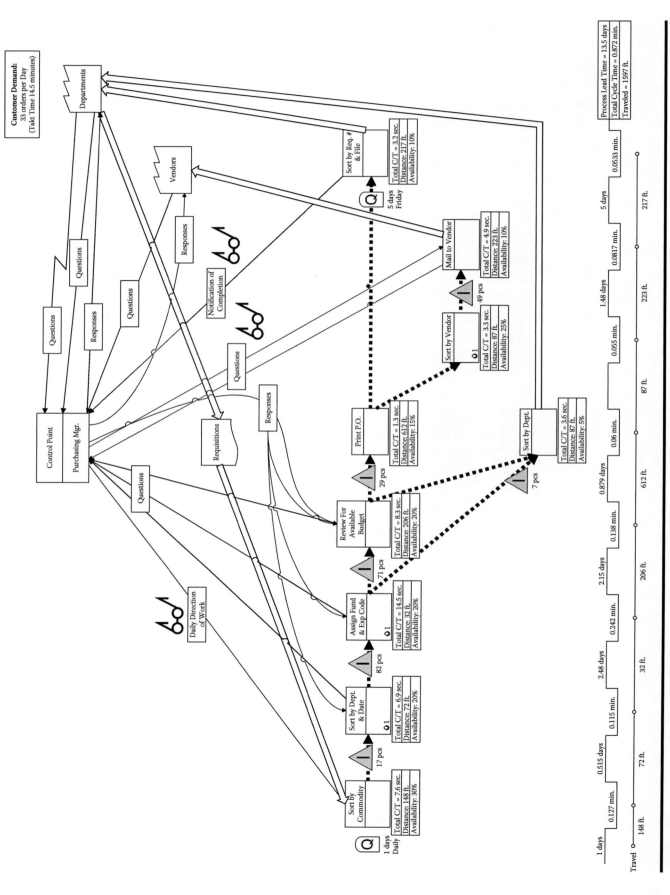

Figure 1.8 A transactional Current State Map where the customer is also the supplier.

CURRENT STATE: UNDERSTANDING AND MAPPING YOUR EXISTING PROCESS

1

Chapter 2

Identifying the Value Stream

> Before everything else, getting ready is the secret of success.
>
> **Henry Ford**

Introduction

One of the greatest challenges for anyone involved with continuous improvement (regardless of the discipline or methodology used) is knowing what to focus on when starting on an improvement project. To provide some guidance to this dilemma, subject-matter experts began creating process maps of the current state as a way to demonstrate what the project team was facing and perhaps even as a way to create a starting point. Showing what the process currently looks like and being able to identify the things that need improving is the starting point for process improvement. But what do you map? Where does it start, and where does it end?

When using Value Stream Mapping (VSM), you can solve this problem, to some extent, by using a product or process matrix. However, not everyone using VSM subscribes to the use of a product matrix. Instead, some organizations prefer to identify the target area and quickly start mapping. Both approaches have advantages and disadvantages:

- The matrix approach's advantages are that it provides great definition to the value stream that is going to be mapped, and it provides the mapping team with insight into how big the map may be. However, one of its disadvantages is that it can take longer to physically get out into the process for the actual mapping exercise. Another disadvantage is that it can bias the mapping team's attitudes and perceptions of what is actually occurring once they begin mapping.
- Organizations that use the fast-hitting approach of identifying the target area and starting the mapping exercise immediately will almost always benefit from staying in step with Taiichi Ohno's "just do it" philosophy. This approach can still be aligned with what James Womack and Daniel Jones explained (in Step 4

of Chapter 11 of *Lean Thinking*), where they emphasized the utility of mapping the entire value stream for all of your product families.

Many companies believe that instead of spending time systematically identifying your value stream, the best approach is to get a team started mapping what they consider to be a value stream, and then rolling out multiple teams to attack remaining value streams not covered in the first exercise. Whichever approach you subscribe to can work, as long as you achieve the ultimate goal: map all of your value streams.

Option 1: The Matrix Approach

Being able to logically capture the starting and end point of the value stream greatly simplifies VSM work. This concept may not capture every known process task within the current state, but it will provide a valuable framework from which to base your map. In the manufacturing world, a product matrix can give clarity to a product family. Many companies have been surprised to see that items that they had considered as part of the same product family can actually have *very few process steps in common*. Likewise, you often find that items categorized in *different* product families should have been grouped in the *same* family, based on the commonality in how they are produced.

Trying to explain how this matrix concept works can be challenging enough when focused on product alone, but to try and explain how to use the methodology for transactional processes at the same time can confuse even the most seasoned process improvement specialist. To simplify the explanation of this pre-mapping work, definitions of production and transactional process matrix, explanations, and examples are presented in the two subsections that follow. Although there is not a significant difference in the two situations, by separating them, it is much easier to understand both the power of the matrix concept and the common mistakes made in both situations.

Production Process Matrix

On the manufacturing floor, this matrix shows a list of all products manufactured by the company, or a subset of these products that the mapper, project team, or Executive Council believes may be a part of the value stream. (The Executive Council is the management team responsible for the overall coordination and success of the continuous improvement initiative.) The simplest way to start this product listing for many people is to list each item that is a part of the product family manufactured on the line, or in the cell, that is targeted for improvement. This list of products is contained in a column down the left side of the matrix. Figure 2.1 shows the start of a product matrix, with the product listing down the left-hand column.

Across the top row of the matrix, you list each process step, or task, that is used in making the product or in performing the service, as shown in Figure 2.2.

Product Matrix

Task / Product	Task #1	Task #2	Task #3	Task #4	Task #5	Task #6	Task #7	Task #8
AB-13402								
AB-15300								
HF-10110								
HC-99955								
HC-88776								
MP-20000								
MP-30001								

Figure 2.1   A product matrix template (ready to be populated) for products sold by a manufacturing company.

Getting the steps or tasks documented can create confusion for many people. This is not a list of *parts*, but of *process steps*. The work performed here can also help you draw the map as you go through the Current State Mapping exercise. This list of tasks will rarely be complete enough to draw a map, and you should never attempt to draw a Current State Map directly from this list, because critical pieces of data will not be accessible to you while sitting in a vacuum.

The challenge comes in how you create this list of tasks for the matrix. A quick and effective way to capture this information is to assemble a team of operators and management that work within the target area. Have this team look at each product listed in the left-hand column individually and think about the basic steps involved in the process. After a quick review of all products, have the team participate in a mental exercise to identify process steps. For the first product listed, give the team 30 sec. to recite the basic steps. Record these tasks on a whiteboard, flipchart, or other medium that is visible to all team members. When the team stops listing tasks, or the 30 sec. has expired, write these tasks in process-step order across the top row of the matrix. Put an "X" in the cell on the row of this first product underneath each process step listed.

Repeat this 30-sec. exercise for the second product listed on the matrix. As new process steps are identified, add the step to the row across the top. Once again, place an "X" in the cells on the second product's row for all process steps that are used in the manufacture of this second product. Repeat this exercise for each product listed in the left-hand column, adding as many additional process steps across the top row as necessary to document the process tasks involved.

Product Matrix

Task / Product	Motor Seal	Shaft Insertion	Spacer Placement	Cord Hang	Case Close	Seal	LED	Test	Package	Band Insertion	Cable Insertion	Switch Connect
AB-13402												
AB-15300												
HF-10110												
HC-99955												
HC-88776												
MP-20000												
MP-30001												

Figure 2.2   A product matrix with tasks assigned, ready to be populated with product information.

Product Matrix

Task / Product	Motor Seal	Shaft Insertion	Spacer Placement	Cord Hang	Case Close	Seal	LED	Test	Package	Band Insertion	Cable Insertion	Switch Connect
AB-13402	X	X	X	X	X	X	X	X	X			X
AB-15300		X	X	X	X			X	X			
HF-10110	X			X	X	X	X	X	X			X
HC-99955			X	X			X	X	X			X
HC-88776			X	X			X	X	X			X
MP-20000		X	X	X	X			X	X	X		
MP-30001		X	X	X	X			X	X		X	

Figure 2.3   A completed product matrix ready for analysis.

After you have completed the matrix, the team may realize that they forgot to list a step or steps for one or more products. Update the matrix as necessary to produce an accurate matrix for decision-making purposes. When completed, your matrix should look similar to Figure 2.3.

After keying this matrix into a spreadsheet application, the next step in identifying what to include in your value stream will become much easier. Sort your products by the tasks listed along the top row:

- Task one is the primary sort.
- Task two is the secondary sort.
- Task three is the tertiary sort, etc.

After completing this sort, it is possible to quickly start identifying the commonality in tasks.

Products that possess high commonality of tasks should be grouped within a single product family and Value Stream Mapped as a single map. As a general rule, focus on commonality of 70% or higher for this grouping. It may be possible to include some products with slightly less commonality if they do not fit within another product family. Figure 2.4 shows several value streams identified in this manner.

When the matrix has been completed and the product families have been identified, you are ready to answer the ultimate question:

Product Matrix with Value Streams Identified

Task / Product	Motor Seal	Shaft Insertion	Spacer Placement	Cord Hang	Case Close	Seal	LED	Test	Package	Band Insertion	Cable Insertion	Switch Connect
AB-13402	X	X	X	X	X	X	X	X	X			X
HF-10110	X			X	X	X	X	X	X			X
AB-15300		X	X	X	X			X	X			
MP-20000		X	X	X	X			X	X	X		
MP-30001		X	X	X	X			X	X		X	
HC-99955				X	X		X	X	X			X
HC-88776				X	X		X	X	X			X

Figure 2.4   A completed product matrix that has been analyzed, and product families identified by the various groupings of products.

Which product family should you map initially?

Although business goals and objectives of the company will most often answer this question, there are ways to answer it if there are no goals or objectives in place to assist with the decision. Consider the following:

- Where is the most pain for the customer?
- Where is the most pain for your employees?
- What is most visible to the workforce?
- Where is the perceived largest return on investment (ROI) for the organization?

After you have decided which product family to map, it is then possible to start the Current State Mapping process. You should file the product matrix for future use, because there will most likely be other value streams identified. Additionally, this matrix may come in handy when trying to identify the approximate number of steps within the product-flow portion of your Current State Map (as discussed in Chapter 3).

Transactional Process Matrix

Value Stream Mapping of *transactional processes* presents a much larger challenge than mapping *production processes*. On the one hand, many perceived transactional processes are nothing more than production processes. On the other hand, just as many transactional processes are service or support functions, which may be similar in appearance but actually contain much different information and are interpreted in a slightly different way.

These differences, however, do not alter the way you should construct the process matrix. Similar to a product matrix, list the processes down the left-hand column and the tasks performed within the value stream across the top row. Start out by listing each possible process (or perceived process) in the functional area (or areas) that you are targeting for improvement. These identified processes should be listed vertically in the column on the left side of the matrix. For example, if you are focusing your improvement efforts on the human resources (HR) department, list all functions or processes performed by HR. This list may look similar to the list provided in Figure 2.5.

Process Matrix

Process \ Task	Task #1	Task #2	Task #3	Task #4	Task #5	Task #6	Task #7	Task #8
Hiring Process								
Job Posting								
Applicant Screening								
Turn-Down Letters								
Insurance Enrollment								
401(k) Enrollment								
Payroll Records Setup								
New Hire Interviews								
Grievance Review								
Job Description Maintenance								

Figure 2.5   A transactional process matrix template with process functions identified in the far left column.

Once this list is complete, you are ready to identify the process tasks or steps associated with each process. Just as in completing a product matrix, a quick and effective way to capture this information is to follow these simple steps:

1. Assemble a team of operators and managers who work within the target area.
2. Have the team look at each process or function listed and think about the basic steps involved for each.
3. Starting with the first function listed, give the team 30 sec. to recite the basic steps.
4. Record these tasks on a whiteboard, flipchart, or other medium that is visible to the entire team.
5. When the team stops listing tasks, or when the 30 sec. has expired, write all tasks in process step order across the top row of the matrix.
6. Put an "X" in the cell on the row of this first process/function underneath each process step listed.
7. Repeat this 30-sec. exercise for the second item listed in the left column on the matrix.
8. As new process steps are identified, add each new step to the row across the top.
9. Once again, place an "X" in the cells on the second function's row for all process steps that are used to complete the process.
10. Repeat this exercise for each process listed in the left-hand column, adding as many additional steps across the top row as necessary to document the process tasks involved.

Somewhat different than with a product matrix, you may discover when working with transactional processes that some functions (or processes) listed in the left-hand column are actually functions *contained within another process* listed in the column. For example, using our HR scenario to demonstrate this situation, you may have listed "background checks" as a process (or function) on your list in the left-hand column. As you start through the 30-sec. exercise, you realize that you have just listed "background checks" as a task for the "hiring process." This is to be expected. As these items are identified, add them to the process steps across the top row, and remove them from the list in the left hand column. Figure 2.6 shows an example.

When the matrix has been completed and the processes and their associated tasks have been identified, you are then ready to determine what should be mapped. Sometimes, the answer is to map "everything in the department." Other times, you realize that the employees within the targeted area work within multiple value streams. When you recognize that there are multiple value streams, pick one to attack first, based on impact on key performance indicators, or some other criterion of the organization. Figure 2.7 shows a completed process matrix.

Process Matrix

Process \ Task	Request Received	Job Description Pulled	Internal Posting	Ad Placed	Application Accepted	New Hire Packet Assembled	Photo ID Completed	Packet Assembled	Applicant Screening	Turn-Down Letters	New Hire Interviews	New Hire Accepts	Employee Completes	Employee Data Entered	Pay Data Entered	Benefit Data Entered
Hiring Process	X	X		X	X	X	X	X			➤	X				
Job Posting	X	X	X													
Applicant Screening									➤							
Turn-Down Letters										➤						
Insurance Enrollment							X	X				X	X			X
401(k) Enrollment							X	X				X	X	X		X
Payroll Records Setup														X	X	X
New Hire Interviews											➤					

Figure 2.6   A transactional process matrix showing where several functions are being reclassified as tasks.

Process Matrix

Process \ Task	Request Received	Job Description Pulled	Internal Posting	Ad Placed	Application Accepted	New Hire Packet Assembled	Photo ID Completed	Packet Assembled	Applicant Screening	Turn-Down Letters	New Hire Interviews	New Hire Accepts	Employee Completes	Employee Data Entered	Pay Data Entered	Benefit Data Entered
Hiring Process	X	X	X	X	X	X	X	X	X	X	X	X				
Job Posting	X	X	X													
Insurance Enrollment								X				X				X
401(k) Enrollment								X				X				X
Payroll Records Setup													X		X	X

Figure 2.7   A completed process matrix ready for analysis.

Attacking multiple value streams simultaneously may cause unnecessary chaos and place added stress on the employees working within the area. Do not try to map or improve multiple value streams at the same time, unless you have a very large pool of employees and time to work through all of the opportunities. Although business goals and objectives of the company may assist you in this selection process, you might just need to listen to the customers of the value stream and start by focusing on the obvious or largest pain as viewed in the customers' eyes.

After you make your decision, it is then possible to start the Current State Mapping process. Again, you should file the process matrix for future use, because there will most likely be other value streams identified. Additionally, this matrix may come in handy when trying to identify the approximate number of steps within the process flow portion of your Current State Map (which is discussed in Chapter 3).

Option 2: Ready, Aim, Map—
Production and Transactional Value Streams

As an alternative to using a matrix to identify all the value streams in your organization, it is possible to use the 30-sec. exercise to identify the basic contents of a value stream, and then go map it.

Regardless of setting, getting mapping teams out into the process is simple when using this technique. Identify a target area or a process that needs improvement. Assemble your mapping team. As a team, conduct the 30-sec. exercise identifying the basic steps in the value stream. Figure 2.8 outlines the methodology of the 30-sec. exercise when used for this purpose.

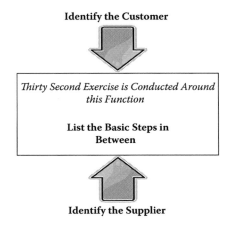

Figure 2.8 Using a 30-sec. exercise can help in identifying the basic process steps of a value stream.

1. **Identify the Customer**

   Prior to conducting the 30-sec. exercise and with all participants involved, identify who the customer is in the value stream. Do not allow this to use more than 5 min. of your time. You are not looking for in-depth detailed analysis of the customer, or how the process works. The purpose is to get everyone on the team and those working within and managing the process on the same page and focused on the customer. It may be necessary to remind the participants that the customer may be internal or external to your organization.

2. **Identify the Supplier**

   After identifying the customer, identify the supplier to the process. Once again, this is prior to conducting your 30-sec. exercise, but it should still take no longer than 5 min. *In a transactional value stream, it is possible that the customer and the supplier are the same entity.* If this is the case, quickly acknowledge this fact to the participants. If it is not acknowledged quickly, others in the meeting may try to explain away the possibility, because production value streams typically show a supplier at one end of the process flow and the customer at the other end. In transactional value streams, it is not uncommon for the customer to also be the supplier. Employees who have not been exposed to VSM and how the supplier icons are used in production mapping may not understand this difference. However, there is nothing that says that you cannot list them in both places, naming them twice.

3. **List the Basic Steps in Between**

   Now you are ready to conduct the 30-sec. exercise:

   ■ Write the supplier at the top of a whiteboard or flipchart and the customer at the bottom.

   ■ Explain to all participants that they now have 30 sec. to list all basic steps in the value stream, from the supplier point to the customer point. Explain that there is to be no discussion associated with this listing of tasks or steps.

   ■ As the team verbalizes the steps, write them down on the list between the supplier and customer. It does not matter if they are in the correct order or, at least, not at this point. Do not allow the team to stray from the exercise by trying to discuss how a particular step works in detail, or whether or not it is actually a part of the value stream.

   ■ At the conclusion of the 30 sec., stop writing and put down the marker. Stop all discussion surrounding this exercise, and if anyone in the room was documenting (i.e., writing as the team was listing steps), pick up their work. You do not want this information out in sight as you explore what was just listed on the board.

   Conduct a short summary session at this point to get agreement on what the basic steps are, and to adjust the order of the steps as required. Thank all participants and explain that this will be the basis of the mapping work to be conducted. Explain that it may, or may not, reflect the actual value stream when the work is complete, because the mappers involved will actually be mapping what they "see" as they work their way through the Current State Mapping exercise.

The mapping team is now ready to begin mapping the current state. However, these mappers should also be aware that this outline may not be entirely accurate as to the functions actually contained in the selected value stream.

In a transactional world, many functional departments consist of numerous and often overlapping tasks and processes. Because of this overlap in duties, many organizations attacking transactional Lean opportunities have begun using this as an easier and faster methodology, instead of creating a process matrix. Many companies with production processes have also adopted this methodology in an effort to avoid "analysis paralysis" caused by teams spending excessive amounts of time overanalyzing tasks within a value stream.

The 30-sec. exercise allows all team members (as well as other employees in the department of area and management) to participate in defining the "scope" of a value stream. This exercise provides the mapper and project team with a starting point (i.e., the point of need) and an ending point (i.e., the customer need is satisfied), as well as a simple overview of what to expect when mapping the current state. With a little planning and forethought, a well-prepared mapper can conduct this exercise very efficiently and allow for all persons in the discussion to express their thoughts without losing the focus of the 30-sec. exercise. The challenge in this technique is to keep participants from overanalyzing the mapping target.

When using this approach to set the stage for mapping your value streams, the mappers as well as your organization's Executive Council must remember that all value streams need to be mapped. This requires understanding what is being captured in the first Current State Map and launching additional teams (or sending this team back out) to identify and capture the current state for the remaining value streams. Although there is nothing to prohibit an organization from mapping all value streams before launching any improvement efforts, the sooner you can begin process *change,* the easier employee buy-in will be and the faster your return on your investment.

Next, in Chapter 3, you will look at what basic information needs to be collected in order to begin developing your Current State Map.

Chapter 3

Collecting Basic Information about the Current State

All we want are the facts, ma'am.

Sgt. Joe Friday in *Dragnet*

Introduction

Value Stream Mapping requires, above all, a strong set of observational skills. When you're mapping, you must be able to observe what is going on within a process, and document it as it occurs. Paint a picture of what it looks like at the time it was documented, not what people *say* or *think* the process should be doing. This picture, or snapshot in time, is truly the power behind the tool. What is most important is being able to explain to employees all of the following:

- What they do
- How they do it
- How they interact with the employees on each side of them in the process
- How the entire process flows

Capturing Basic Information

Before going out into the process to map, your mapping team should sit down and work through a series of questions designed to open your eyes to the value stream so that you can observe the process clearly, with an open mind. Having worked through a product matrix, you have the basic steps in your mind already. But, you must understand that what you see when you enter into the value stream to document most likely will look somewhat (if not entirely) different than your team documented in the matrix.

Additionally, the mapping team needs to gather some basic data about the value stream being mapped. This data is intended to provide foresight into the control, flow, and demand of the process, as well as customer expectations and supplier abilities. Have the mapping team in a group setting go over this set of questions and data needs before embarking on your journey into the depths and details of the value stream. If you do not have the subject-matter experts in the room to answer all of these questions, then your team should hand out assignments to various teams to go and gather this information from the proper sources. This may necessitate a discussion to identify the subject-matter experts that need to be approached. The knowledge you gain through this work will be invaluable as you walk through the process, mapping the current state. Figure 3.1 lists the basic data to gather during this meeting.

Begin to Map Your Process

With this basic information in hand, the mapping team has the necessary background information to start mapping the process. Although this data will provide insight to certain issues and conditions that may exist within the value stream, your mapping team members must remember to not only look for situations that *support* what they now know, but also *to keep an open mind* and map what they see when they walk and map the process. Capturing basic background data upfront can give you some great clues, but don't allow it to taint your view of the value stream.

In the event that there are strong preconceived ideas around what is wrong with the value stream, the mapping team might want to conduct a simple brainstorming session prior to actually mapping the current state. By allowing all team members to brainstorm the perceived pain, problems, and issues, any preconceived notions will come to the surface, and discussion will help the team to pinpoint these issues.

However, you should not stop with this brainstorming list and discussion. Conduct a follow-up exercise by having each team member independently work through the brainstorming list to categorize each problem into the eight wastes of Lean (see Quality Glossary at the end of the book). Each team member should write down which of the eight wastes apply to each problem listed. More than one waste can be assigned to a problem.

Once everyone has had the opportunity to assign waste, you can then total up the number of times each Lean waste appears, as well as the number of total wastes that appear for each problem. From this exercise you can oftentimes eliminate these preconceived ideas and refocus on what the team as a whole believes is the biggest problem (based upon the number of wastes listed next to each problem) and which Lean waste should receive the most focus.

Caution: *You must be extremely careful using this exercise prior to actually mapping the current state. While it can and often does eliminate preconceived ideas from tainting the mapping process, it can also alter the thoughts of the mapping team to the point that the Current State Map being drawn now has added emphasis on something that came out of the exercise, regardless of how big the issue is in reality.*

Pre-Mapping Data Collection Needs

Customer Data
- Who is the customer?
- What is the actual customer demand? (Quantity of orders received or amount required by the customer).
  - As a product family or by individual product model
  - By the day, week, month, quarter, or year
- If there is more than one product, what is the mix?
- How often does the customer order?
- Does the customer provide a forecast?
- How often do you deliver to the customer?
- What is the customer delivery window?

Supplier Data
- Who is the supplier?
- How often do you order?
- Do you provide a forecast?
- How often does the supplier deliver?

Value Stream Work Data
- How many shifts are worked within the value stream?
- What hours are these shifts?
- How many breaks and for how long?
- Do automated processes stop during breaks?
- Do manual processes stop during breaks?
- Are there any pre- or post-shift meetings and for how long?
- Is there clean-up time scheduled during the shift and for how long?
- Is lunch paid or unpaid?
- How long is the lunch break?
- Do automated processes stop during lunch?
- Do manual processes stop during lunch?

Value Stream Control Data
- Who, or what, controls production?
- Is this control point a single person or department?
- Is this control point a group effort from different departments?
- Are you using an automated system to control production?
- Is the automated system an MRP or ERP system?
- Is the automated system comprised of spreadsheet files/reports such as Microsoft Excel or Lotus 1-2-3?
- What hours is this control point operating?

Figure 3.1   This list provides a sample set of typical data needs, broken down by category, that should be answered prior to actually mapping the value stream.

This is not the time to pull out your laptop or tablet PC, if you are planning on using software to document your Value Stream Maps. These software solutions are intended to be used for postfloor exercise documentation. It is extremely difficult to keep up with the process step flow and order while trying to process step data using a computer as you walk the value stream. Many engineers, project mangers, and analysts who have conducted process-mapping exercises in the past tend to fall back on their traditional methods to document process flow.

With VSM, just as with most Lean tools, the rules have changed. You should no longer lock yourself in a room. To map the current state using VSM, *you must walk the process.* You must observe and document how the process is actually functioning at the time you are walking through the value stream. Documenting what you see and how it operates in the "real world" is extremely powerful. As such, you need to be able to draw quickly, as you see it. Your first-pass map does not have to be pretty, just functional. Whether you are mapping as an individual or as a team, you will go back and draw a clean version before you review it with the workers within the value stream.

For small value streams (that is, value streams that the team perceives to have few tasks or process steps), it is possible to actually begin drawing the communication part of your map on the top of your paper. Start by placing a title block in the upper left-hand corner or along the right side of your paper. In this block, the mapper should document basic information about the map, the value stream, the date, the mapper's name, etc. Figure 3.2 shows a simple title block completed for a Current State Map. Title blocks can be as simple as the example shown in Figure 3.2 or as complex as what you see on technical or architectural drawings.

CURRENT STATE MAP	
Company Name	Path Links Pathology Services
Value Stream Name	Histology Laboratory (Lincoln)
Drawn By	Mick Chomyn
Date	11 Oct. 2005

Figure 3.2 Simple Current State Map title block.

Even if you use software to document your value stream after this initial mapping exercise on the floor, you should place this completed title block on your paper. Keeping these floor exercise maps in a file after the mapping is completed should be a part of your standardized work rules associated with VSM. Having the work papers to go back to in case of an issue or questions can often mean the difference between buy-in from the workforce and total disagreement from workers or managers in the process. Being able to go back and show exactly what you drew when can stop arguments and discussions rooted in the "that's not the way we do it" tactic. File away any and all preliminary drawings and working papers for future use. When you redraw the current state at some point in the future, you can then keep the map version that earlier change was based on, throw out old work papers, and use the map originally presented to the workforce as the baseline for all change.

For these small maps, you can then place a **control point** box at the top middle of your paper and label it showing who or what controls the value stream, and if an automated system is involved, you can also show it on the bottom portion of the box. For most manufacturing operations, this control point is *production control*. If this is the case, that is how you would label the box. If this control is made of multiple persons or departments, you can show each one at the bottom of the control point box.

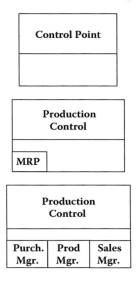

On the far left side of your paper, you can draw in the supplier (or suppliers) to the value stream. Using an **external** or **internal source** icon to identify your suppliers, you can get as detailed as necessary in order to communicate this information. However, it is highly recommended that you do not draw an excessive number of these icons, in the event that you have a high number of suppliers to the value stream. Drawing each and every supplier and customer icon when there are large numbers of each merely takes additional time that could be better used discussing the opportunities identified. If a project team member, manager, or some other employee demands that multiple icons be used, work toward a compromise that limits the number used.

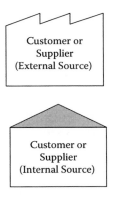

On the right-hand side of the paper at the top, draw in your customer. Once again, use the internal or external source icon, as shown above, and label the icon as "customer" (or "customers") or write in the customer's name. The customer icon and the supplier icon should be lined up horizontally on your page, as a way to quickly see them as the page is read and interpreted by others.

Use your customer and supplier data that you have gathered to connect the three areas—supplier, control point, and customer—with manual or electronic communication lines. Multiple lines may be used between each of the icons and should show, but are not limited to, sales orders, forecasts, and purchase orders.

Figure 3.3 shows what the top of a typical Current State Map will look for a simple value steam before starting the mapping exercise on the floor. However, many Current State Maps have more process steps than will comfortably fit on a single sheet of paper. In those cases, it is recommended that you not complete the top of the map until you have documented the process steps in the value stream.

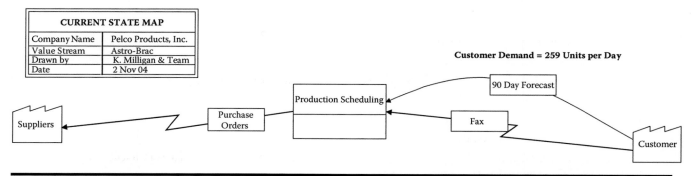

Figure 3.3   Title block, supplier, customer, and control point information excerpted from a Current State Map.

Calculating Takt Time

Using the customer data collected, it is possible to start understanding customer demand and its effect on your value stream. Take the customer-demand data and convert it to a daily demand rate. If your team has captured individual product models, it is recommended that you merge this information into a single number for ease of use on the first pass through the value stream. If you are converting annual data, divide the total demand by the number of days the production floor actually worked during this period. A similar calculation can be done to convert quarterly, monthly, or weekly demand to a daily number. *This daily demand rate may be the single most important piece of data you gather prior to mapping.* Write this number on the top of your mapping paper on the right-hand side, as shown in Figure 3.3.

With the daily demand rate in place, it is now possible to calculate the *Takt time* for the value stream. *Takt* is a German word that means *beat.* In essence, Takt is the beat of the line or cell; it is the speed that this value stream must operate at to keep pace with demand. To calculate Takt time, use the following formula:

$$\text{Takt time} = \frac{\text{Net available time for identified time period}}{\text{Customer demand for the same time period}}$$

The time frame used to capture customer demand data and calculate Takt time can fluctuate from "by the shift" to a 12-month number. The most common forms that customer-demand data is found in are daily, weekly, monthly, or yearly. Regardless of how you receive this data, you can calculate Takt time as long as you know what the net available time is during this same period. *Customer demand* is defined as *customer sales* or *customer requirements* during a specified period of time. Understanding what customer sales or customer requirements actually are is the difficult part of this data gathering.

In a sales-focused environment, you should not look at scheduled amounts as customer demand, because it may be possible that your sales department is "pushing out" scheduled orders, thus increasing the lead time for delivery to customers as sales increase. In this situation, customer demand should be calculated as the total sales volume of the product in the value stream that is received during the designated period, regardless of when the order is scheduled.

The lone exception to this is when you are receiving blanket purchase orders, or 12-month or multiyear orders that spread delivery to a customer over a period of time. In this situation, count these timed orders within the appropriate time frame (e.g., a 12-month contract with only 9 months' worth of deliveries in the sampled time period would reflect only the 9-month total).

When customer requirements (whether they are internal customer requirements or external customer requirements) dictate demand, you should look specifically at what the customer of this value stream requires. This concept holds true for manufacturing processes where parts or subassemblies are being produced to meet the demand of a final assembly line, or some other internal customer. It also holds true for most transactional value streams. Understand what your customer wants and when they want it.

The *net available time* is the time that the doors are open and the value stream is operating. Start with the total time that the doors are open and the lights are on. Subtract out any time that the value stream is not operating due to meetings, breaks, lunch, or other scheduled downtime. If the process continues to operate during breaks, lunch, or other scheduled downtime, do **not** subtract this time. Idle time—or any other time that the process is not operating, but is waiting on something … anything—should also remain in the net available time. Just because you are not running the value stream does not mean that you do not count the time. You are looking at "time available" to run the value stream, **not** actual run time.

As shown in the equation above, dividing the net available time by the customer demand gives you the Takt time. If your net available time is stated as a daily number, then you should divide it by the average sales on a daily basis. It is recommended that you calculate your Takt time on a per-shift or per-day basis. If you run multiple shifts, then you may want to calculate it based on per-shift numbers. If you only run one shift, then calculate it on a daily basis. Using this strategy makes it much easier for employees working within the value stream to understand how you got the Takt time you are reporting, and it is in a time frame that makes sense to them.

In a transactional value stream, you should always calculate Takt time. Even though you may be mapping a value stream that runs only on an as-needed or on-demand basis, and even if it is very infrequent, you should perform this calculation. The Takt time you come up with may make no sense at all on first look. But as you dig into the various process steps within the value stream, you may come up with a cycle time that far exceeds the Takt time. This is a signal that something may be wrong. For example, Figure 3.4 shows where Takt time in a transactional setting is used in this manner.

Hiring Process	
A. Gross Time (8:00 AM to 5:00 PM)	9 hours
B. Less non-processing time (lunch only, staggered breaks)	30 minutes
C. Equals *Net Available Time* (A – B = C)	8.5 hours
D. New employees hired last year	129
E. # of work days in year	260
F. Less holidays	10
G. Equals net work days	250
H. *Customer Demand* as daily rate (D ÷ G = H)	0.52
Takt Time Calculation	
J. Net Available Time (C) divided by	8.5
I. Customer Demand (H) Equals	0.52
K. *Takt Time*	16.4 hours

Figure 3.4   Example of Takt time calculation.

The fact that the Takt time is 16.4 hours, or slightly more than two days, has absolutely no bearing on the way a hiring process actually works. Your organization hires new employees when they need to: either when someone resigns, or when you terminate employment with someone, or when you are expanding or growing. Your HR department does not plan on completing a new hire every two days. The objective is to hire as quickly as possible once the request to hire, other paperwork, or a verbal need has been communicated. However, you can use this Takt time to review process steps in the value stream and determine if the time spent is acceptable. If there are minor steps in the process that take longer than the two-day Takt time, then opportunity exists for improvement. Likewise, if major steps in the value stream exceed this Takt time, the project team should analyze the step and determine if the time allotted or required can be reduced.

Due to legal requirements or company policy, you may never be able to reduce the time a job opening is posted internally or through employment agencies or advertising. Because of these built-in time periods that take extended time, you must be able to flow the work through the remaining process steps as timely as possible. To accomplish this, you can use the Takt time as a benchmark to target maximum cycle times at these "other" process steps. Any step that has no fixed time requirement, such as posting, should not have a cycle time that exceeds the Takt time. If the cycle time does exceed Takt time, then you have an opportunity to improve the process. (For more information on cycle times, see Chapter 7, "Interpreting and Understanding Basic Product Flow.")

Takt time is a critical piece of data that provides great insight into the needs and capabilities of the value stream. As you work on creating your Current State Maps, the basic information you have gathered to this point—and in particular the Takt time—will help experienced mappers understand why certain tasks and functions are performed in certain ways. These observations then not only strengthen the picture painted of the current state, but they also start the process of thinking about the future state.

Next, in Chapter 4, you will learn to document your value stream from receipt of materials to product delivered specifically in a manufacturing setting.

Chapter 4

Documenting Manufacturing (or Production) Process Flow

I start where the last man left off.

Thomas A. Edison

Introduction

When mapping any process, the first challenge encountered is always identifying what you are documenting. The definition of the value stream, from receipt of raw materials to finished product delivered to the customer, must be in place in order for you to be successful when mapping a process. Figure 4.1 shows a simple example.

In a production setting, this typically involves identifying the individual product or product family (see Figure 4.2). As Value Stream Mapping (VSM) has continued to gain popularity as a process improvement tool in its own right (i.e., separate and apart from Lean), it is often necessary to also list the reason for mapping the value stream in the first place. With this information in hand, the more difficult part of starting a map set can then be addressed.

Determining the proper level of detail to be included in the production flow portion of the map is critical to capturing, analyzing, and explaining the opportunities in the value stream. Although many process and quality improvement professionals have been led to believe that VSM only provides a *high-level* look at processes, the reality is that this could not be further from the truth. The power of VSM lies in the *detail*. You can map a value stream at several levels of detail:

- You can map at a *very high level* with little detail.
- You can *drill down* to provide as much detail as required to satisfy the reasons for creating the map.
- You can provide detail *at a very finite level*, breaking a process step down into a map of its own.

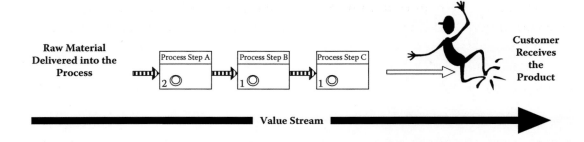

Figure 4.1   The product or process flow of a Value Stream Map extending from the receipt of raw materials to the customer receiving the finished product.

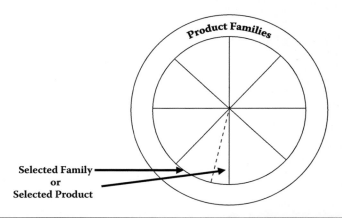

Figure 4.2   Before mapping begins, the product family or specific product must be defined from all products or product families within the company.

The level of detail should be determined by the problems or issues being addressed and the audience to which the map set will be presented; Figure 4.3 illustrates these options.

Identifying and Mapping the Main Flow

A primary goal of any value stream Current State Map should be to capture how a process or value stream actually operates: *in practice*, not theory. Another

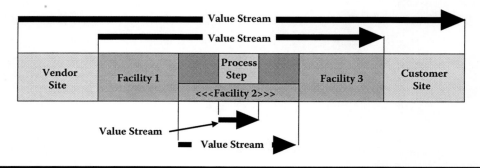

Figure 4.3   Selecting the level of detail at which to map can go from crossing multiple companies boundaries, to focusing in and providing very specific detail of a single process step.

equally important goal of a Value Stream Map is that it be drawn in such a way as to be understood by anyone. Because a Current State Map is a snapshot in time, the viewer should be able to look at the map, and within a relatively short time frame with minimal explanation, understand the value stream. Because of this goal to have everyone understand the Value Stream Maps produced, there are very few rules that exist with this discipline. Therefore, when you are (or anyone else is) mapping, we encourage you to be creative and to use the VSM tool in such a way that it is possible to clearly communicate to all operators, management, suppliers, and customers. This does not, however, mean that you can draw anything and any way you like. The tool itself allows for flexibility to work within any setting, and yet (just like most Lean concepts), boundaries still exist.

The rules that do exist focus on the following:

- Standardization of icon use, as much as possible
- The basic layout of the map
- Creation of a structured method of documentation and presentation to make the results clearer to the audience

Capturing the main process (or product) flow in an organized manner is critical to success in a mapping exercise. After you have determined what to map, you must now get down on paper what the product flow actually looks like. To do this, start with the main flow through the value stream. Figure 4.4 summarizes the steps you should take.

When you're mapping in a production setting, you should always walk the process and map exactly what you see. You should conduct your first-pass walkthrough of the value stream by walking the process in reverse order; from delivery to the customer to receipt of materials. You should capture what you actually see, with pencil and paper. Even though there are many software packages now available to assist with VSM, using paper and pencil still provides the fastest way to capture what is observed during this initial pass.

Capturing the Main Flow

- Document how the value stream *ACTUALLY* operates
- Draw the map so it can be explained to anyone
- Focus on the main flow first
- Use paper and pencil
- Walk the process backwards

Figure 4.4 The basics of capturing the main flow.

Identify each process step by using a **process box**. The process box is a basic icon, also used in traditional flowcharting, that is used to show where flow starts and stops within the process.

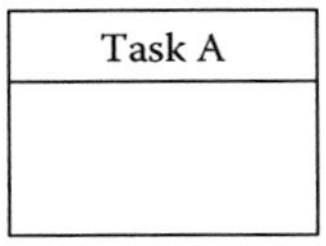

Task A

> **Key Items in the Main Flow**
> • Where flow starts and stops
> • How product is moved from one
>   process step to another
> • Where the inventory is located
> • Where the people are located

Figure 4.5   Summary of key items in the main flow.

When you're walking the process and observing how the process actually operates, you should ignore traditional departments and boundaries, and focus instead on where flow occurs. Flow typically starts at the point where labor (value-added or non-value-added) is applied to product or where machine time is initiated, excluding material handling. As discussed in Chapter 1, non-valued-added (NVA) is anything the customer is not willing to pay for. In contrast, value-added tasks add market form or function to the product or service; simply put, they *are* what the customer is willing to pay for. Flow stops at the point where the product comes to rest. The easiest way to see product "at rest" is to look for piles of inventory on workstations, in baskets, on pallets, etc. Operations that use batch and queue production methods will usually have significant amounts of product "at rest."

As you're mapping and moving from one process step to another, there are three other critical items you should look for: how product is moved, where inventory is, and where the employees are. These three items, along with the earlier discussion of flow, are summarized in Figure 4.5.

Map How the Product Moves from One Step to the Next

The first thing you should look for is how the product moves from one step to another. Is it moved on to the next step in the process without thought or consideration as to whether the next step is ready and waiting for it to arrive? When work is moved in this manner, it is being "pushed." To show a "push" on a Value Stream Map, use a **push arrow** to signify this move. A push arrow is drawn as a fat striped or dashed arrow. This shape is used to differentiate it from other types of product movement and information flow.

Figure 4.6 shows the product flow of a basic Current State Map with push arrows throughout the flow.

Materials might also be moved using a FIFO lane, where the material is moved and consumed in a "first-in–first-out" methodology.

$$-FIFO\rightarrow$$

In organizations that are already focused on flowing material through the process, and that move material only when the customer (either an internal or external customer) asks for it, you should map this using a pull arrow. The pull arrow is

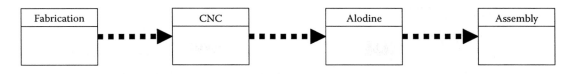

Figure 4.6   Production flow from a Current State Map, with push arrows showing the process flow.

drawn as a fat, solid, white-filled arrow. Although this is a very common occurrence in Lean enterprises, this is rarely seen in traditional production settings.

Map Where the Inventory Is

The second thing you should be looking for is inventory. The **inventory icon** is represented by a triangle with an "I" in the middle. This symbol is very appropriate because the triangle, often called a "delta," represents change in many settings. Because Current State Maps are snapshots in time, there is no better way to acknowledge that the inventory level observed and documented on the map will change.

Inventory is what manufacturers live and die for. Inventory is obviously the heart and soul of the production process. If you have too little inventory, parts shortages begin to occur. When this happens, the process can come to a grinding halt. If you have no inventory, then you have no product to complete, and no finished goods to deliver to the customer. To combat this situation, traditional manufacturers bring in large quantities of raw material and/or component parts inventory. However, because each and every vendor is not linked together to coordinate delivery dates and quantities, once a vendor misses a delivery date or ships too small of a quantity, the manufacturer suffers from a similar problem. There is plenty of raw material, dollar value-wise, but not the right materials. The result is piles of inventory. That is when you can show the power of this relatively small icon on the page.

By showing on your map where the inventory is located and how much exists, you have the ability to tell a story about how material flows through the process. If multiple stacks of material exist between two process steps, you may choose to show it as two separate inventory icons. By quickly counting the amount of inventory that exists at a specific location, you can label the inventory icon with a quantity while mapping and then convert it to lead time after the mapping on the floor is complete. This conversion is discussed in Chapter 12. The thing to remember when mapping the current state is that, although it is not

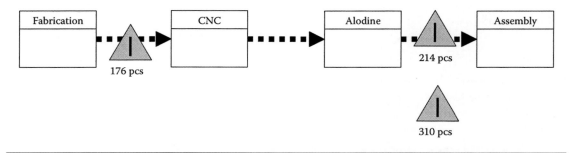

Figure 4.7   Basic flow with multiple piles of inventory.

essential to get the inventory count 100% accurate, it is important to show *what you actually saw when you were walking and mapping the process.* Figure 4.7 demonstrates what a basic flow looks like with multiple piles of inventory documented between two steps in the process.

Map Where the Operators Are Located

Finally, you should be looking for and documenting where the operators are located within the value stream. The **operator icon**, represented by a circle with a half-circle underneath, as if looking down on the operator's head and arms, is used to show where the operators are *actually* located when the process is mapped. Do *not* place operator icons where someone says the operators are *supposed* to be, or *usually* are, or even where they are *budgeted or assigned.* Instead, mapping the operators should be based on an actual observation: once again, a true picture of what was observed.

When multiple operators are seen within one process step, the actual number of operators should be placed next to the symbol, and the symbol should be placed inside the process box.

Putting It All Together

Putting this all together, the main flow should look similar to the example shown in Figure 4.8. The push arrows shown in this example might not always be the method used to move material through the process. There may be a FIFO lane in place, or the value stream may even contain a pull that moves the material when the customer is asking for it. When you're mapping, you should spend adequate time observing the process to determine where flow starts and stops, as well as to determine how the inventory moves through the process.

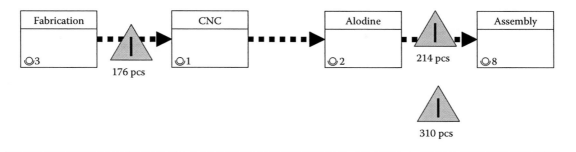

Figure 4.8 **Example of the main flow showing inventory and operators located throughout the process.**

Mapping Subtasks and Parallel Flows

As you follow the main flow of a value stream to create a Current State Map, you may often find forks in the road, i.e., places where two or more process flows come together or move apart. Where these branches in the flow occur, you may find subtasks or parallel flows in the value stream:

■ Subtasks occur where subassemblies or other feeder processes exist to provide parts or components to the main flow of the value stream. Subtasks typically start from a unique point in the value stream and feed into the main flow.
■ Parallel flows exist where there are multiple options in the value stream that occur through different parallel paths or when various tasks are completed simultaneously through different paths and then come back together at a single point in the main flow.

When you're mapping subtasks or parallel flows, the challenge is in knowing when to follow their paths. This often requires abandoning the main flow in pursuit of the newly found path. Although it is possible to follow and map this newly found path, and then return to the main flow once the subtask or parallel flow has been documented, it is usually easier to denote the existence of the path directly on your mapping pad at the point in the value stream where it was identified, and then return and capture it on the map once the main flow has been completed. By writing directly on the map, as shown in Figure 4.9, when you find an alternate path, it makes it easy to go back and find where the starting or ending point was identified, and then pick up the mapping process at that point.

Mapping Subtasks

Subtasks are often identified with subassemblies or component manufacturing that feeds a main flow, and they typically start at a point disconnected from the main flow of the value stream. When you're mapping the current state, you will

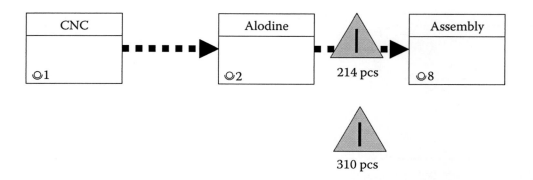

Figure 4.9   Mapping exercise showing note about alternate path.

usually find where subtasks join the main flow when you ask where parts come from to get to a process step that you are documenting. When operators explain that subassemblies or components are manufactured elsewhere on-site and join up with the flow at this step, you should recognize the additional path and prepare to come back and capture this information. However, on occasion, you may overlook a subassembly path on your first pass through the merge point and not discover it until you get to the start of the process or later. Either way, once you document the main flow, you should use the same technique of walking the process backwards to map this additional flow. Figure 4.10 demonstrates what a subassembly path might look like from the starting point up to the merge point in the main flow.

Mapping Parallel or Alternate Paths

Parallel or alternate paths through a value stream represent variation and decision making within the process. There are several schools of thought that suggest that VSM only provides a macroview strategic look at the process. These "other" schools of thought state that to dissect a process in detail, you must use

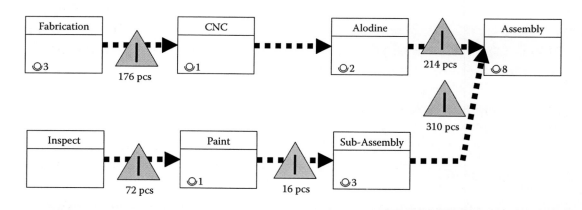

Figure 4.10   Example of a subassembly path merging with the main flow.

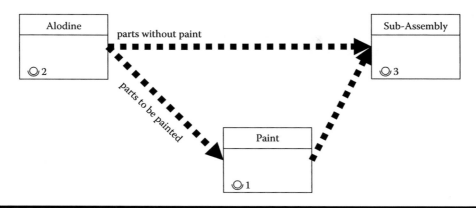

Figure 4.11 **Main flow and subpath with labels on push arrows showing when to follow each path.**

flowcharting. In flowcharting, decision-making diamonds are used to show where optional paths and decision making occur.

However, this concept of not being able to use VSM to provide detailed analysis of a process could not be further from the truth. The Lean Enterprise Institute discusses this matter in general terms in its *Value Stream Mapping Workshop Participant Manual,* which presents the various "levels" at which you can map a value stream:

- Across companies
- Within your own walls door-to-door
- Detailed at the process step level

The power in VSM is that a visual representation can be used to show these decisions. If you need to show which decision follows which path, simply label the flow arrows following each path (for example, see Figure 4.11). Alternate paths often branch off from the main flow and then rejoin it later in the process. In some instances, the process branches off into two or more parallel paths, such as when more than one assembly line is set up to run identical parts through the process. In this occurrence, the paths may not rejoin until the parts reach a warehouse or the shipping dock. Figure 4.12 shows a representative sample of a Current State Map where a subtask feeds into the main flow before the process branches out into three parallel assembly lines.

Lining Up Process Steps

In order to provide a Current State Map that workers can accept, the picture you paint must be clear and concise. The easiest and most effective way to achieve this is by proper alignment and flow of the process steps on the map. When you ensure that the top level of the process flow is the main flow through the process, you set the stage for gaining this acceptance. Subtasks,

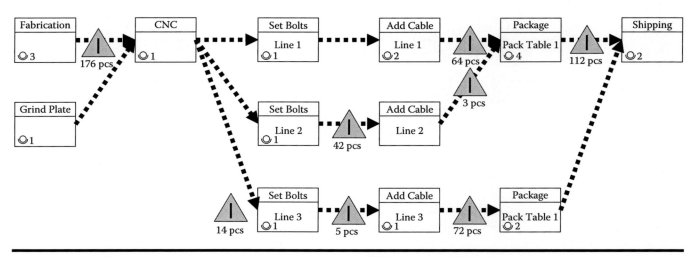

Figure 4.12   Example of a main flow with subtasks and parallel processes.

parallel paths, rework, etc., must be relegated to the area beneath the main flow. The main flow in Figure 4.13 has been highlighted to demonstrate how this should look.

In order to clearly show the main flow and to make it easier to understand the relationship of the subtasks and other flows within the map, you should align the process boxes both horizontally and vertically. If you fail to adhere to this basic alignment concept, workers within the process will more often than not fail to "see the picture."

Aligning the Process Horizontally

The need to align the process boxes horizontally accomplishes multiple goals:

1. The first goal is to isolate and provide visualization of the main flow.
2. The second goal is to group and prioritize subtasks and other process steps that are not a part of the main flow.

Each subtask flow may occupy its own layer beneath the main flow. However, this is not a requirement to create a visual picture that is easy to explain. Just as often when you're mapping, you can allow multiple subtasks to occupy the same line beneath the main flow as long as they do not interfere with each other's flow. The challenge is to place each subtask in such a manner as to provide an easy, visual depiction to the audience.

In the example shown in Figure 4.13, the push arrows used to show the flow (or the lack thereof, as the case may be) do not cross over each other. An effective map will attempt to prevent, whenever possible, push and pull arrows from crossing over one another. This merely eliminates one possible point of confusion for workers within the value stream trying to understand the map.

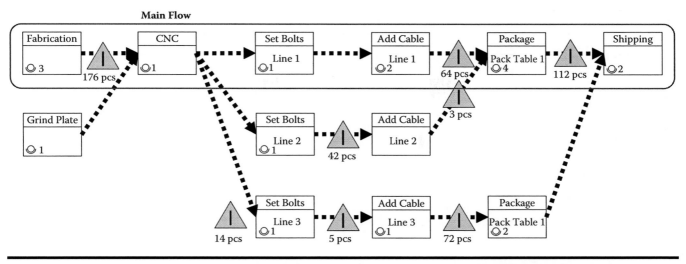

Figure 4.13 Production flow portion of a Current State Map, with proper horizontal alignment of the main flow shown.

Aligning the Process Vertically

Aligning process boxes vertically is even more important, because one of the primary purposes of a Value Stream Map is to show process lead time. To show the amount of work "sitting" within the value stream, it is critical that process boxes be aligned vertically and that all work (whether it is piles of inventory or work queues) is allowed to stack on top of each other to "capture" process lead time. (This is discussed in detail in Chapter 12.)

By aligning process boxes both horizontally and vertically, as well as providing proper unobstructed vertical alignment of inventory, as shown in Figure 4.14,

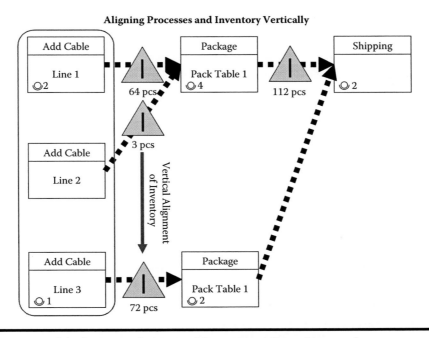

Figure 4.14 Example of process boxes and inventory aligned properly.

you greatly simplify the job of explaining the Current State Map to an audience. By thinking of proper alignment as synonymous with focusing a camera on the subject of a photograph, the purpose becomes clear. The workers within the process, as well as management, must have a clear understanding of the current state in order for the project team to be successful.

The Power of Speed

The power behind VSM is in the project team's ability to quickly identify the issues and opportunities and gain agreement on them, so that through open and honest discussion, project work can start. With the basic concepts of product flow understood and documented, it is then possible to focus on refining the flow, collecting appropriate data, and observing and documenting communication or information flow.

Next, in Chapter 5, using the same concepts, you will see how transactional processes are mapped.

Chapter 5

Documenting Transactional Process Flow

A rose is a rose is a rose.

Gertrude Stein

Introduction

Regardless of the type of process being mapped, Value Stream Mapping is still Value Stream Mapping. It doesn't take on a different look or become a different tool just because you leave the manufacturing floor. As a matter of fact, many "transactional" processes are actually production processes that are misidentified. Just because a process exists in an office, that doesn't make it transactional. You must observe what the value stream is actually doing before making a determination as to the type of process, i.e., whether it is production or transactional. Figure 5.1 shows the overlap between production and transactional processes.

Regardless of whether it is a production or transactional value stream, you should still use the same basic technique to map the current state. The primary difference is whether a *product is being produced* or a *service is being provided*. It doesn't really matter what scenario you encounter when you're mapping. You should take into consideration all facts as you observe the value stream. For many people, what adds confusion to the mapping process is the fact that support processes can be either production or transactional in nature. When mapping, you should always start with the product or process flow. You still map it back to front. You still need to get into the environment where the value stream operates and document what you see.

This is not to say that there are not differences in how you use the tool when mapping transactional processes. There are differences. But although many people have been promoting what appears to be an entirely different technique, when

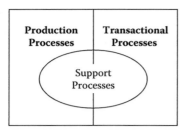

Figure 5.1 Support processes for value streams oftentimes overlap between the production and transactional worlds.

you get down to it, the concepts as first utilized by the Japanese are still valid regardless of the process setting.

The challenge when using Value Stream Mapping in a transactional world lies in recognizing where subtle differences alter the technique used to document the current state. Although these subtle differences provide great insight into a transactional value stream, the process used to create the map starts exactly as it does for production processes.

"The Product" in a Transactional World

For many people, the simplest way to identify the value stream is to think about the final output of the process as a "product," whether it is actually a product or a service. By using this thought process as a starting point, you can then start at the end of the value stream and work your way backwards. This concept is often quite helpful, because many people working within a transactional process struggle to understand that processes actually exist in their world, much less that a finished product or service is delivered.

Choosing the Level to Map

Just as with a production process, you must determine at what level you will map. With transactional Value Stream Mapping, it is important to quickly identify this level, as well as where you start and stop the map. This is critical, because it is very easy to drift in and out of other value streams, due to the intertwined, multitasking world of employees who work in and with transactional processes. This is somewhat more difficult than production processes, because many support functions within an organization depend on each other for success, as shown in Figure 5.2.

Understand the Focus of the Value Stream

The workflow in a transactional process represents what traditional flowcharts would show as a process map. To map the workflow, you must be able to differentiate the process flow from communication or information flow. For example, the process may be to provide information about road conditions

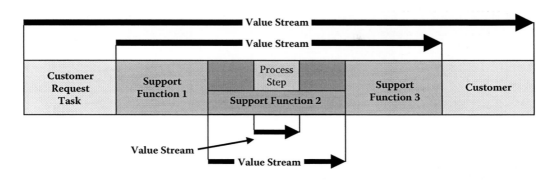

Figure 5.2   Selecting the level of detail and focus for a Value Stream Map can be more complex in transactional settings than in production environments.

during a winter storm. You have to separate the process from the information that exchanges hands as part of the process. The data about road conditions may be in effect materials feeding into the process, just as parts are in the manufacturing process. But the communication between persons involved in providing this information is just that—communication within the value stream. When you're mapping this, you must take time to understand what the workflow is and what information or communication flow exists in support of the process.

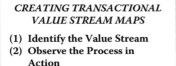

CREATING TRANSACTIONAL
VALUE STREAM MAPS

(1) Identify the Value Stream
(2) Observe the Process in Action
(3) Determine the Work Flow
(4) Identify Communication
(5) Understand the relationship between Work Flow and Communication
(6) Create the Current State Map

Figure 5.3   The basic steps leading up to a transactional Current State Map.

By first identifying the value stream and then observing the process in action, you can begin to make valid decisions about the current state. You must determine what is workflow and what is communication, and then understand the relationship between the two. Having this knowledge prior to documenting the current state through a map makes it much easier for you to stay focused on capturing an accurate picture of the process flow on the initial walkthrough. Figure 5.3 summarizes the steps involved in creating transactional Value Stream Maps.

Start with the Workflow

Just like mapping production processes, you should start with the workflow through the value stream, mapping back to front. Focus on the main flow first, and then just as with production value streams, go back and pick up parallel and feeder flows that branch off of or feed into the main flow. Figure 5.4 provides an example of the main workflow.

Figure 5.4   The main workflow of a transactional Current State Map.

This basic flow looks no different than that of a production value stream. However, as you observe the transactional value stream and capture the workflow, the differences begin to emerge. The first challenge you face when mapping a transactional value stream is in understanding the difference between the workflow of the process and the information being communicated.

You must differentiate between the process and information being communicated. In the transactional world, many times people mistake information that is being shared between persons working in the value stream for the process or workflow itself. You must be able to sift through the many exchanges of information, or communication, and find the actual task that should show on the process flow.

Unlike production processes (where physically walking the process provides the best method of documenting the value stream), transactional value streams do not always lend themselves to this methodology. Although, quite often, it is possible to walk the process back to front, just as likely, you may find that the value stream is contained completely within a single workstation or office, making the walking unnecessary. This does not, however, let you off the hook completely. You must still document the map by being in the area where the work occurs, even if that means sitting in the middle of the room, or standing over an employee's shoulder and watching what goes on around you. This discussion is diagramed in Figure 5.5.

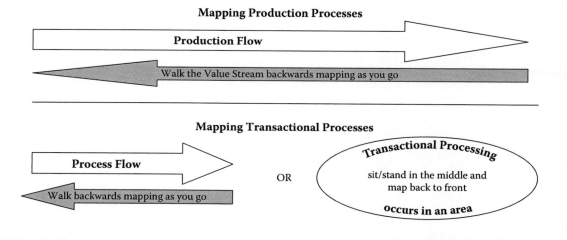

Figure 5.5   Transactional Current State Mapping can use the same drawing method as production value streams or may utilize a much simpler observation and documentation technique.

Additionally, some value streams flow at such a slow pace, or so infrequently, that it is not always possible to map the process flow when it is occurring live. In these situations, you may need to immerse yourself in the area where the value stream exists and verbally walk through the process with the subject-matter expert(s) who operates the value stream. In this case, it is recommended that you use the same methodology as production mapping, working back to front to challenge the operators' thinking.

Once you believe you have a reasonably good main flow, you should then ask the operator(s) to perform some sample runs to demonstrate the process, which will enable you to capture further insight and data about the process.

Mapping Subtasks and Parallel Tasks

Once again, the similarities between production value streams and transactional value streams are much stronger than many people using VSM as a process-mapping tool would like you to believe. The greatest challenge facing you when mapping transactional processes is in dealing with the timing of events or tasks. It is not uncommon that a value stream begins, and then subtasks or parallel tasks spin off the main flow. As the value stream follows one of these alternate paths, a time delay may affect the speed at which one or more paths operates. When an overnight delay (or even a delay caused by interoffice mail or the availability of a single person) slows down the speed at which the value stream operates, you need to try and figure out how to represent this flow on your map.

Without even looking at the data, the best method for resolving these types of issues is to try and place each task on the map from left to right as close to the actual sequence as possible. Where these subpaths or parallel paths have a common task, it is best to stretch or adjust the map, as necessary, to have each of the paths pass through a single process box. Figure 5.6 shows how this occurs when multiple forms are being used for production approval in an information technology project management office. As the common tasks occur, the parallel paths feed into this single point and then out again as the different forms run their distinct routes through the value stream.

Using this method alone will provide proper sequencing and provide a greatly improved picture of what is actually going on in the value stream. This technique further demonstrates the importance of always drawing left to right on the page and lining up your process boxes both vertically and horizontally. Without this alignment and single flow direction, it can be very difficult for employees and managers alike to follow the flow and understand what is happening with the current state.

Next, in Chapter 6, you will see the importance of flow and how to clearly document it.

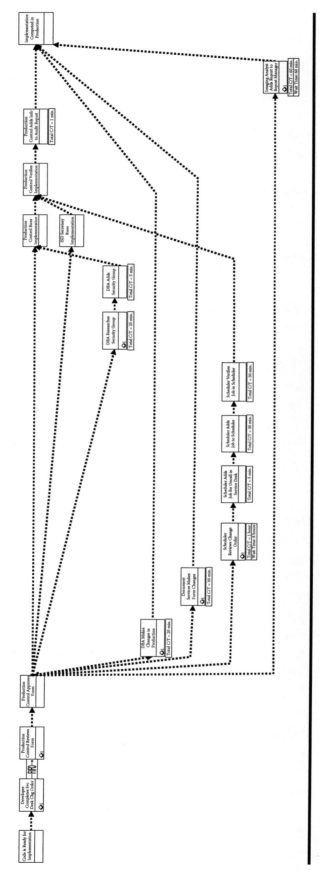

Figure 5.6 An example of stretching or adjusting the map to accommodate subtasks and parallel tasks coming out of and into single process steps.

Chapter 6

Showing the Flow Clearly

We have met the enemy and he is us.

Pogo (Walt Kelly)

Introduction

When mapping a current or future state, the first and most important step is to clearly show the flow of the value stream. Without a clear picture of what the process currently looks like, or a simple yet comprehensible vision of the future, it becomes extremely challenging to explain your maps to the audience. Buy-in and insight from the audience provide a critical ingredient for Value Stream Mapping (VSM) in a Lean transformation. The audience's interpretation, comments, and ideas are where much of the power of Lean begins to show. Without this clear picture, the speed at which change can be made can be greatly inhibited.

To draw a Current State Map that is clear and concise, the first step is to understand how to draw the flow. Chapters 4 and 5 provided great insight into the basics of this concept. However, even though some examples of more complex value streams are used to demonstrate the technique, these chapters do not address the fact that the world is an imperfect and often complex place.

A simple or very high-level value stream can be documented all on one path or flow. This is how many people who do not understand the power of VSM think all Value Stream Maps look. Figure 6.1 shows a simple linear flow for a Value Stream Current State.

Providing Definition to Subtasks and Parallel Paths

However, unless you are mapping at a high level, and not documenting the details of the value stream at a level that operators and employees within the value stream understand, these types of Current State Maps (like the one shown in Figure 6.1) are the exception, not the rule. More often, Current State Maps will possess some

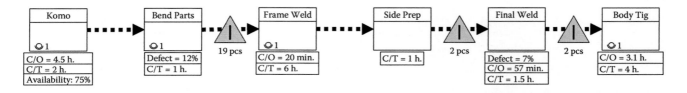

Figure 6.1   The current-state product flow for a simple value stream.

amount of subtasks or parallel paths that the process can follow. For example, Figure 6.2 shows the current-state main process flow, subtasks, and parallel paths that a value stream follows in creating a technical document to be posted to an Internet website. The real world rarely plays out according to theoretical concepts; therefore, when you are mapping, you must determine how to paint a clear picture of what is *actually* occurring *simultaneously* at several points in the process.

Mapping the Reality of Rework

But no matter how simple or complex a value stream may be, there is and always will be one issue that mappers and employees working within a value stream must address: *defects*. No matter what the process is, or what the setting might be, errors and defects exist. In an effort to catch these errors before customers see the defect, organizations have a habit of building multiple inspection points into the process. When errors and defects are found, the work is either scrapped or rework occurs.

As you can see in Figure 6.3, when rework occurs, the product or work-in-process flows backwards against the main flow of the value stream. In a block diagram such as the one shown in Figure 6.3, this is an easy depiction. But when mapping this situation in a Value Stream Map such as shown in Figure 6.2,

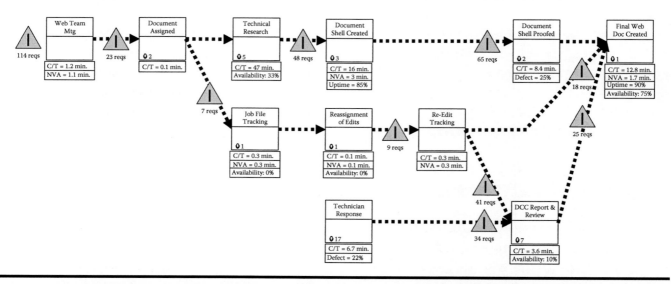

Figure 6.2   The process flow of an actual Current State Map, showing the main flow as well as subtasks and parallel paths.

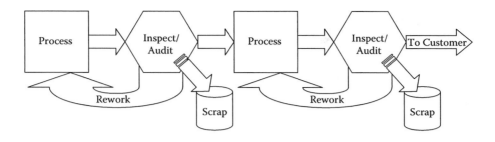

Figure 6.3   A process flow that includes rework to fix defects.

where you are attempting to show process flow from left to right on your page and then adding the communication that occurs, this can become confusing very quickly for the audience and even for experienced mappers.

Using Terminators to Clarify Rework in the Flow

To combat this problem, Value Stream Mapping has evolved to include a new use for an old tool. **Terminators** (also called *terminal points*) from traditional flowcharting have been integrated into the Value Stream Mapping world to specifically address situations where work is required to go back to another process step earlier in the flow. Where inspections or audits are conducted and rework is required or work is scrapped, you can flow out of the process box where the identification occurs, and then move the work to another point in the process using one of several techniques.

Terminator

The first and most common use of a terminator for rework is to draw a push arrow out of the process box where the defect is found and connect it to a terminator aligned properly underneath the process box where acceptable work in the process moves. A "Rework" label is applied to the arrow connected to the terminator. Figure 6.4 shows how this technique works. The terminator itself is labeled to show where the rework occurs in the process. This is usually done by writing the word "To" in the terminator followed by the label from the process box where the rework takes place. In Figure 6.4, the terminator is labeled "To Check Info Keyed."

Figure 6.5 demonstrates how to use a terminator in conjunction with a rework station as a stand-alone step in the process, and then return the work to a point to continue in the process.

By using terminators within the process flow, it is possible to move the work back in the value stream without having to draw lines that go against the direction of the main flow. This technique provides a simple way to draw the map

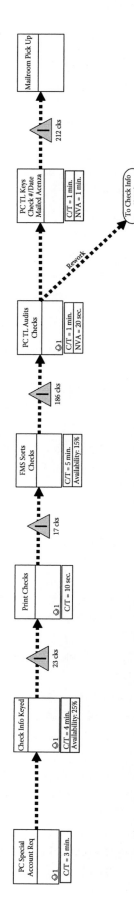

Figure 6.4   Using the terminator icon to show how rework is handled.

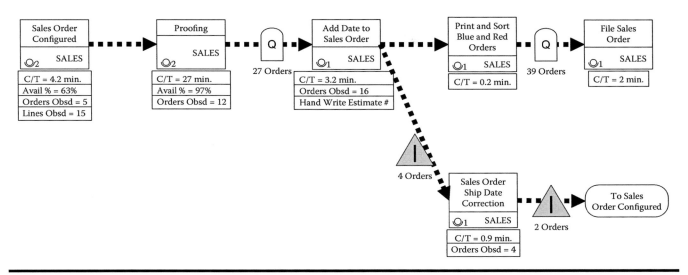

Figure 6.5   An example of a rework step in the process flow using a terminator to return the work to the correct point in the value stream.

when real-world situations such as rework occur. But you still must explain the flow to your audience. When you include situations like this in your map, the simplest way to explain them is to:

> focus on the explanation of the main flow first;
> then explain the subtasks and parallel flows;
> and then explain all rework situations last.

By isolating these flow situations until the end of the process flow discussion, the audience can grasp the big-picture details first, and then you can handle the exceptions with as little (or as much) explanation as is required. Quite often, this means taking the discussion off line so that those who understand how the flow is altered can begin working on change as soon as possible.

Traditional flowcharting uses terminators to show when a process ends, or when it is continued on another page. Terminators can be used in much the same manner with Value Stream Mapping as well. Besides using terminators to go back to a process box on a Value Stream Map, you can also use these icons to connect value streams together. It is not uncommon to find outputs from the process flow, or communication, that are inputs into other value streams and are not the main product or service being produced by the value stream. The most common occurrence of this scenario is support functions within the organization that provide data, files, drawings, material, etc., to a primary value stream of the company.

To show where these value streams tie together on a map, when the output is not the main product or service, use a terminator icon as the next step in the map, and state what value stream it goes to. By labeling the terminator through standardized wording, it becomes a very visual and yet simple way of explaining

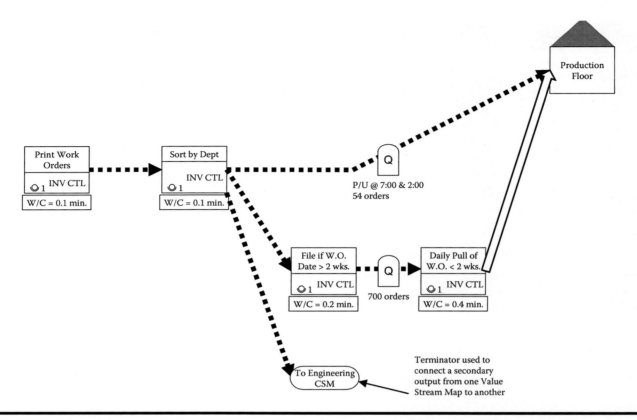

Figure 6.6   An example of how to connect multiple Value Stream Maps using terminators and labels.

to the workforce where the information, material, etc., is going. When you start the label with "To," followed by the name of the other Value Stream Map, and end the label with "CSM" (Current State Map) or "FSM" (Future State Map) the terminators that are used this way adopt the Lean methodology of simple visual controls to assist in the explanation of where to look for this continuation of information. Figure 6.6 shows how you can apply this type of labeling and the use of terminators.

The Power of Simplicity

The power and detail that can be added to Value Stream Maps through the use of terminators can be readily seen when explaining maps to employees within the process. Being able to add in rework steps and scrap process steps without having to repeat them throughout a map reduces the number of process boxes on the page, and allows the audience to focus more easily on the process flow (or lack thereof). Using terminators to move the work backwards to start through the flow again provides this much cleaner method for picturing the value stream. Moreover, by adding the use of terminators to tie multiple value streams together, you can paint a much clearer picture of the process. By doing so, you achieve the following benefits:

- Employee buy-in comes more easily.
- Brainstorming for solutions becomes simpler.
- Change can be initiated much faster.

In Chapter 7, you will discover that once flow has been documented, it must then be understood and interpreted.

Chapter 7

Interpreting and Understanding Basic Product Flow

A process cannot be understood by stopping it. Understanding must move with the flow of the process, must join it and flow with it.

Frank Herbert

Introduction

It is not enough to know how to picture flow on a Value Stream Map. When you're mapping flow, you must understand what is included in each process step of the value stream. To accurately draw a Value Stream Map, you need to show and explain what happens within each process box and how the material or work-in-process moves from step to step.

Showing Where Flow Starts and Ends

Each process box should represent where flow starts and when it stops. The push or pull arrows in between the process boxes represent the movement between steps. When observing the value stream in operation, you should pay close attention to each task within a perceived step so that you can draw a true depiction of the process. When the first operator (or employee) begins to apply value-added or non-value-added (NVA) activity to the product, that is the first step of work-in-process (or service). When the last employee in the process step sets the work down or stops working after adding value or performing non-value-added activity, that is when the process step ends. A label should be added to the process box that accurately describes the activity taking place within this process step. Figure 7.1 illustrates.

When working with production value streams, identifying the starting and ending tasks in a process step is relatively easy to do through direct observation.

Identifying what is within a Process Step

(a) Initial task (when work is initiated)
(b) Second task performed without interruption
(c) Third task performed without interruption
(d) Etc.
(e) Etc.
(f) Final task performed without interruption

Process Step Name

Figure 7.1 Dissecting the concept of "from the time flow starts until the moment that flow stops."

By watching the process flow in this type of setting, you can determine when work enters the process step and when it exits. Watching the way work moves into and out of each process step also provides great insight into how the value stream flows.

The Traditional Mindset: Pushing Work

In traditional manufacturing organizations, production work is usually performed according to schedules or forecasts. Each step of the process works independently at the pace of the operator. Each operator's focus is solely on the individual goals and demands of the single step in which he or she works. This mindset is referred to as "island mentality." What happens elsewhere in the value stream has no bearing on how or when an operator works within this island mentality.

When work is "pushed" onto the next step in a value stream in this manner, it is represented on a Value Stream Map with a **push arrow**.

At the beginning of each process step, where pushes occur, is where most large piles of inventory, or bottlenecks, appear. The work is pushed forward and piles up without regard to what is happening downstream. Figure 7.2 illustrates the process flow of a portion of a Current State Map, where material is pushed through the value stream, and accurate and descriptive labels have been applied to the process boxes.

The Lean Concept of Pull Systems

In a Lean organization, material is controlled throughout the value stream. Work is only performed and moved on to the next step in the process when the customer (i.e., the ultimate customer, whether external or internal) requests it. To control this movement of material and the associated work, every effort is made to set up the value stream to *pull* the work whenever possible. When work is

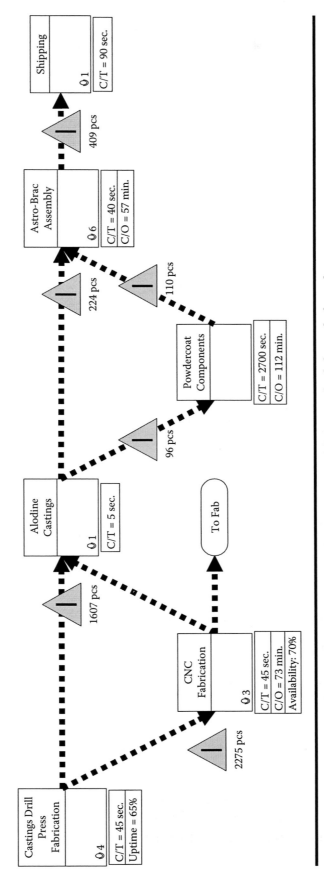

Figure 7.2 The process flow of a Current State Map showing material being pushed through the value stream.

completed and delivered to the customer when requested, this "pull" is shown with a **pull arrow** on the Value Stream Map.

Figure 7.3 provides an example of how to show a pull within a Current State Map. Although it is not uncommon to see a majority of pull arrows on a Future State Map, the expectation on Current State Maps is to see a mixture of pushes and pulls.

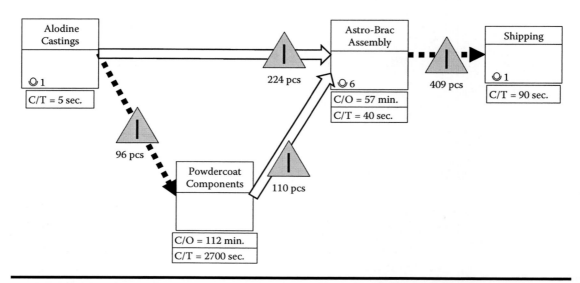

Figure 7.3   Current-state process flow showing material being pulled through a value stream.

Controlling Material When Pull Is Not Possible

When it is not possible to create a pull, a Lean company will create a system for controlling the materials throughout the process. The most common form of controlling inventory is with **FIFO lanes**. FIFO (First In, First Out) relies on a controlled area, where material is most often moved into a lane at one end and pulled out at the next process step at the other end of the lane in order to always use the oldest material first. The controls are based on the maximum number of pieces of work allowed in the lane at one time.

When the maximum is reached, a signal tells the process step feeding the FIFO lane to stop producing and wait until there is room to add more work. If the lane remains full for too long, this should be interpreted as a signal of a potential problem downstream, and the next step in the process should be looked at to see if a problem exists at this point or beyond. Figure 7.4 shows how a FIFO lane is drawn and used in the future state.

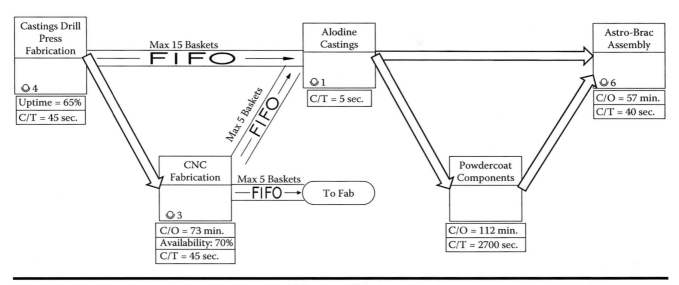

Figure 7.4   A future-state process flow using FIFO to control the flow of materials.

Calculating Customer Demand and Takt Time

As you develop a Current State Map for a value stream, one basic piece of information that you should include as early as possible in the mapping process is the calculation of *Takt time*. *Takt* is a German word meaning "beat": it is the speed or pace that a value stream must operate at to meet customer demand. The earlier you can calculate Takt time, the better, because it provides great insight into what customers' expectations are, and it allows for better observations during the initial mapping process.

Takt time is calculated using the following formula:

$$\text{Takt Time} = \frac{\text{Net available time for identified time period}}{\text{Customer demand for the same time period}}$$

Net available is defined as the time that the doors are open and the value stream is operating. For example, if the value stream does not start up until after the start of a shift meeting, you should not include the time allowed for the meeting. Likewise, if the process stops at breaks and/or lunch, you should also exclude the time taken for those breaks or lunch. Also, the net available time should not include cleanup time or time set aside at the end of shifts for meetings or other purposes.

Customer demand during the same period is the amount of product, components, etc., that the value stream's customer (either external or internal) requires during the same time frame used to calculate net available time. The most common time frame used for this calculation is a daily snapshot of time. When mapping, you should start with whatever available demand data that is accessible,

---

Example 7.1: Takt Time Using a Five-Day Work Week

Assembly process in an electronics component manufacturing center. *Net time available* in the value stream calculation:

> One 8-h. shift daily Monday through Friday 8:00 a.m. to 4:30 p.m.
> Two 15-min. breaks each day where all processes stop
> 30-min. unpaid lunch
> 15-min. shift startup meeting
> 15-min. cleanup at end of shift

Net time available = 480 min. daily (lunch unpaid: excluded from gross available time)

Less	30 min. for breaks
Less	15 min. for shift startup meeting
Less	15 min. for shift cleanup
Equals	**420 min. net time available per day in the value stream**

Customer demand during the same period calculation
Sales data available from sales department:
Last quarter sales for product family mapped = 218,400 pcs

Customer demand = 218,400 pcs ÷ 13 weeks = 16,800 pcs per week
16,800 pcs ÷ 5 days = **3,360 pcs per day**
Takt time = 420 min. ÷ 3,360 pcs = 0.125 min. or 7.5 sec. per piece
Takt time = 7.5 sec.

Based on this Takt time, the production cell must complete one piece and have it ready to ship on the average of every 7.5 sec. This does not mean the cell must build a piece in 7.5 sec.; instead, it means that one must be completed on the *average* of every 7.5 sec.

---

and then reduce or expand it to a daily requirement. While the current day, week, or month is the preferred snapshot in time, often the only accessible data is historical. Examples 7.1 and 7.2 illustrate the concept.

In the two examples shown, there is a 0.1-sec. difference in the Takt time, even though there is a 40-h. work week in both examples and the amount required is identical. The difference in Takt is created by differences in the time removed for breaks, shift startup, and shift-end activities.

If you know this type of information before you walk the process and map it, that knowledge gives you insight into how the process should be flowing to meet customer demand. From this information, it is possible to quickly identify where constraints in the process exist that need attention in order to create flow.

When you're mapping, you should calculate Takt time even when you're working with transactional value streams. Although the Takt time calculated for some transactional value streams may appear to have no useful meaning at the

---

Example 7.2: Takt Time Using a Four-Day Work Week

Assembly process in an electronics component manufacturing center. *Net time available* in the value stream calculation:

> One 10-h. shift daily Monday through Thursday 6:30 a.m. to 5:00 p.m.
> Two 20-min. breaks each day where all processes stop
> 30-min. unpaid lunch
> 15-min. shift startup meeting
> 15-min. cleanup at end of shift

Net time available = 2,400 min. weekly (lunch unpaid: excluded from gross available time)

Less	160 min. for breaks	
Less	60 min. for shift startup meeting	
Less	60 min. for shift cleanup	
Equals	2,120 min. available per week or	
	530 min. net time available per day in the value stream	

Customer demand during the same period calculation:
> Sales data available from sales department:
> Last quarter sales for product family mapped = 218,400 pcs

Customer demand = 218,400 pcs ÷ 13 weeks = 16,800 pcs per week
16,800 pcs ÷ 4 days = **4,200 pcs per day**
Takt time = 530 min. ÷ 4,200 pcs = 0.126 min. or 7.6 sec. per piece
Takt time = 7.6 sec.

Based on this Takt time, the production cell must complete one piece and have it ready to ship on the average of every 7.6 sec. This does not mean the cell must build a piece in 7.6 sec.; instead, it means that one must be completed on the *average* of every 7.6 sec.

---

time it is calculated, you should nevertheless conduct the exercise and post the Takt time on the Value Stream Maps. (An in-depth discussion of how to use Takt in these transactional settings is provided in Chapter 9.)

Showing Inventory

Throughout the value stream, inventory will exist that needs to be represented on the map. To show this inventory, Value Stream Mapping uses the **inventory** icon. This icon is a triangle with an "I" in it.

Anywhere you see inventory sitting in the value stream, you should use this icon to identify the material, components, parts, and/or finished goods. Place this icon on the Value Stream Map directly on, or near, a push arrow or pull arrow. You should never place the icon inside, above, or below a process box, because the placement of the inventory is used to show process lead time. When mapping, you need to keep inventory separate from the process boxes because there is data associated with the process step that has a different meaning from the process lead time.

As you walk the value stream and see inventory, you should physically count all inventory associated with the product or product family you are mapping. Although counting finished goods is a straightforward concept, it becomes much more difficult when counting parts and raw materials. Therefore, you must determine what to count from the raw material warehouse to the final assembly step in the process.

Although there is no hard-and-fast rule about how to count parts and material, there are some strong suggestions about how to tackle this issue. When looking at raw material, it is recommended, as a general rule, that you exclude small, very low-cost commodity parts (such as screws, washers, rivets, etc.). The most expensive material, or the material that is transformed into a major component in the product, can be used to calculate inventory levels. Another way is to count the total inventory for each raw material and then adjust for what percentage of the material is estimated to be used for the specific product or product family. For sheet or roll stock, it is important to determine how many parts can be manufactured from a sheet or from a foot of roll stock, etc. Once this adjustment has been made, you can add all the counts from each part, and then include the total averaged over the number of parts included in the count. Example 7.3 illustrates this approach.

Another way to count "parts" when dealing with raw materials is to count only the most expensive part or the main part, such as a housing, case, shaft, etc. Regardless of the method you select for counting the raw materials, the counts will be close enough for Value Stream Mapping. This "close enough" concept is based on the general rule that if the data collected for a map is 70% accurate, you are close enough to get started.

As you count inventory between steps in the value stream during the mapping process, you can document it on the map as a single inventory icon with a total count, or you can show it as multiple icons if the inventory is physically located at different locations within the facility. Figure 7.5 demonstrates the use of inventory icons as single icons between process boxes and multiple icons representing various locations for the inventory.

As you count inventory on the floor while you're walking a process, it is recommended that you record the physical count on your map. Once you have completed the initial mapping exercise to capture the process flow, your mapping team can then use the daily customer demand to calculate how many days'

Example 7.3: Counting Raw Materials Using All Components

If the total number of components used in a product is five (excluding screws and washers), and one part is stamped from a 10 × 100-ft. roll of sheet aluminum, the amount of inventory present would be calculated as follows:

Part A: stamped from the sheet aluminum at the rate of 10 parts per ft. (75% of the two rolls present is estimated to be used for the product being mapped)

Part B: 80 cartons of 12 parts each

Part C: two locations of parts; one location has 410 units, and the other has 615

Part D: one rack with 1080 pieces

Part E: two trays with 550 motors each

Totaling all parts:

2 rolls × 100′ × 75% × 10 parts per ft. = 1,500 parts of Part A

80 cartons × 12 each = 960 parts of Part B

410 units + 615 units = 1,025 parts of Part C

1 rack × 1,080 pieces = 1,080 parts of Part D

2 trays × 550 motors = 1,100 parts of Part E

Total number of parts = 5,665

Divided by 5 parts = 1,133 units of inventory

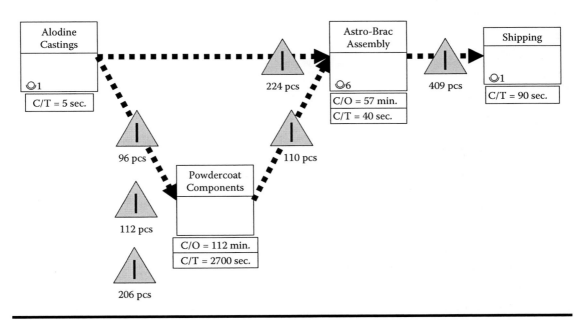

Figure 7.5   Process flow showing areas within the value stream where inventory exists in a single location, as well as an area where inventory is stored in multiple locations.

> ### Example 7.4: Calculating Inventory as a Unit of Time
>
> Inventory counted between process step A and process step B = 100 pieces
> Daily customer demand (same number used to calculate Takt) = 50 pieces
> 100 pieces of inventory ÷ 50 pieces demanded each day = **2.0 days of inventory**

worth of inventory is in between each step of the value stream. Example 7.4 shows how to calculate inventory as a unit of time:

This inventory amount, calculated in days, can then be added beneath the physical count shown under the inventory icon. Figure 7.6 shows the updated map with the additional information under the inventory icons.

By adding together all of the days' worth of inventory shown in the value stream, you can see the amount of time before the value stream will run out of parts if no new materials are added to the beginning of the process. This total number of days is also known as the *process lead time*. (A detailed discussion of process lead time is provided in Chapter 12.)

Capturing Cycle Time

> *The average elapsed time from the moment one good piece is completed until the moment the next good piece is completed.*

The final piece of information that needs to be captured as you document the process flow of the value stream is the cycle time for each of the documented

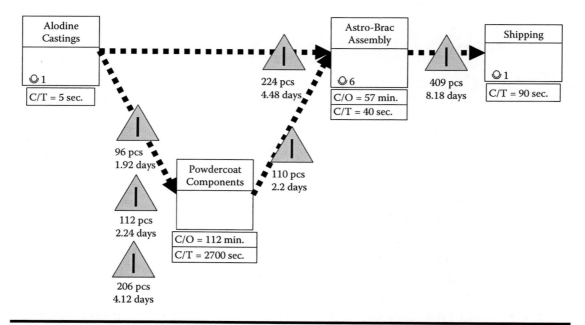

Figure 7.6   Showing inventory amounts and how long it will last based upon current customer demand.

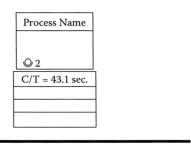

Figure 7.7   Documenting cycle time on a Value Stream Map.

process steps. Figure 7.7 illustrates how to show cycle time on a Value Stream Map. Cycle time is measured at the last process step in the value stream, and it shows how often one acceptable unit of product can be completed and provided to the customer. Within the value stream, cycle time is used to show how often one unit of "good" work-in-process is completed and moved to the next process step in the value stream.

Cycle time is perhaps the single most important piece of data that is captured in Value Stream Mapping. From this single piece of information associated with process steps throughout the value stream, you can see how the production process flows at the most basic of levels. Obviously, there are other things that happen throughout the value stream that affect this flow. But with just this one piece of information shown and compared to the Takt time, it is possible to see if there is an opportunity to meet customer demand.

There are numerous other pieces of information and data that can be captured and added to the map. However, to create a map with the basic information required to understand what is going on within the value stream, you must capture cycle times and apply them to data boxes underneath each process box on the map. The data box is located directly underneath the process box, and it can contain any information that you believe is important to the process.

When capturing cycle time, you and your mapping team should rely on actual observations and simple time studies, *not* on historical or system times, or on manufacturer (user manual) times on equipment. The amount of observation time required to determine cycle time depends on the number of repetitions you observe. However, if you observe 20–30 units (or 10–20 min. of observation time), that will usually provide adequate information. Starting a stopwatch and letting it run for a predetermined amount of time while counting the number of units of good work completed at the process step is the preferred method for establishing cycle time. At the conclusion of the predetermined time, divide the time by the number of units, and then insert this average cycle time into the data box using the abbreviation "C/T =" followed by the calculated time.

It is important to remember that cycle time is based on good work being completed at the process step observed. If defects are being created at the process step observed, do not include them in the count of units. Instead, you should also add this additional information pertaining to defects as a percentage into the data box, using the label "Defects =" followed by the percentage of defects observed. Example 7.5 illustrates the concept.

To document cycle times in an effective and efficient manner, if you are mapping as part of a team, you can assign one mapper to remain at a process step to capture cycle time; that person can then catch up with the team further along in

---

Example 7.5: Capturing Cycle Time and Defects

During a 10-min. observation at one step in the value stream, 85 good units of work were observed, and 15 defects were observed.
Cycle time is calculated as 10 min. × 60 sec. = 600 sec.
600 sec. ÷ 85 good units = **7.06-sec. cycle time**

Defect rate is calculated as 15 defects ÷ 100 total units (i.e., 15 defects + 85 good units)
15 defects ÷ 100 total units = **15% defect rate**

---

the value stream. "Leap frogging" in this manner provides a fast way to keep the process flow documentation moving without having to slow down or come back after the fact to capture cycle times.

Alternatively, if you are mapping alone, or if you prefer that your mapping team stay together, you can document the entire value stream process flow, and then team members can go back into the process steps documented and complete the cycle time observations.

In the event that a value stream (or a process step within a value stream) is not operating when the mapping is occurring, it is best for you to return when the process is functioning. If this is not possible, there are two possible options for documenting the cycle times:

Set up a test run at the process step(s) not operating at a long enough duration to determine cycle time.

Through a question-and-answer session with operators, estimate the cycle time, and then use the estimate with a notation that shows an estimate was used.

Summarizing Basic Process Flow

To provide a basic picture of the process flow, it is important to capture the flow and draw it in such a way that any audience can understand the value stream. To successfully complete this process flow documentation exercise, you must define each process step in the value stream, and then you must understand and document whether material is being *pushed* or *pulled* through the process. You should calculate Takt time before going out into the value stream to document, so that you can be looking for possible constraint points. Finally, you must capture cycle times for each process box on your map and then add them to the data boxes underneath each process box. With this information in hand, you will be well on your way to providing a clear picture of the value stream to any audience.

Case Study in a Manufacturing Environment

Current State Map
Case Study: Pelco Products, Inc.
Manufacturing company
The Current State Map shown in Figure 7.8 is a real-world manufacturing value stream from Pelco Products, Inc. Pelco manufactures traffic signal hardware, ornamental lighting, and utility hardware. The Astro-Brac product family was mapped by a Lean project team as a first attempt at using Value Stream Mapping as a tool to initiate change. This Current State Map provided critical information to the team concerning the amount of inventory throughout the process, pinpointed bottlenecks and unbalanced flow issues, as well as highlighted multiple problems associated with excessive amounts of communication. The results of the Pelco team's Value Stream Mapping efforts and associated Lean improvements are discussed in Chapter 16.

In Chapter 8, you will learn what role data needs to play in implementing Lean and specifically how it is used in mapping manufacturing processes.

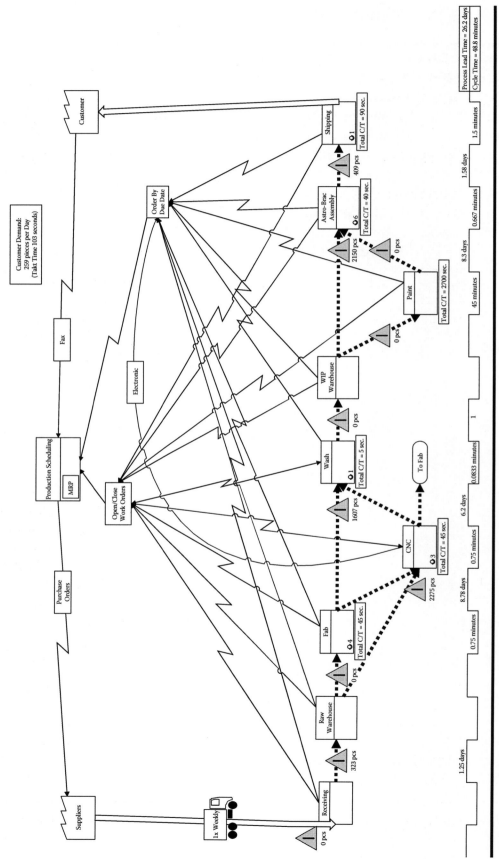

Figure 7.8 *Actual* Current State Map from Pelco Products, Inc. (manufacturing company.)

Chapter 8

Utilizing Data in Manufacturing
How to Add Power to Your Map with Facts

It is a capital mistake to theorize before one has data. Insensibly one begins to twist facts to suit theories, instead of theories to suit facts.

Sir Arthur Conan Doyle

Introduction

Even though many quality- and process-improvement practitioners continue to discount Lean as a serious continuous improvement discipline, Lean has gained ground in many industries and sectors outside of the manufacturing world. The major complaint registered by the misinformed is that Lean does not use data as a basis for process change, but instead relies on the opinions of the workforce. However, these statements could not be further from the truth. Value Stream Mapping is the perfect argument for Lean practitioners to show where data comes into play, how it is collected quickly and efficiently, and how Lean project action plans are created from this data. Mappers who learn to collect available data without the need to stop and analyze on the spot, but instead wait until a first pass at a Current State Map is complete, can show the power of Lean data to any audience.

As you gain experience walking the manufacturing value stream and capturing the process flow, looking for data becomes easier. Looking for process steps where changeovers exist, where equipment is shared or breaks down, or where defects are generated becomes second nature over time. Repetition is the key to recognizing each of these situations. Until you gain this experience, you should continually ask questions regarding each of these situations: questions should be part of your standardized mapping process at each and every step in the value stream.

When Value Stream Mapping in a manufacturing environment, there are five pieces of information that you should review at every process step:

The number of operators
The cycle time
Changeover time
Uptime (showing the reliability of your equipment)
Availability of equipment (shared equipment)

The number of operators at each step of the process should be captured and entered into the process box. In an effort to ensure that the other four data points are reviewed, it is recommended that underneath each process box on the Current State Map, a data box with each of these four data point labels should be added as the first pass of the process flow is drawn, as shown here.

Process Name
C/T =
C/O =
U/T =
Avail:

If you can quickly capture the data, you can add the information immediately. If not, as the mapping team reviews and consolidates its work into a single or "clean" map of the process flow, then you can assign some team members to go back out into the value stream to observe and collect the necessary information. This chapter describes each of these five pieces of critical information in more detail.

Record the Number of Operators for Each Process

Record the actual number of operators observed within a single step of the value stream at the time a process step is documented, regardless of what they are doing or whether they are budgeted or assigned to the process step or value stream.

As you walk the process and document each process step on the page, the first piece of information that you should add at each step is the number of operators you observe in the process. The number of operators, or employees, documented on a Current State Map is the *actual* number you see at the time you are drawing the process flow of the map.

There is no *portion* of an employee, or full-time-equivalent (FTE), when you map using VSM. The amount of operators is not what is *assigned* or *budgeted* to perform the task, but the *actual* number of employees you see within the process step at the time you are mapping. Document this number by placing the **operator** icon with the number of employees you observed inside the process box, as indicated below.

This single piece of information may create more discussion and debate than anything else you draw on a Current State Map. Whether you see no employee in the area or you see ten, the truth will emerge. If there are five employees assigned to a process step, but you see only two during your mapping exercise, that will start a discussion. If there are ten employees in the area instead of the assigned five, that will start a discussion. This is exactly what is needed for project teams to identify problems and opportunities for improvement.

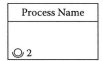

Sometimes, there is an explanation that is valid, such as when employees are floating within the value stream when they have no work to complete at a particular time. At other times, though, the answer is simple: management moved personnel to expedite an order or clear a bottleneck at a given point in the value stream—usually at the expense of another portion of the process.

By documenting operators in the Current State Map, you (or your mapping team) have the power to demonstrate where the misuse of the workforce hinders flow and creates imbalances in production. This piece of information—although very simple and basic—is extremely powerful and important to the success of a Value Stream Mapping exercise.

Record the Cycle Time of Each Process Step

The cycle time is the average elapsed time from the moment one good piece is completed until the moment the next good piece is completed.

The concept of cycle time is illustrated in Figure 8.1.

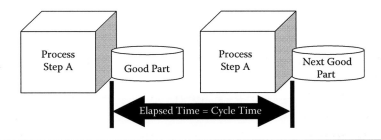

Figure 8.1   Cycle time is the elapsed time from one good piece of work to the next good piece.

As stated in Chapter 7, cycle time is perhaps the single most important piece of data that is captured in Value Stream Mapping. From this single piece of information associated with process steps throughout the value stream, it is possible to see how the production process flows at the most basic of levels. Obviously, there are other things that happen throughout the value stream that affect this flow. But with just this one piece of information shown and compared with the Takt time, it is possible to see if there is an opportunity to meet customer demand. (For a complete explanation of the concept and how to capture and report cycle time, refer to Chapter 7.)

Record the Changeover Time from One Process to Another

Changeover time is the elapsed time from the moment the last good piece of one product run is completed to the moment that the first good piece of a different product is completed.

The concept of changeover time is illustrated in Figure 8.2.

"Good piece to good piece": this simple statement should be explained to and comprehended by all employees, including operators, supervisors, managers, and engineers. It is unfortunate that many employees do not understand that changeover time is more than just the time it takes to change out a blade, bit, die, etc. One of the greatest opportunities for improvement for many manufacturers is with changeovers. This is why capturing and reporting accurate changeover time (or C/O, as it is commonly labeled in the data box) is so important in Value Stream Mapping.

Process Name
C/T =
C/O = 10 min.
U/T =
Avail:

There are many instances where a changeover should be reported, but none are "scheduled" during the allotted mapping exercise time. The tendency of many mapping teams is to hold a mapping session with operators in the value stream and estimate this changeover time. This may be the least accurate piece of information that you can estimate from this type of session. Many operators historically greatly under- or overestimate changeover time, depending on the situation explained. Many operators will underestimate because they think that the time is just what it takes to change out the tooling. However, the studies of Shigeo Shingo (explained in his book *Single Minute Exchange of Dies*) show that this equates to only about 5% of the actual changeover time if no work to reduce this time has been performed. Other operators will greatly *pad* the time reported because they think this will allow them adequate time to perform these duties in the future.

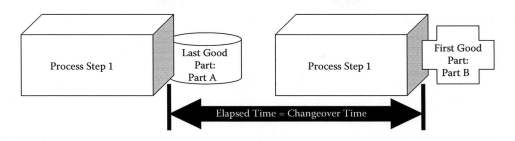

Figure 8.2   Changeover time includes not just the time it takes to make the change, but all the time from the last good piece from the previous run to the first good piece of work from the new run.

In other words, there can be too great a variance, and the confidence level of the audience may not accept what is reported through estimations. Although this may be the only way to start discussions about an individual process step, you should never move on without flagging the data line in some form such as placing an "E" (for "estimate") in front of the "C/O =" label and highlighting it or placing a cloud around the line to remind the team that this number is an estimate. You should determine when the next changeover is scheduled and ensure that there is someone associated with the mapping exercise at the process step to observe and capture accurate actual data.

To accurately capture changeover time, you should be physically located at the process step in time to start the clock at the moment the last good (i.e., defect-free) piece of work is completed. The clock should be stopped at the moment the first good piece of the next product is completed. In the event that the changeover time is exceptionally long (e.g., greater than one hour), you may want to use the concepts of Shingo, and capture split times for the various parts of the changeover. From this additional data, Lean improvement teams can get a jump start on attacking the waste in the changeover.

When changeovers occur, the changeover time within one process step will delay delivery of parts or work-in-process to the next step in the process by the time it takes to complete the changeover. When changeover time is relatively small, this may not be an issue that requires the inventory time value on the Value Stream Map to be adjusted. However, if the changeover time is unusually long, you should adjust the time value of the inventory shown in the value stream. The most common form of making this adjustment is to add the changeover time to the inventory immediately in front of the process step where the changeover occurs.

Record Uptime, or the Reliability of Equipment

Uptime is the percentage of time that a piece of equipment works properly when the operator uses it for the prescribed task.

The fourth piece of information mappers look for is uptime, or reliability of equipment. This data is generally labeled in the data box with the symbol U/T. When searching for genuine uptime, the question you should ask operators is: *"What percentage of the time when you need this particular piece of equipment does it actually work as intended?"* When capturing this information (which is displayed as a percentage), you should generally start with the historical knowledge of the operator(s), and then search for additional information to validate this data.

Process Name
C/T =
C/O =
U/T = 10%
Avail:

The issue of equipment uptime can be a difficult concept for operators to grasp, if they have never previously been exposed to it. Asking someone how often a piece of equipment works or doesn't work when he or she walks up to use it can be a confusing question for many people. Typically, operators want to discuss the percentage of the total time (i.e., the total time that the doors are open and the lights are on), rather than the percentage of time that equipment does or does not work.

When searching for supporting data, there is rarely anything found unless a log is kept of the equipment that documents every single time the machine is used. This is the primary reason why you should start with the "tribal" knowledge of the operator. To validate the percentage reported in the data box, you can use a simple log sheet and make tic marks to show the number of times the equipment works and the number of times it does not work, as shown in Figure 8.3.

Uptime Log Sheet	
Works	Doesn't Work
̶I̶H̶L̶ ̶I̶H̶L̶ III	III

Figure 8.3 Example of a simple uptime log sheet.

The concept of "does not work" should be explained to the operator as "when you activate the machine, it does not work *properly.*" This could mean that the maintenance department needs to be called in, or it could mean that the operator must stop the task at hand and adjust or repair the machine. By capturing this information on a log sheet for as little as one shift, you can find extremely useful information.

For many organizations, equipment reliability is a hidden opportunity. Companies that do not want to invest capital dollars in new equipment have a tendency to give a mandate to operators and the maintenance staff to keep existing equipment running … period. Over time, this mandate becomes a process of using bubble gum and baling wire. Operators accept equipment failure as just a part of the process, without realizing the hidden cost of downtime. Value Stream Maps can become a very useful tool in combating this mentality. When you show management the cost of downtime in lost labor dollars and repair costs, management and owners alike can make informed decisions about replacing equipment, with the long-term goals of Lean as the guiding principle.

Uptime will have an effect on the performance of the value stream at the step in the process where the equipment problems exist. The most common problem (similar to what is experienced with long changeovers) is the creation of bottlenecks immediately before the affected process step. The impact on the time value of this inventory is based on the uptime percentage of the equipment. For example, if the uptime of a machine is 85%, then the inventory time value immediately before this step in the value stream would be the time value of the inventory divided by the uptime of the equipment. In other words, if the inventory prior to the process step in this example was 1 day, then the adjusted time value would be:

$$1 \text{ day} \div 0.85 = 1.18 \text{ days of inventory.}$$

Additionally, any observer watching this step in the process might expect the average cycle time of the process step to also be affected in the same manner. This situation requires you and your mapping team to review your data and ensure that the cycle time you are calculating and reporting includes this equipment reliability issue. If there was no occurrence of equipment failure when the cycle time was calculated in the example above, the cycle time would also need to be divided by the uptime to create an updated cycle time approximately (in this example) 17.6% longer.

Record the Availability of Equipment

> The availability of equipment (AOE) is the percentage of time that a piece of equipment shared between two or more value streams is available for production of parts in the value stream being mapped.

The final piece of basic data collected in manufacturing value streams is the availability of equipment, represented in the data box as "Avail." This data is important for any process step that uses equipment. When there is no equipment, you can omit this line, or you can simply report it as 100%.

Process Name
C/T =
C/O =
U/T =
Avail: 10%

The purpose of this data point is to show where equipment is shared between value streams and what impact that sharing has on the performance of the value stream being mapped. When you present this information for each process step you enable operators, managers and project teams to "see" the impact of what happens when equipment is shared among production lines or cells. Because proper timing of parts production and the arrival of those parts at the next step in the process are critical to the success of a value stream, understanding the effect of this type of equipment use is very beneficial.

For example, if a machine is shared among three separate products, and one product that is included in the value stream being mapped has this machine available for parts production for 5 hours each week, then the availability of the equipment is 12.5%. The challenge facing schedulers, expeditors, and managers is to determine how they can best utilize these 5 hours to always have parts available for the next step in the value stream.

Determining the amount of availability is straightforward:

- Review production logs or schedules for some period of time.
- Then calculate the percentage of time that the equipment is used for the selected value stream.
- Do not adjust for any maintenance or other activity (or inactivity) that may present itself in the logs or schedules.

Figure 8.4 shows an example.

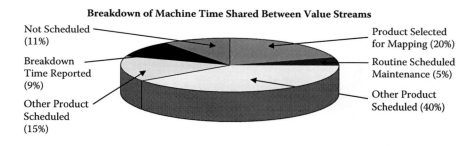

Breakdown of Machine Time Shared Between Value Streams

Not Scheduled (11%)

Breakdown Time Reported (9%)

Other Product Scheduled (15%)

Product Selected for Mapping (20%)

Routine Scheduled Maintenance (5%)

Other Product Scheduled (40%)

Figure 8.4 By analyzing production schedules in the scheduling office and production logs at the equipment, usage for the selected machine was reported as shown in the given pie chart. The product being mapped accounted for 20% of machine time. Therefore, the availability equals 20%.

When equipment is not shared among different product families, availability is 100%, and you should report it this way even if there are breakdown issues, maintenance time requirements, etc. Evaluating these opportunities takes on an entirely new life and direction for the Lean project team focusing on change. Until such time as equipment is dedicated to a single value stream you should calculate equipment availability in this manner, because the time element that you are attempting to explain to your audience is the net time available to the value stream.

Record Work Content and Non-Value-Added Time

Work content is the total amount of actual value-added and non-value-added labor time associated with a process.

In addition to the four basic pieces of data captured in data boxes, another useful piece of information is work content (sometimes called *labor content*). Work content is the actual physical labor associated with a process step. This content includes both value-added and non-value-added labor.

Work content is sometimes confused with cycle time, so it is important that you explain to operators and audiences very clearly and precisely the difference between the two concepts. Although cycle time is *not* concerned with the number of employees working the process step, work content *adds together* the labor time used by each employee working within the process step.

Early in the process improvement journey, most effort is focused on reducing cycle times. Once progress has been made in this area, project teams shift their focus toward the actual amount of labor being applied to the value stream. Once this shift occurs, you should begin adding work content to your maps, labeled as W/C, in the data box, as shown here.

Process Name
◎ 2
C/T =
C/O =
U/T =
Avail:
W/C = 10.2 min.
NVA = 0.7 min.

Along with this information, you may also include any non-value-added time observed and enter it on another line labeled NVA. This non-value-added time becomes an immediate focus of project teams as they look for ways to remove waste from the value stream. Figure 8.5 shows two examples of how to record work content.

Record the Defect Rate

A defect is a unit of work that is scrapped or reworked within any step of the value stream.

One additional data point that you should collect during the process flow portion of the mapping exercise is defect rates. Shown in the data box as "defects" and

Two Examples of Work Content

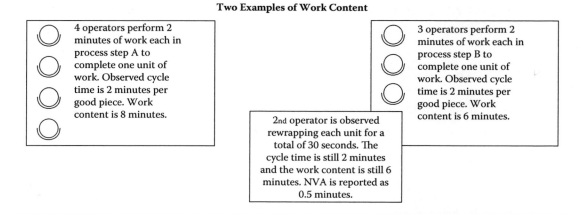

4 operators perform 2 minutes of work each in process step A to complete one unit of work. Observed cycle time is 2 minutes per good piece. Work content is 8 minutes.

3 operators perform 2 minutes of work each in process step B to complete one unit of work. Observed cycle time is 2 minutes per good piece. Work content is 6 minutes.

2nd operator is observed rewrapping each unit for a total of 30 seconds. The cycle time is still 2 minutes and the work content is still 6 minutes. NVA is reported as 0.5 minutes.

Figure 8.5   It is possible to record work content as a single number, or the data collected can be reported as work content (value-added time) and non-value-added time.

reported as a percentage, this piece of information shows where the process flow is slowed down by quality problems.

Process Name
C/T =
C/O =
U/T =
Avail:
W/C =
NVA =
Defect = 12%

The defect rate is calculated by dividing the *number of units work scrapped or reworked* by the *total number of units processed* through the process step. Although many companies track quality numbers in great detail and can provide the defect rate for each step of the process, there are just as many organizations that either do not track defects at all or, for any number of reasons, report them inaccurately.

Even if defective units of work-in-process are reworked, value is added, and they are moved on in the value stream, *the defect still occurred*. Therefore, you should record them, and you should initiate corrective action to eliminate the defect in the future. Unfortunately, this does not always occur. However, you can start the process of eliminating the waste of defect by capturing defect rates and reporting them on the Current State Map.

Just as uptime of equipment affects the throughput of a value stream, so do defects. The immediate impact of defects on the value stream is felt at the process step where the defect occurs. If the defect rate is relatively small, you may choose not to adjust inventory time values on your map. In the event that it is a significant defect rate, however, you should adjust the inventory time value immediately preceding the process step where the defect is reported. This is done by dividing the time value by the inverse of the defect rate. For example, suppose the amount of inventory is reported as 1 day, and the defect rate for the process step immediately following the inventory is 15%. The adjustment to the inventory time value would be

$$1 \text{ day} \div \text{inverse of the defect rate } .85 = 1.18 \text{ days}$$

Other Data You Might Want to Record on Your Map

The information discussed so far in this chapter covers the *basic* data needs and other routine sources of process data used in Value Stream Mapping; however, it is by no means the *only* data or information that may be included in data boxes. You should include anything else that you and your mapping team deem is important, as you identify it. It is always possible to go back and delete information later. But it is not always possible to remember or recapture everything a team sees over the course of a few hours to a few days.

Here are a few examples of other information that you may want to include in your data boxes:

- 5S scores from 5S system audits (see Quality Glossary at the end of the book)
- Safety risk assessment scores
- The number of pieces of paper found in the process step
- The number of components or parts used at the process step
- The room temperature (e.g., in food processing companies)

As your organization gains the experience of mapping its own value streams, other significant items of information specific to your environment will become visible. Do not overlook these opportunities. They may become an integral piece of basic information that your organization's Value Stream Mappers will collect in the future.

In Chapter 9, you will apply the tools you have learned to transactional processes.

Chapter 9

Basic Process Flow in a Transactional World

Furious activity is no substitute for understanding.

H. H. Williams

Transactional versus Manufacturing Process Flow

Much ado has been made about the differences between transactional Value Stream Mapping and manufacturing Value Stream Mapping. *Learning to See* remains the gold standard for Value Stream Mapping of manufacturing processes. Numerous books have also been written specifically about Value Stream Mapping for office and service processes, as if that were a totally different and unique concept. However, the reality is that there are very few differences when mapping, whether you are mapping a manufacturing setting or a transactional environment.

Regardless of the setting, the purpose of Value Stream Mapping is to document the current state, showing where flow occurs and where the work-in-process stops. The icons used and the amount of detail is identical. In a manufacturing setting, the process flow documents a product being built. In a transactional setting, the "product" being built is often paperwork, with the final product being reports, purchase orders, services delivered, etc. But there are also many value streams in transactional settings that are actually production processes, just like in the manufacturing world. For example, claim processing, print shop services, and laboratory testing are just a few of the value streams in transactional environments that are true "production" processes.

The actual differences in manufacturing and transactional Value Stream Mapping are few. The speed (or the lack thereof) in many transactional processes presents a challenge when you're mapping, as do extremely low-volume value streams, such as the hiring process in some companies with low turnover rates. And perhaps the greatest difference in the two settings is that many employees working in office environments multitask every day, switching from one value stream to another throughout the day in an attempt to complete all of their assigned duties as quickly as possible.

Yet in spite of these differences, the same challenge exists for Lean practitioners: how do you visually document a current state where work does not flow, employees work with the island-mentality mindset, and constraints and non-value-added activity exist throughout the value stream? When you focus on the similarities of the two environments and then find ways to address the minor differences, you can develop effective Value Stream Maps and explain them to the employees within the process.

Difference 1: Speed of Transactional Processes

Whereas most manufacturing processes move at a fairly regular and brisk pace, the challenge when you're mapping many transactional value streams is the extremely slow pace at which they operate. For example, the hiring process in many organizations takes months to complete. Add to this fact the low turnover rate experienced by some organizations, and it very quickly becomes a challenge to walk the actual process from back to front and "see" the value stream operating as you walk. With posting periods for both internal and external applicants lasting from 3 to 30 days, there are often long lag times between periods of activity in this value stream.

So how can you effectively document an extremely slow-moving value stream such as this? You would map this environment in a similar fashion to the way you would map in a manufacturing center for specialty parts being manufactured once a month, quarter, or year. Several options on how to achieve this are described in the following sections.

Option A: Map the Process by Using the Employees' Knowledge of the Process

The most common solution is to hold a mapping session with employees of the value stream in an area where the value stream operates. Use the tribal knowledge of these employees to estimate process steps' cycle times and other pertinent data. Use the built-in delays for posting times, etc., as the amount of work-in-process (i.e., inventory) that is sitting between process steps.

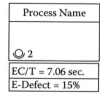

Process Name
⟲ 2
EC/T = 7.06 sec.
E-Defect = 15%

If there is a disagreement over the cycle times reported (or over other data shown in the data boxes), it may be necessary to create simple log sheets for employees to complete. From these log sheets, you can work with those persons

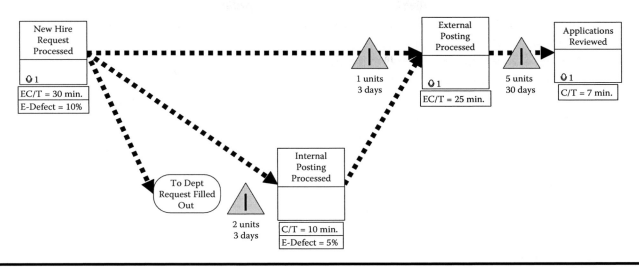

Figure 9.1   A transactional current-state process flow showing estimated cycle times and estimated defects, as well as actual cycle times.

who disagree to establish estimated data points that can be agreed on. Label the data in data boxes as "estimated," or expected, times by placing an "E" in front of the data labels, such as EC/T for estimated cycle time, as shown in Figure 9.1.

Option B: Map the Process by Working Backwards from the Last Process Step

While walking or standing in the middle of the value stream (because many transactional processes all take place in a single room or office), map as much as possible, working backwards from the last process step. When a process step is not operating, set up a simple experiment and have operators of the value stream work a sample as if it were actual work. Repeat as necessary to capture cycle time. As in Option A, use the built-in delays for posting times, etc., as the amount of work-in-process (inventory) that is sitting between process steps.

Option C: Use Both Options A and B

Use a combination of Options A and B, as necessary, to document the value stream. It may be necessary to create simple log sheets as in Option A to update cycle times and other data if some employees or management do not agree with the data.

Difference 2: Transactional Employees Sometimes Do Not See a Process

Unfortunately for mappers, many employees working within a value stream do not understand that they have a process to follow. When asked to explain the process they use, many employees respond with the statement, "I don't have a process.

I just do what it takes to get it done." This lack of understanding that everything we do in an organization has a process can frustrate even the best mapper.

The first challenge with this problem is in explaining that a process exists; it just may not be documented. This may take many different forms. However, the most common practices include demonstrating that repetitive tasks do exist or asking questions of employees to show them that they do have a process. Once you have overcome this hurdle, you will still face the challenge of convincing the employee(s) that the Current State Map that you've drawn and presented is really what their process looks like. This can be made substantially easier if the value stream has written policies or procedures to follow and use as discussion points while reviewing the map.

Difference 3: Takt Time in Transactional Value Streams

Calculating Takt time is an essential part of mapping any value stream. Even in very slow-moving, infrequently used value streams, you should go through the exercise of calculating Takt time. The resulting calculation may at first pass seem utterly ridiculous and appear to have no meaning.

For example, in a government permitting office, there is a value stream that processes applications for building hydroelectric dams. Anecdotal data suggests that this permitting value stream currently takes more than 4.5 months to approve a single permit. During the past year, four applications were received and processed. As water resources throughout the western United States become scarce, it is expected that this number will increase, yet no one knows by how much. While mapping the current state, the mapper calculated Takt time as follows: 2,080 hours of net available time divided by 2 applications equals a Takt time of 520 hours, or 3.1 months.

To the mapper, this number seemed absolutely useless. However, as he was capturing cycle times and work-in-process (inventory) levels, he recognized that the only employee in the permit office who conducted part of the background and environmental checks was a regional employee who only worked in this office one week every four months. The employee was also responsible for conducting background checks and investigations for three other value streams. Very quickly, the mapper recognized that if a single step of the value stream could not be completed due to a constraint that held applications for up to four months at a time, this value stream was in trouble. There was no way to work to the pace of the customer, never mind the expectations of the customer.

Although Takt time may have little meaning when looking at the value stream on the surface, it may be a valuable tool in explaining to employees working at a single step within the value stream why they continue to face an ever-growing backlog of work. The smart approach is to calculate Takt time, document it on the Current State Map, and then use it if and only when necessary. Recognizing when to use one of these tools is the critical component. Trying to use a tool such as Takt when it makes no sense can only diminish the perceived skills of the mapper in the employees' eyes.

Difference 4: Work Queues versus Piles of Inventory

The fourth and perhaps the most difficult difference to understand is the concept of queues versus piles. In the manufacturing world, inventory is often moved from workstation to workstation in an uncontrolled manner. These piles of inventory are documented on the Value Stream Map as a triangle with quantity and "day value" listed underneath. This situation also occurs in transactional settings. However, there is another way of moving work-in-process in transactional worlds that makes it somewhat unique.

Work queues appear regularly in transactional processes. These queues are situations where the work is placed in a pile, inbox, folder, etc., and are worked on a regular schedule by the employees operating the value stream. Typical scenarios of this type are working things "once a week," or "Tuesday and Thursday afternoon after lunch." These work times also typically include the amount of time set aside to do the work, such as 30 minutes, 1 hour, or all afternoon.

To show this difference in how work is held and released from the queue, Value Stream Mapping uses the **queue** icon.

This icon differentiates it from piles of inventory and shows the audience that the work is processed at certain times. By adding above or beneath the quantity the work time(s) of the queue, the audience can easily understand how, when, and what effect this queue has on the flow of the value stream. Figure 9.2 demonstrates how a queue is used in a typical transactional value stream.

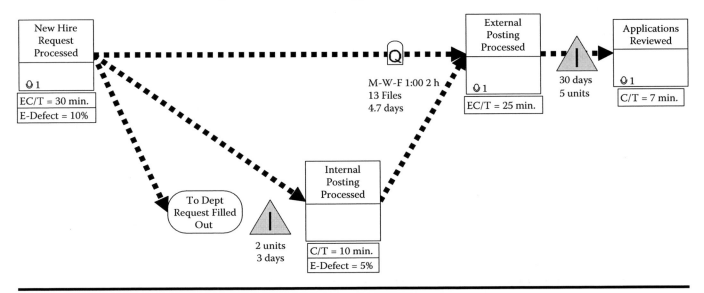

Figure 9.2   How a queue is used in a typical transactional value stream.

Example 9.1

A queue is worked every Monday, Wednesday, and Friday from 1:00 p.m. to 3:00 p.m. When the current state was mapped, there were 13 files in the queue. The process step following the queue has an observed cycle time of 25 min. To calculate the time value in days of the queue:

13 files × 25 min. (cycle time) = 325 min. of work

325 min. of work ÷ 120 min. allotted = 2.7 days to complete

2.7 days to complete + 2 days not working queue = **4.7 total days**

When looking at the example shown in Figure 9.2, notice that piles of inventory and a queue both exist in this Current State Map. This is not unusual. This is one of the major reasons why bottlenecks occur in transactional value streams; workers throughout the value stream use an "island mentality" and work at their own pace.

The other critical piece of working with queues is in calculating the time value of the work sitting in the queue. Unlike piles of inventory where we calculate the time value by dividing the quantity by the daily customer demand, we use the cycle time of the process step following the queue combined with the scheduled time the queue works to determine the time value as demonstrated in Example 9.1.

The formula to determine the time value in days is:

Quantity × cycle time (of the following process step) ÷ Time allotted to work the queue + number of days in between days that the queue is worked until it is empty = Time value in days

By accurately calculating work-in-process when queues are utilized, you can greatly enhance the power of Value Stream Mapping. This one change away from the manufacturing calculation for days of inventory will reflect a much more accurate picture of the value stream. Without this tool and the formula for calculating the time value, you may struggle greatly when you attempt to convince your audience of the process flow.

Data in the transactional world is different ... right? Chapter 10 will discuss this data debate.

Chapter 10

Transactional Data Is Different ... Or Is It?

Collecting data is only the first step toward wisdom, but sharing data is the first step toward community.

Henry Louis Gates Jr.

Introduction

When creating a Current State Map for a transactional value stream, it would be a totally different concept from Value Stream Mapping for manufacturing if you believed much of the information that has been presented on the subject. However, Chapter 9 laid out the basic process flow similarities and differences in the two environments, so it should now be obvious that the actual differences are subtle.

The way you document the process flow is not really different; instead, there are only slight variations and adjustments in technique. The same can be said for the data that you collect and display in the data boxes on a transactional Value Stream Map. All of the data discussed in Chapter 8 is valid; it can and should be used; and it forces workers in a transactional world to think about the processes they deal with every day from a new and different perspective.

If you think about it long enough, it becomes very clear that making a widget in a manufacturing facility is not really any different than processing an application to issue a permit: raw material in ... finished product out. Whether your organization is processing paper or providing a service, your ultimate goal is to provide something to your customers that they want now, of the highest possible quality, and at the best available price.

Although the data points discussed in Chapter 8 should all be considered as available in a transactional world, there are some variations and changes in how you use certain concepts. The information in this chapter is intended to expand on your knowledge base already gained from this book.

Recording the Number of Employees in a Transactional Setting

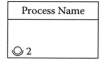

Documenting employees in a transactional setting is essentially the same as in a manufacturing setting. The only challenge is in determining if an employee who is sitting (or standing) in an office or room with other employees is actually a part of the value stream being mapped. Because many employees in a single office perform duties in multiple value streams, it can be difficult to separate one value stream from another when it comes to employees.

The burden on the mapper in a situation where multiple persons are working in the same area is to ask each individual if he or she performs the process step that is currently being documented. This can turn into a laborious exercise, because you must ask this question for each and every process step in the value stream.

Documenting Cycle Time

Process Name
C/T = 10 sec.
C/O =
U/T =
Avail:

In a transactional world, capturing cycle time can become quite challenging, too. For example, there are many high-volume processes that exist in large claims payment departments, purchasing departments, and billing departments. Documenting cycle time in these environments is obviously no different than in a manufacturing center. However, how do you determine cycle time when the value stream does not flow all the time? How do you gain this knowledge when the tasks in a value stream are all being done by a single person, and that person is also required to perform tasks that are part of another value stream?

> **Option A:** The simplest method is to ask the employee performing the process step to accumulate enough work to enable the mapper to observe an extended period of flow as multiple pieces are processed.

Cycle Time Log Sheet

Process Step Name:_____ Date:_____
Employee Name:_____

Start Time	End Time	Quantity

Figure 10.1   Cycle time log sheet for a transactional process.

Option B: Provide a log sheet that the employee(s) can complete that captures the amount of time working the process step and the quantity worked each time they performed the duties. In Figure 10.1 you can see that a log such as this has three columns: start time, end time, and quantity. At the top of the sheet, you list the name of the process step, and provide a space for the name of the employee who is performing the process step and the date.

It is important that you (or your mapping team) not turn this exercise into a multiday or multiweek affair. Instead, you should conduct it in a single day, and then you should remove the log sheet. If for some reason the volume is too low to make a valid decision on cycle time, bring a new log sheet in at the next available day to perform the work. And because this logging of data is non-value-added, it is important that the log sheets not become a permanent part of the process step.

When using log sheets, it is important to get the employees who are being tracked to understand the importance of the exercise. Emphasize the importance of capturing accurate start and end times. Explain to the employee(s) how to make a pile of work as it is completed, so that accurate counts of the quantity can be captured before the work is moved on to the next process step. This explanation is critical, because this is where inaccuracies will occur if an experienced mapper is not involved hands-on throughout the exercise.

Documenting Expected (Estimated) Cycle Time

Process Name
EC/T = 7.3 min.
C/O =
U/T =
Avail:

On some occasions, the value stream being mapped is one of indeterminate quantity and indeterminate demand. In other words, the value stream may produce one unit of work or 100, and may run only once a year, or every day. The employees working within the value stream just do not know when the need will arise. All the employees know is that when the need presents itself, they must perform the assigned duties.

When a value stream functions in such a manner, the ability to observe the process in action may not align itself directly with the need to review and improve the value stream. When faced with such a situation, you should conduct a meeting with all employees who work in the value stream and explain the mapping project goals and objectives. Set up a walkthrough to document the process flow by taking a completed unit of work and walking it backwards through the value stream, while documenting each process step along the way.

Once you have established the process flow, you should move from process step to process step and ask the employee to complete his or her task. You should time the task and add it to the data box as an expected, or estimated, cycle time, using the label "EC/T," as shown in this section.

There are times, however, that it may not be possible to even run a single unit exercise from which to estimate cycle time. When such a situation presents itself, you should turn to the old standby concept of brainstorming. Hold a brainstorming session with all employees who perform the process step, and ask each person how long it takes to perform the task. Average the answers to get an estimated or expected cycle time. Add this information into the data box with the EC/T label. Ask employees to operate the value stream and time themselves on how long the task actually takes. Then invite them to update the Current State Map once they have a timed experience.

Documenting Changeover Time

Process Name
EC/T =
C/O = 12.5 min.
U/T =
Avail:

Believe it or not, there are changeovers in the transactional world. Actually, there are many *more* changeovers in transactional settings than on the manufacturing floor. Every time an employee changes tasks in the office, a changeover occurs. It may not take nearly as long as manufacturing changeovers, but it can become very disruptive to the flow of the process.

Therefore, as you observe and document the current state in a transactional world, you should look for changeovers that take an unusually long amount of time. When these long changeovers occur, you should document the changeover time on the Current State Map. It is generally recommended that you *not* document short changeover times (e.g., less than 2 or 3 minutes) in the data box, because that may create unnecessary and often confusing discussion, which probably will not result in any substantive change.

The proper way to identify these transactional changeovers is to watch for the conclusion of one task, e.g., an employee getting up from his or her desk or workstation, picking up a pile of work and filing it, and finally returning to the desk with a new pile of work that is not the same subject as what was previously being completed. Another good way to identify these changeovers is to watch for when an employee exits from one software program (or a group of screens from a software package) and opens a new program (or new set of windows). When you see changeovers such as these, the correct way to capture this information is no different than in a manufacturing setting. (For additional information on this data point, refer back to changeover time in Chapter 8.)

Documenting Uptime or Reliability

Process Name
EC/T =
C/O =
U/T = 93%
Avail:

Another basic concept in the Lean world is uptime or reliability of equipment. Transactional value streams are no different from manufacturing value streams when it comes to experiencing reliability problems. For example, personal computers break down every day. File servers fail. Adding machines quit working, or the adding machine tape jams. It happens just like in a manufacturing setting.

There is, however, one additional item in a transactional setting where uptime has become an even bigger issue: connectivity to the network. This applies not just to the organization's internal network, but also virtual private networks (VPNs), and of course connectivity to the Internet. Employees relying on network connections in a transactional world experience the exact same frustration as the

Uptime Log Sheet	
Works	Doesn't Work
~~THL THL~~ III	III

Figure 10.2　Sample uptime log sheet.

manufacturing equipment operator when a failure occurs. If this failure continually happens, the flow of the value stream can be greatly affected.

Unfortunately for most mappers, there is little or no data readily available to turn to for uptime data. Very few (if any) organizations track office equipment failure as a routine matter. For office equipment, the simple answer is to track failure through a simple log, just as in the manufacturing world. Figure 10.2 shows an example. Once the information is captured for the Current State Map and associated continuous improvement projects, it should be eliminated, because it is a non-value-added activity.

For connectivity uptime issues, some organizations track this type of network information, but most do not have it in an easily accessible format that can provide fast answers to the question. As a result of this, the starting point for uptime (U/T) information is usually through a brainstorming session with the employees performing the process step. If uptime is an issue, start with the percentage of time that the employees believe the network connection works when the process step is needed. Emphasize that the data needed is only in relation to when the network is needed for this process step, not whenever they get on the network for whatever reason.

Post this uptime percentage in the data box, and then ask the information technology (IT) department to validate the information in whatever manner they have available. If the data returned from IT is substantially different from the estimate, bring the IT staff and the employees working the process step together to try and determine why the two numbers are so far apart. Do not stop the mapping process to solve this issue. Keep moving and come back at a more suitable time to address the issue, perhaps through a continuous improvement project.

Documenting Availability of Equipment (AOE)

Process Name
EC/T =
C/O =
U/T = 93%
AOE

When mapping on the manufacturing floor, value stream mappers use the concept of availability as a way to explain what percentage of a machine's time that a particular value stream has access to. This concept still holds true for transactional value streams, but it is not encountered nearly as often.

For example, large printers, such as those found in a company's print shop or IT center, as well as document-scanning stations and even large-volume shredders are equipment typically found in transactional environments. And as you create Current State Maps of various value streams in a transactional organization, you may find other situations as well where you need to document the availability of equipment that is necessary to a process.

However, the concept of availability goes well beyond that of equipment in transactional environments. As such, the label that transactional mappers use for "availability of equipment" is more often seen as "AOE," as opposed to the manufacturing standard of "Avail." This change in labeling can help you prevent confusion with your audience when discussing the concept of availability. (For a complete discussion and information on how to calculate availability of equipment, refer to Chapter 8.)

Documenting Availability of Personnel (AOP)

Process Name
EC/T =
C/O =
U/T =
AOP: 20%

As Value Stream Mapping moved from the manufacturing floor in the United States to the office and eventually to all transactional and service environments, one of the largest and most difficult issues that mappers had to face was how to accurately present the number of employees and the amount of time each employee spent working within a particular value stream. The problem that has continually come before mapping teams is how to show this "availability" of the employee in a setting where employees as a matter of routine practice multitasking all day long. Employees in transactional value streams regularly perform more than one duty for their employer. It has become second nature to most office employees to continually "shift gears" throughout the workday to complete all of their assigned duties.

Trying to convince a staff of office employees that a Current State Map is an accurate depiction of how a value stream operates can become one of the most frustrating tasks you must do when mapping the transactional world. To solve this problem, the concept of availability has been expanded to the workforce itself; see Figure 10.3.

Availability of personnel (AOP) is now a very common method of not only showing how employees work in the value stream, but it also has become a very valuable tool in convincing transactional employees that they have a process and

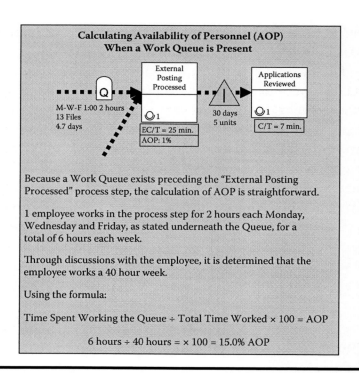

Figure 10.3   Calculating availability of personnel (AOP) when a work queue is present.

that there is a way to accurately depict what the employees do and when they do it. Using this expanded concept of availability now makes it a much easier task when explaining a map set to a group of transactional employees.

To determine and map AOP, you must use a combination of knowledge about the process flow and some direct interaction with the employee(s) operating the process step. By knowing how much time an employee spends performing the assigned task through an understanding of any work queue that is present immediately in front of the process step, you should have a basic idea of how much time is spent in a day or week working on this process step. Then, when you take this time element as a percentage of the total workday or workweek, you can see the approximate percentage of time that that employee is available to complete the task. Figure 10.3 illustrates this procedure.

When you're trying to map a setting where no work queues precede the process step, you must rely on the knowledge of the incumbent employee(s) performing the work. Just starting out with a best-guess estimate is often enough to paint the picture effectively. Even if a discussion develops over how much time an employee really has to perform the duties, the mapping exercise has fulfilled its goal of getting all issues out on the table for discussion.

Another positive benefit from using the employee's perceived time frame as the reported percentage is that using this number as a starting point often creates fast buy-in from the employee on the accuracy of the Current State Map. Anytime you can find an employee working within a transactional value stream to champion the validity of a map, you and your mapping team should work to firmly *retain* that employee's buy-in. This can make the continuous improvement process much easier once the discussion begins to focus on change.

Just as with availability of equipment (AOE), AOP can greatly reduce the ability of a value stream to flow. The impact of queues, and how to calculate and report this effect, was discussed in detail in Chapter 9. But there is also an effect on the ultimate performance of a process step when AOP is an issue. If AOP equals 50% for a process step, it should be expected that the work will only flow 50% of the time from this step in the value stream. Therefore, although the cycle time may be reported as 1 min. when the process was operating and data was captured, in reality, you should not expect over the long run to see anything better than a 2-min. cycle time due to AOP.

How to Document Tasks That Supervisors and Managers Demand Be Performed Immediately

There is one situation that almost every organization in the world faces from time to time and must be addressed when discussing AOP. It is not uncommon that, within a value stream, a certain process step exists where the employee assigned to the task spends the majority of his or her time working within other value streams. However, management has stated that whenever work appears on this employee's desk for this value stream, all other duties will cease until the process step is complete.

How exactly do you report AOP in this situation? The very simple answer is AOP = 100%. It does not matter how much time is allotted each day or week to perform the function, the company procedure is that anytime this work appears, it has the highest priority. Therefore, you must be extremely vigilant in a transactional world to look for situations where this occurs as demonstrated in Example 10.1. Anytime a discussion is held about available time and there is no queue present to manage the flow, you are well advised to ask about mandates and procedures that set priorities on work.

One interesting fact about AOP that you must understand is the relationship (or the lack thereof) that these percentages have with the total breakdown of

---

Example 10.1

To summarize, here's how to document AOP when the organization's *policy or procedure requires immediate processing* of some task:

- Employee A estimates that she spends 20% of her time working on process step 1.
- Employee A's supervisor requires Employee A to immediately process any work appearing on her desk for process step 1.
- Employee A availability appears to be 20%.
- Due to procedural mandate, AOP = 100% because it must be worked as soon as it arrives.

an employee's allotted time for all of his or her duties in a day, week, or month. Because the general thought process wants us to break down an employee's time and account for 100% of this time, what happens when you start changing the AOP to 100%? And what happens if there is more than one function that must be performed each and every time work appears?

First and foremost, it must be understood that when a prioritization of task appears in a transactional world, all logical associations of time and effort for each and every task performed by the employee cease to exist. For example, suppose an employee has 10% of his time available to perform function A and 90% of his available time is to be spent on function B. The standard operating procedure states that anytime work appears for function A, it must be performed. Even if, over the course of one year, this percentage of allotted time holds true, what happens when work for function A appears nonstop for one month? At that point in time and any other time work appears, AOP for function A is 100%.

As you are mapping a value stream where this scenario exists, the AOP of the deferred task is not important unless it is also a process step in this value stream. When this happens, then you are faced with the exact *opposite* situation.

The exact opposite situation occurs when an employee is told to not work a certain process step if there is work from another process step or value stream still demanding her attention. When this occurs, you should take the discussion further and try to understand the normal amount of time available to work the process step being mapped. From this, you should then explore the situation to the point that there is agreement on what percentage of the time work shows up and is not processed due to the other value stream's interruption. From this, it is then possible for you to multiply the available time by the percentage of interruption. The resulting percentage is the AOP.

As Example 10.2 demonstrates, this type of interruption can have a dramatic impact on an employee's ability to perform her duties to the satisfaction of

---

Example 10.2

To summarize, here's how to document AOP when *policy or procedure prevents processing*:

■ Employee A estimates that she spends 20% of her time working on process step 1.
■ Employee A's supervisor requires Employee A to never process any work appearing on her desk for process step 1 if work from value stream C is available to process first.
■ Employee A estimates that this situation occurs 15% of the time when process step 1 work appears.
■ Calculate AOP as

% Time spent on process step × % Time interrupted by higher priority work
= AOP 20% × 15% = 3.0% AOP

management. In most situations like this, management is not even aware of the adverse impact its decisions on prioritization of work have on the process.

By using AOP to show availability of personnel, Current State Maps often visually portray what employees have attempted to explain with less-than-successful results for long periods of time. Anytime an employee's work is prioritized at the expense of another task and work is available to be processed, a value stream will slow down or completely stop flowing.

Documenting Defects

Process Name
EC/T =
C/O =
U/T =
AOP:
Defect = 12%

Although the issue of defects and how they are reported in a data box is absolutely no different than on a manufacturing process's Current State Map, this chapter adds emphasis to this topic to remind you that defects are a serious issue, regardless of the setting. It is unfortunate that, for many transactional organizations, the issue of quality is not held in as high esteem as it is in manufacturing settings. As a result of this failure to promote quality, there are many employees in transactional environments who do not even understand the cost of defective output.

Therefore, you should look closely at each step of the value stream as you map the current state and attempt to capture defect rates for each process step. The simplest way to identify many defects is when employees tell a mapping team about the mistakes made by the customer when they submit information up front. Although this quickly raises a red flag for Lean practitioners and other continuous improvement teams, without explanation, many employees will never recognize the opportunity to improve a process.

Capturing Other Data

Building on the various data types explained in this chapter and Chapter 8, it begins to become apparent that mappers are finding new data points every day. As soon as someone discovers a way to calculate and report this information in the data box, there is another situation appearing, just waiting on someone to find a way to explain it on a Value Stream Map.

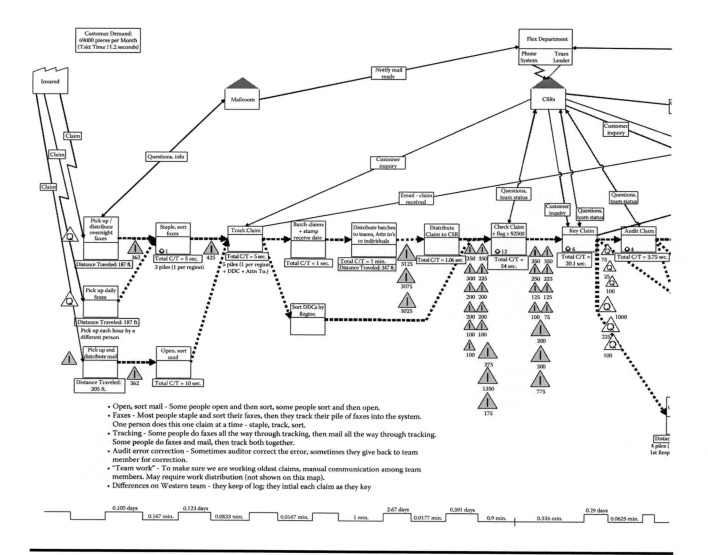

Figure 10.4 *Actual* **Current State Map from American Fidelity Assurance Company (insurance company—claims processing)**

There is one major thing that many mappers find captivating about transactional Value Stream Mapping. When you create a Current State Map, you not only have the opportunity to use every single VSM concept that is used for manufacturing value streams, but you also find there are additional concepts that help paint the picture. From this snapshot in time, there is a new and uniquely different way to look at the processes we have always performed.

The list of other items that can be placed in the data box in a transactional map is endless. As the Current State Map is developed, you can add to the box anything that appears to be even remotely important. Remember, you can always take it out later. Some of the "other" items that are seen on transactional maps include:

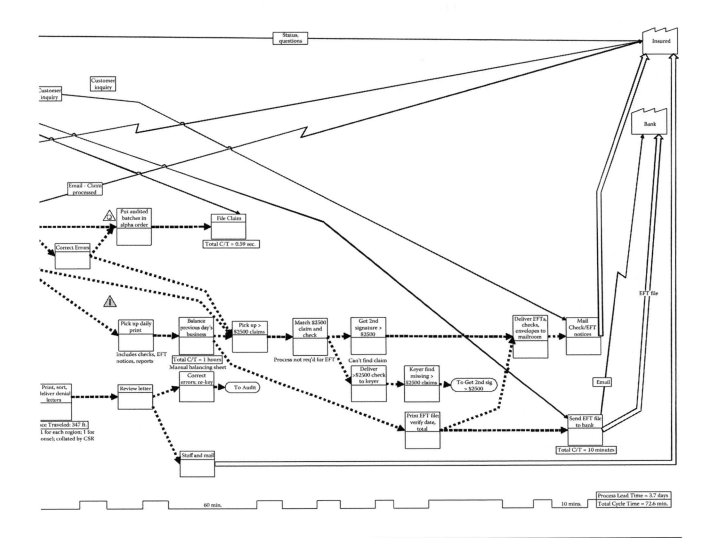

Figure 10.4   (Continued).

- The number of forms utilized
- The routing of paperwork or process
- The number of approvals required
- The number of copies
- Locations where paperwork is filed

As you draw your maps, remember to be creative. Listen to the employees in the value stream. Add the items to the data boxes that are important to the employees. From this faster buy-in and pride of ownership, the development of champions within the process can become a reality. Figure 10.4 shows a Current State Map created by a team of mappers at American Fidelity Assurance Company for one of their claims-processing value streams.

Case Study in a Transactional Environment

Current State Map
Case Study: American Fidelity Assurance Company
Insurance company—claims processing

The Current State Map (see Figure 10.4) is a value stream from American Fidelity Assurance Company. This map detailed the waste within a claims benefit processing department. Through the mapping exercise, the mappers and Lean initiative team (as they are known within American Fidelity) identified multiple bottlenecks, as illustrated by the multiple inventory icons shown in the map. The multiple paths through the value stream highlighted the unnecessary processing, excess travel, and excess motion found in this process.

The results of the American Fidelity Lean initiative team's Value Stream Mapping efforts and associated Lean improvement initiatives are discussed at the conclusion of Chapter 17.

In Chapter 11, you will learn how to understand and capture travel distance on your map.

Chapter 11

Capturing Travel Distances throughout the Value Stream

Time is the longest distance between two places.

Tennessee Williams

Introduction

When Tennessee Williams spoke his famous quote about time and distance, he wasn't referring to business processes and the precious time associated with distance in the process. But he might as well have been. Time is a precious commodity in the business world: once it is used, a cost has been incurred. Good use of this time generally results in favorable outcomes for the business; bad use often leads to financial trouble, or worse.

This basic concept in business is what has driven many organizations using Value Stream Mapping to begin to document travel distance on their maps. The time and cost associated with this travel is non-value-added (NVA) regardless of the value stream, and organizations should make every effort to reduce or eliminate travel distances. Adding this information to your Current State Map provides additional insight about the value stream that can be extremely beneficial to a project team as you work to identify and eliminate waste in the process.

Measuring Travel Distance in the Value Stream

When discussing travel distance in a value stream, several different "travel distances" can be the subject of the discussion. As such, it is extremely important to properly identify and communicate the focus of the travel. The travel distance could be referring to the travel path of the product, the travel path of the employee(s), or a combination of both. To ensure that all participants, both mappers and audience, are on the same page, the subject of travel must be clearly

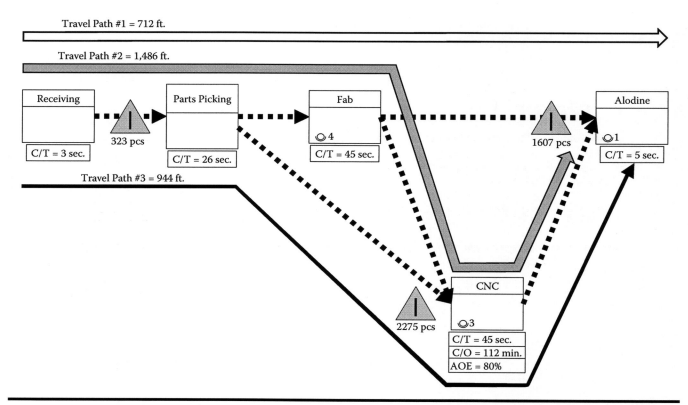

Figure 11.1   Being able to explain which travel path is being used, and why, is critical when looking for ways to reduce travel in a value stream.

communicated up front. The next three sections clarify the difference between each of these types of travel distance.

Measuring and Documenting the Travel Path of the Product

The physical path of the product, service, or paperwork (in a transactional world) is the most common travel distance measured and reported on a Current State Map. This travel distance is the physical path of a single unit of work. The preferred way to measure this path is to follow the product through the longest possible path of the value stream, as illustrated in Figure 11.1.

What this means is that you must measure and document the travel path of all possible paths through the Current State Map. Then you must conduct a review of all possibilities to determine the path reported. When measuring the travel distance of components or other pieces of work from one process step to another on the map, it is possible that these components may be coming from multiple storage or staging locations. To determine the travel distance in situations such as this, measure from the approximate center or midpoint of all locations where work is stored or placed after the first process step to the location of the next process step, as shown in Figure 11.2.

If these components are coming from multiple process steps within the value stream, you should measure the distance from each step, and then use the

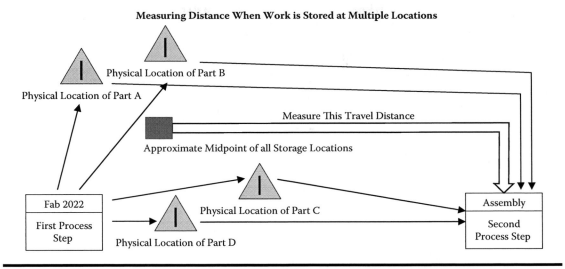

Figure 11.2   When work is stored at multiple locations, find the midpoint of the storage locations and measure the distance from this point to the next process step.

distance of the work coming from farthest away. As an alternative to using the longest distance, you can measure the distance of each component and then calculate the average travel distance from the first steps to the second, as shown in Figure 11.3.

Measuring and Documenting the Travel Path of Employees

The second possibility for reporting travel distance is in relation to the employee(s) in the value stream. Although this is somewhat more difficult to measure, this

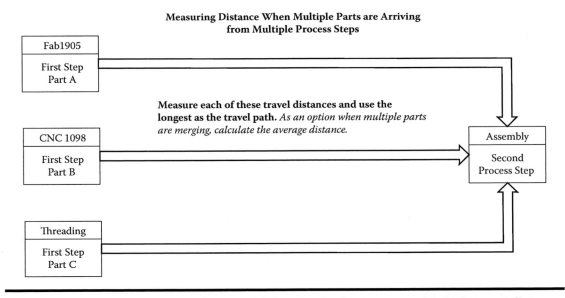

Figure 11.3   When parts arrive from multiple steps in the process, use the longest distance traveled or average distance traveled as opposed to measuring from a midpoint.

travel distance can tell a very compelling story. By direct observation, it is possible to capture the travel utilized by each employee in a process. This requires identifying each employee in the process and tracking his or her movements during the completion of one unit of work. The challenge is to ensure that any prework travel to pick up work-in-process, other materials, tools, or supplies is documented. Likewise, you must also document the postwork travel, which might include delivering the work-in-process to the next step in the value stream, as well as returning tools, supplies, and/or materials to other locations.

Because of this complexity, many organizations choose to look only at the travel path of the product, but there is a fast alternative to capturing this information. By measuring the travel path of the product and estimating the travel path of the workforce as twice that of the product, that provides a reasonable travel distance for employees. This estimate is based on the concept of employees moving work from one process step to another and then returning to their assigned workstation, desk, or work cell empty-handed, as is often the case observed in a Current State Map.

Physical Measurement of Travel

To physically measure the distance traveled in a value stream, you (and/or your mapping team) must get out into the process, walk each path, and document what you find. Although the only way to ensure that the distance you report is accurate is to staple yourself to a unit of work or to an individual employee (if you are measuring the travel distance of the employees), the methods for gathering the actual data vary. The three most common ways to physically measure travel distance are described in the following paragraphs.

Method 1: Using a Measuring Wheel. The measuring wheel is perhaps the most accurate method for measuring travel distance. These devices come in many shapes and sizes; however, the result is the same: an accurate measurement between steps in the process.

Method 2: Using a Pedometer. A pedometer is a device used to measure travel distance of individuals moving from one point to another on foot. Nearly as accurate as measuring wheels, pedometers are often found in the toolkits of Lean facilitators and Value Stream Mappers, alongside masking tape, measuring tapes, chalk, etc.

Although some people find it difficult to make adjustments to the device, in order to accurately measure the stride of the wearer, the most challenging part of using a pedometer is often trying to find the right place to wear the device. It is recommended that it be placed on a belt on the wearer's hips; other places that may measure distance more accurately includes clipping it to the top of a boot or to the shoe laces on the front of a shoe or boot. Most pedometers can count both steps and feet, so you must remember to check the setting on the device before starting. If in fact the steps option is used, it is relatively easy to convert to feet, as is discussed in the following paragraph.

Method 3: Counting Steps. Counting steps is still the most common form of measuring travel distance through a value stream. By simply walking from one process step to another and counting the number of steps you take, you can determine the approximate distance traveled between steps in the value stream. Because the normal stride of a normal person is 2.5 feet per step, you can determine distance by multiplying the number of steps by 2.5 to arrive at the distance. If the individual walking the process is shorter than 5′ 6″ tall, you may want to consider reducing the 2.5 feet per step to 2.0 feet per step. Likewise, if the person doing the measuring is taller than 6′ 3″, you may want to lengthen the distance per step to 3.0.

Finally, here are a few other ways to measure distance, although there are more than just these listed:

■ Odometers in trucks, automobiles, golf carts, tractors, etc.
■ Handheld global positioning system (GPS) units
■ Measuring tapes

Showing Travel Distance on a Value Stream Map

As you walk the process from step to step, you should write the distance you've traveled between the process boxes, usually immediately above the push or pull arrow, as shown in Figure 11.4.

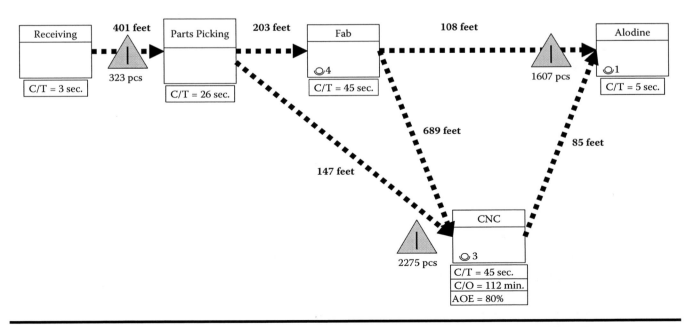

Figure 11.4   Documenting the travel distance between process steps on the process/product flow portion of your map.

To ensure that this information can be differentiated from other information on your map, remember to label each data point with "feet" or "steps," depending on the method you are using to measure the distance. If you use steps, then once you are finished capturing steps in the value stream, you can convert the distance to feet (as described in the previous section). For clarity, it is best to decide on one mode of measurement and use that method throughout your value stream.

After you have documented all distances, you must then identify the longest path through the value stream and show this information on your map. Follow each possible path through the value stream, and add up the distances along the way. Once you have determined the longest path, you can then document it on the map underneath the Takt time.

An easier way to determine the travel distance is to pull the longest distances captured between steps down to the bottom of the map and create a travel distance line. Where there is only one path, identifying the distance is straight-forward. Where there are parallel or alternate paths running parallel on the map, you must select the longest path. Draw a line below and parallel to the process lead time and total cycle timeline at the bottom of the map. Place a mark at the midpoint beneath each column of process step boxes. Copy each of the longest paths down to the bottom, as shown in Figure 11.5, and then total on the far right-hand side of the map.

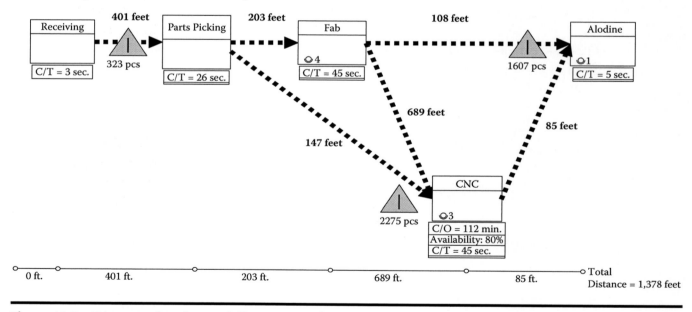

Figure 11.5   Documenting the total distance traveled in a process.

Documenting Long Travel Distances within a Process Step

Occasionally, you will measure travel distance between steps and discover, as you are walking the process, that inside a single process step, there is a long travel distance of its own. Closed-loop manufacturing processes (such as found in the food processing industry) provide excellent examples of this scenario. Raw materials are introduced at the beginning of a process step, such as in a blender or grinder, and are extruded into forms some distance away. When this type of scenario occurs, many times, you don't know how to reflect this travel distance that is internal to the process step.

Therefore, to include distances such as these, you should separately measure the travel distance of the process step. Once you have determined this distance, you can add one half of the distance to the travel feeding the process step and one half to travel leading away from the process step.

You may also find situations similar to this in the transactional world. For example, when information is entered into a computer screen, processed through the system, and then printed out on a printer at another location in the facility, the transactional value stream faces the same dilemma. Adding the travel distance that is required to retrieve the printout is no different than pulling work-in-process from one end of an extruder after it has been ground, mixed, liquefied, and extruded into a form (as described in the manufacturing example).

As an alternative, it is possible to capture and report the travel distance within the process step. Instead of placing a mark at the midpoint of each column of process steps, place a mark on the line at the left and right corner of each column of process step boxes. Record the longest distance between process steps in between the columns and the longest distance within a process step in the space directly beneath the column, as shown in Figure 11.6.

Check for Hidden Travel in Transactional Processes

Following the flow in transactional processes, it is easy to lose sight of all the hidden wastes that exist. As you focus on capturing the travel of the main flow, it is possible that you may overlook other unnecessary travel that occurs regularly as a part of the process. Transactional value streams can possess substantially more waste than production value streams, as documented through two studies.

The first study was conducted by the National Institute of Standards and Technology (NIST)/Manufacturing Extension Partnership (MEP) and is used extensively in the NIST/MEP Lean Training Program. This study shows that as much as 95% of all process lead time is non-value-added (NVA) in manufacturing processes. This study was followed by a second, similar study that David LaCourse presented at the 2004 Institute of Industrial Engineers Lean Management Conference. LaCourse revealed that transactional value streams often have more than 98% of their process lead time attributable to waste.

One of the most common wastes overlooked is when employees take multiple copies of paperwork, sort it and then file it, never reference it again other than to retrieve it later, move it to another location to do additional non-value-added work, and finally move it again to throw it away or destroy it. Often, this

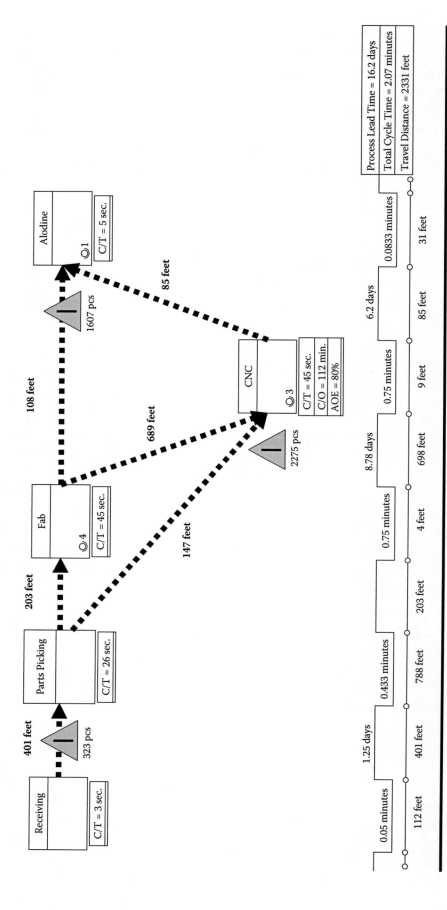

Figure 11.6 It is possible to capture and report travel distance within process steps by breaking the travel line at the bottom of the map down into smaller pieces showing distance inside process steps, as well as between them.

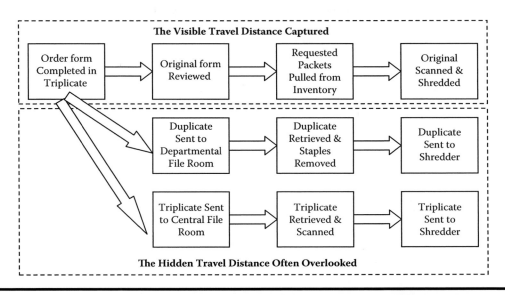

Figure 11.7   Be sure to look for hidden travel distances associated with support tasks or other less obvious paper task paths in the value stream.

paperwork is stored long distances away from where the process work occurs. Figure 11.7 illustrates these hidden distances.

Therefore, as you gather travel distances in transactional value streams, you should be aware of these hidden travel paths. Keeping this possibility in front of you often helps you discover additional steps in the value stream that perhaps were overlooked during the first-pass mapping of the current state. When such occurrences present themselves, you should make sure you include these hidden distances on your Value Stream Map and in your travel distance total.

The addition of travel distances to Value Stream Maps has become an excellent tool to assist project teams with improvement opportunities. By accurately identifying and documenting the travel path through a value stream, one more method presents itself to help project teams explain to employees where the problem, pain, and issues exist in their process. Because not everyone hears and sees things the same way, this provides another option to get the message across to all employees of the organization.

In Chapter 12, you will look at what "value" is created from the process flow. After all, Lean is all about creating value and eliminating waste.

Chapter 12

Showing the "Value" from the Process Flow

> Vision is the art of seeing the invisible.
>
> **Jonathan Swift**

Introduction

The purpose of Current State Maps is to provide a vision of reality. All too often, employees within a process will explain their work as they perceive it—from their small slice of the world. Therefore, in organizations that use traditional methods for mapping their processes, the outcome can very easily become a stitched-together picture of each worker's own perception added to all the other employees' thoughts as to how the process works. *This is neither accurate nor beneficial* to change agents who are seeking truth and insight into what is *actually* occurring on a day-to-day basis.

To see reality, you must be able to see the invisible: in other words, see what is in front of your face but not obvious to the observer. Current State Maps create a vision of the real value stream. These maps show what many people do not see, and what others *choose* not to see. Without this vision, it is difficult to move ahead quickly. Not seeing the whole picture can result in "analysis paralysis," or it can create a situation where project teams are constantly suboptimizing processes by attacking only what they *think* is important.

Capturing an accurate Current State Map with all of the components in place can create great value and synergy for a project team. "Accurate" is in the eye of the beholder, but to experienced Value Stream Mappers, if the map is determined to be 70% accurate, that is close enough to begin. Experienced mappers subscribe to the mindset that "if everyone on a project team agrees that there is a problem, then how accurate do you need to be?" An accuracy of 70% typically gets the major points covered, avoids analysis paralysis, and allows teams to move quickly to make change.

Also, because Value Stream Maps are living, breathing documents, they are intended to be updated. As team members or other employees in the value stream see additional information or corrections that need to be addressed, they should be updating the map … every day! This map should become a living, evolving documentation of the process.

An obvious value of the Current State Map is the chaos and confusion that is visually shown on the map. When the initial mapping is shown to the audience, it typically reveals all of the following problems:

- Excessive communication (which is discussed in Chapters 13 and 14)
- Overly complex process steps
- Non-value-added (NVA) steps
- Bottlenecks

However, it is the calculations used to explain "time in the process" that show the most invisible waste. Just like travel distance (discussed in Chapter 11), these calculations provide an incredible amount of knowledge that is often overlooked when analyzing processes. Therefore, this chapter takes a closer look at all of the components of process time.

Measuring Total Cycle Time

As you collect cycle time and place it in data boxes on the Current State Map, a picture begins to emerge. By reviewing each process step defined in a process box, it is possible to compare the cycle time of the process step against the Takt time to see if the task can be completed within the required time frame necessary to meet customer demand. However, an even clearer message begins to emerge when the cycle times from all process boxes are brought down to a common timeline on the bottom of the map.

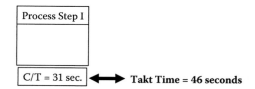

Start by drawing a line parallel to the bottom of each process box all the way across the map, as shown in Figure 12.1. This dashed line is the placeholder for each of the cycle times on the Current State Map.

Next, copy the reported cycle time for each step to the corresponding line position, as shown in Figure 12.2. Immediately, you see where steps in the value stream could be causing flow problems. Large variation in cycle time from one step to another clearly shows where bottlenecks may occur. Anytime you have a relatively short cycle time followed by a substantially longer cycle time, it is possible for bottlenecks to occur.

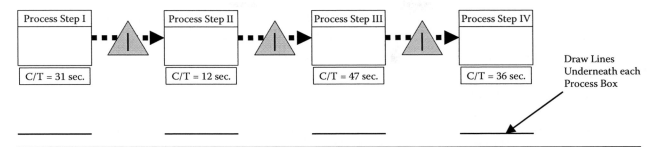

Figure 12.1 To document the cycle times on your timeline, use visual placeholders by drawing lines underneath each process step at the bottom of the map.

There is one additional piece of information that also comes from this timeline: the total cycle time. The sum of all cycle times shown at the right side of the map provides a very powerful piece of data for the project team. Total cycle time represents the amount of time required for one unit of work to be processed through *all* steps of the value stream, without any waiting time between steps. In other words, it shows how long it would take to complete a unit of work if each step were completed in order immediately after the preceding step. Figure 12.3 shows an example of how total cycle time is reported.

The total cycle time label in the box at the right side of the map can also be shown as "TCT." This abbreviation can come in handy when maps are being drawn on flipchart paper or whiteboards and space is limited.

As you and your project team are reviewing total cycle time on the Current State Map, remember that this number is the amount of time required to produce a single unit of work based on how the value stream currently operates *without regard to waiting or other non-value-added time between process steps*. It is *not* how often one good unit of work is completed and delivered out of the process. To see how often one good unit of work is completed and delivered, simply look at the last process step cycle time.

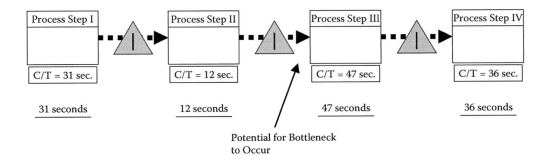

Figure 12.2 By pulling cycle times down to the timeline, it is easy to quickly see where problems may exist.

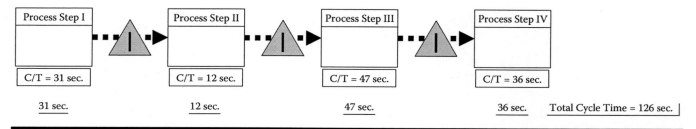

Figure 12.3 **The total cycle time timeline shows how long it should take to produce a unit of work if there are no interruptions or waiting between process steps.**

Interpreting Parallel or Subtask Cycle Times

Capturing the total cycle time for basic, single-path value streams is very simple and straightforward. But what do you do when you have parallel or subtask flows within the value stream? The challenge is to produce a picture of the value stream that accurately depicts the process as it actually operates. To accomplish this, when two or more process boxes are stacked vertically, as shown in Figure 12.4, you should show the longest cycle time on the timeline.

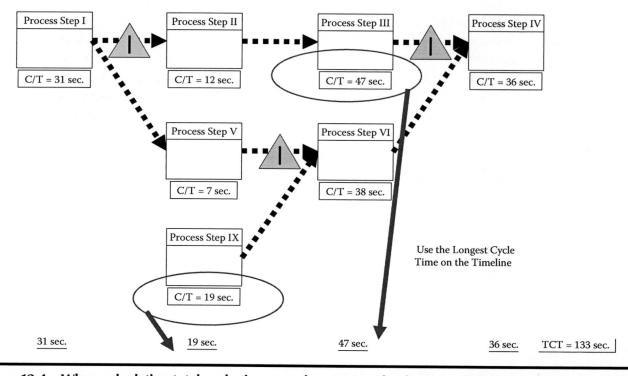

Figure 12.4 **When calculating total cycle time on value streams that have parallel process steps, always use the longest cycle time from each vertical column of process steps.**

Measuring Process Lead Time

In addition to total cycle time (TCT), the second standard piece of data contained on the timeline is process lead time. *Process lead time* (often referred to as PLT) is the total expected elapsed time from the moment raw materials are received (or, in a transactional environment, that work is requested) to the time the finished good or service produced from this raw material or request is shipped or delivered to the customer:

- In manufacturing settings, this is synonymous with inventory turns, i.e., the number of times a manufacturer completely cycles through all materials from raw to finished goods in a year.
- For transactional value streams, this is a concept that has rarely been explored in these terms in the past. This information is shown on a Value Stream Map in similar fashion to total cycle time data.

By understanding the level of customer demand on the value stream, the mapping team, the project team, and the organization as a whole can gain great knowledge about how long material, or a request for service, stays in the value stream. To determine process lead time, you must first determine customer demand. The easiest way to explain customer demand to an audience is on a daily basis, i.e., how many units of work are required by the customer daily.

This single piece of information (which was discussed in the Takt time sections of Chapters 7 and 9) unlocks another critical piece of the puzzle. Using this data with the amount of inventory (a.k.a. materials, requests, forms, finished goods, service units, etc.) within the value stream provides the final aspect of the process flow contained in the visual map that Rother and Shook discuss in *Learning to See*.

M-W-F
1:00 - 1:30
186 pcs

1,250 pcs

Underneath each inventory triangle or work queue icon shown on your map, you should have already documented the number of units of work observed when mapping the process flow. If not, this is the time to capture that data. Then take the amount of inventory or work observed and divide it by the daily customer demand; this enables you to calculate the number of days' worth of materials or work between each step in the value stream:

Daily volume of work = quantity of work or materials ÷ daily customer demand

Some Value Stream Mapping (VSM) software packages do not require you to manually calculate this number. Instead, when you input customer demand, the software automatically calculates the amount of inventory between steps in the value stream and places it on the timeline for you. If you must manually determine this number, however, document each data point directly beneath the inventory or work queue icon.

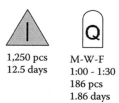

1,250 pcs   M-W-F
12.5 days   1:00 - 1:30
            186 pcs
            1.86 days

Once again, a much clearer picture begins to emerge. Excessive amounts of work or materials in the value stream begin to become visible when these quantities are translated into daily amounts of work. If there are extremely large (in terms of number of days) volumes of inventory between process steps, then team members can begin zeroing in on issues and opportunities and making decisions quickly.

Just as you did with individual cycle times, you should pull down these daily units of work (which you documented beneath the inventory and work icons) to a corresponding timeline at the bottom of your map. For example, assuming that customer demand for the given value stream equals 100 units of work each day, then the day's worth of work shown in Figure 12.5 would range from 0.17 days to 12.5 days. The process lead time timeline should be offset from the total cycle time timeline. It is often shown as a staggered line, as in Figure 12.5.

Once you've added the demand stated in days to the line, you can then add up all of the numbers across the timeline, and then add this total to the total cycle time to determine process lead time (PLT):

PLT = total of all days' worth of inventory (work) + total cycle time

You should record this at the right side of the timeline, just as you documented the total cycle time. Figure 12.6 illustrates how this is documented and how it looks in relation to the TCT and the process flow of the map.

This not only enables the project team and any other audience assembled to see both the process lead time and the total cycle time; it also enables anyone

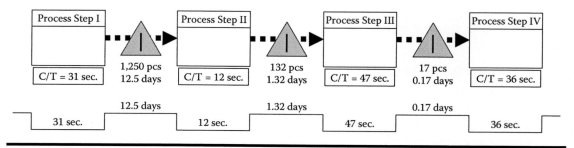

Figure 12.5   Once you have the amount of inventory calculated in days, pull this calculation down to a timeline raised above the cycle time placeholders on the timeline.

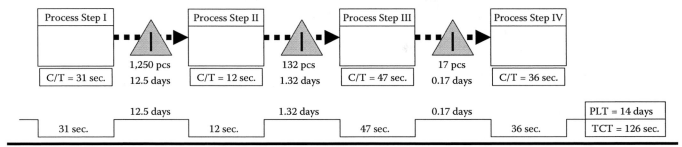

Figure 12.6 Calculating process lead time (PLT) using the amount of inventory and cycle times.

observing the map to then start asking the obvious question that most often comes from this exercise: *Why does it take so long to move work through this value stream if the total cycle time is so much shorter?* As in the example shown in Figure 12.6, why does it take on average 14 days for work to flow from start to finish if it only takes 2 min. and 6 sec. to actually process a unit of work through all of the process steps? This one single comparison—which is often invisible until this timeline is completed—can bring about the most profound change in attitude of management and employees alike once it is seen.

Addressing Multiple Locations of Inventory as Well as Parallel or Subtask Paths

Many mappers visually show inventory/work where they find it. If there is work or materials in multiple locations between two process steps, they show multiple inventory or work queue icons to represent the various piles observed. When this occurs (whether it occurs because of multiple locations, or when parallel or subtask paths created situations where multiple icons are stacked vertically on a map), you should use the "total of all piles" to calculate the number of days shown on the timeline. **Do not use the largest amount**. Inventory is different from cycle time, and the calculation is performed differently. Figure 12.7 shows an example of how this concept works.

Measuring Value-Added Time: An Alternative to Total Cycle Time

Cycle time of a process step can be broken down into two pieces: value-added (VA) time and non-value-added (NVA) time. Value-added time—which is time for any activity that the customer is willing to pay for—is the only time on a Value Stream Map that Lean practitioners want to see. Any time (i.e., activity) that the customer is not willing to pay for is non-value-added time, which is a waste and which is the focus of Lean improvement: to identify and eliminate waste.

Even though it may not be possible to eliminate all non-value-added time from a process, making NVA time visible provides additional insight into the opportunities that exist in the value stream. To create this visibility, when capturing cycle time,

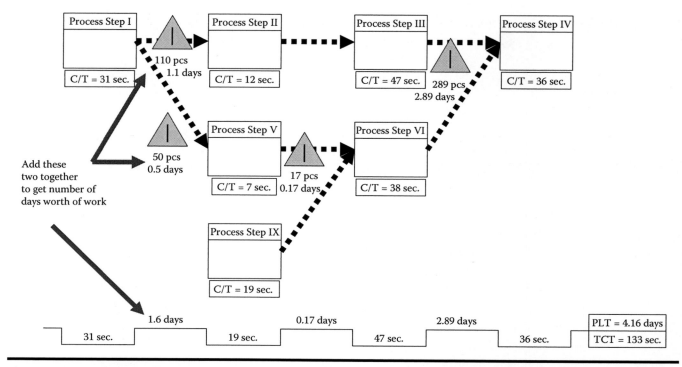

Figure 12.7   When working with multiple piles of inventory in a vertical column, always add the amounts in each column together to get the number of days worth of work (process lead time).

you must break down your observations and document the time for both VA and NVA activity. Typically, observations of this type take more time, but the power of the information obtained cannot be denied. Both workers and management alike can make some very definite decisions related to NVA within a process step.

To display this information on the Current State Map, you should record both the VA and NVA time in the data box beneath each process box. The most common abbreviations used in the data box to show this data are "VAT" for the value-added time and "NVA" for the non-value-added time. Once you have collected this information and added it to your map, you must translate the information to the timeline at the bottom of the map.

Figure 12.8 shows how to report this information on the timeline. By placing the VA on the timeline where cycle time is usually reported, the "processing time" required to produce a unit of work is still being reported in the same manner as when cycle time is used. You should then draw a line over the top of the VA time and record the NVA above this line. Utilizing this concept, you are essentially placing the NVA time on the same line as the NVA portion of the process lead time.

Measuring Total Travel Distance

Chapter 11 discussed how to capture the travel distance within a value stream. Documenting travel distance on your map provides insight and discloses where excess travel exists. However, just like many other pieces of information on the Current State Map, the data may get lost within the chaos displayed on the map.

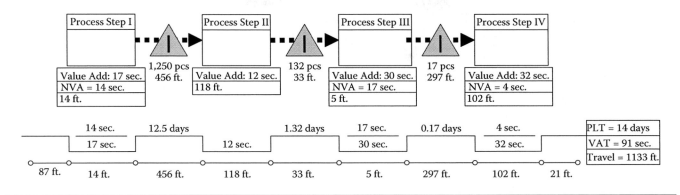

Figure 12.8 When capturing non-value-added time in the cycle time, document it directly above the cycle time of the appropriate process step box.

To combat this visibility problem, you can treat travel distance in a similar fashion to the timeline, and create a travel distance line below the timeline on your map.

The most common form of a travel distance line is a straight line drawn across the bottom of the map, with hash marks or other icons identifying the start and end of travel distance in relation to process steps in the value stream.

Figure 12.9 shows how this travel line can be added beneath the process flow and process time timelines. This example shows a situation where travel distance is measured from the middle of one process step to the middle of the next process step. The start and end points for each measured travel distance are drawn directly underneath and at the midpoint of the process step box.

Once you have added the travel distance line, you can then copy down the distances reported on the map onto the corresponding position on the line, just as you did with cycle times and inventory time. Figure 12.10 shows a completed process flow section of the Current State Map with all of this information in place.

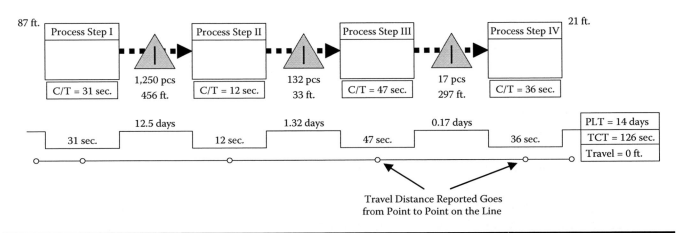

Figure 12.9 To make the tracking and explanation of travel distances easier, create a travel distance line directly beneath the timeline.

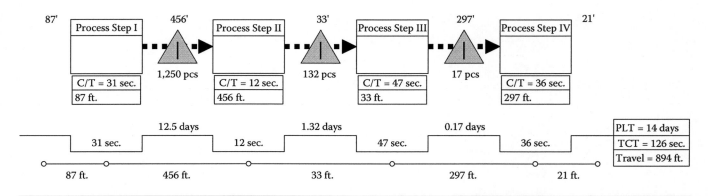

Figure 12.10 An excerpt from a Current State Map showing the completed time timeline and travel distance timeline.

When there is substantial travel distance inside a process step, the easy way to show this on the travel line is to draw the start and end points for each travel distance lined up with the corners of process step boxes. For example, this situation is often seen in closed-loop processes and/or some office processes. Figure 12.11 provides an example of how this looks.

As you can see in Figure 12.11, the travel distance documentation has been placed in the data boxes and underneath inventory icons in an effort to make it more visible. But, until it is shown on the travel distance line, the real impact of this travel is not fully seen.

Documenting Total Work Content Time

When working with labor content or work content (as discussed in Chapter 8), you can display this information just as you do cycle time. In place of the cycle time timeline, you can insert the work content data. The major difference

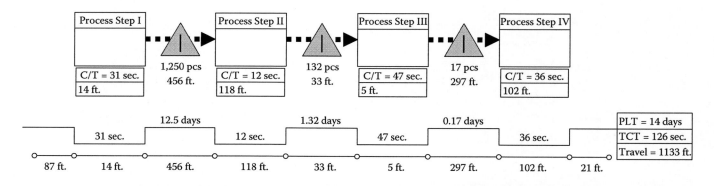

Figure 12.11 When large amounts of travel distance exist within a process step, it is generally easier to break down the travel distance line further to show this travel inside the task.

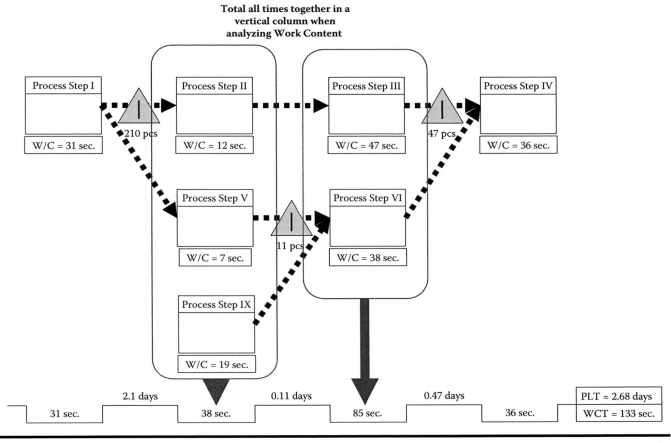

Figure 12.12   When reporting work content (total labor) on the timeline, as opposed to cycle time, you total work content for all process steps in the vertical column.

between cycle time and work content on the timeline is what data you pull to the line.

As discussed earlier, with cycle time, you only report the longest cycle time on the timeline when process boxes are aligned vertically due to parallel or sub-task paths. In contrast, with work content time, you sum all work content times together when they are aligned vertically, and place the total on the timeline, as shown in Figure 12.12.

When summing the values on the line, show the total work content time in the position where you usually report total cycle time. The abbreviation for this total work content time is typically shown as "WCT," "TWC," or "TWCT."

Chapter 13 will show the role communication plays in the value stream specific to a production setting.

Chapter 13

Capturing Communication Flow in a Production Setting

*Communication is something so simple and difficult that
we can never put it in simple words.*

T. S. Matthews

Introduction

While the process flow portion of a Current State Map provides great insight into how the value stream operates, the top or *communication* portion of the map can provide just as much information about waste. Communication is any and all information flowing within the value stream between employees, suppliers, customers, and equipment. In a production setting, many project teams focus their efforts on the process flow, at the expense of communication problems. Suboptimization of the value stream occurs during early process improvement associated with these efforts simply because of the chaos caused by excessive and/or ineffective communication throughout the process.

To avoid suboptimization, project teams should include the communication that occurs in a value stream. Mapping the communication can be accomplished simultaneously while documenting process flow. Capturing both portions of the map simultaneously requires a great deal of focus to ensure that you not only identify all pieces of both process flow and communication, but also that you document them accurately.

An easier approach is to follow the methodology presented in this book, and document the process flow first; then go back into the value stream and capture communication. When creating a Current State Map, you should capture both formal and informal communication. Obtaining this information requires observation and investigation. You must not only keep your eyes open for paperwork, reports, orders, routers, drawings, and other forms within the value stream; in addition, if you are going to truly uncover all of the communication, you must also ask questions of operators and other employees in the process.

To develop this portion of the map, you must start out with three basic components before adding in communication data: draw the customer, supplier, and control point on your map before you obtain this communication data. By understanding who the customer and supplier are, and how the process is controlled, you can ask better questions while you discover where communication exists. Additionally, this knowledge will give you better observations, because knowing who the players are in the value stream makes it easier to watch for interaction between these entities. The next three sections of this chapter describe these three components in more detail.

Identify the Customer

Just as you do with the process flow, you should start at the end of the value stream and work backwards, collecting data as you go. Before you (or your mapping team) enter into the value stream to collect communication data, you should have a conversation to identify the customer. This customer may be the ultimate customer, or end user, or it might be a third-party distributor, broker, or an internal customer. It should not matter to you who the customer is, as long as the customer is identified.

Once you've identified the customer, place an icon in the upper right-hand corner of the map, designated as the customer. If the customer is *external* to the organization in which the value stream lies, the most commonly used icon is the **external source**, shown here.

This icon makes it very simple and clear that the customer is external. The importance of this fact should never be overlooked by the project team, or by employees within the value stream. External customers' demands and expectations change regularly, and there is little that can be done to alter this fact other than react.

On the other hand, if the customer is *internal* to the organization (such as another department or production cell), then the proper icon is the **internal source** icon.

Whereas the external source icon is shaped like a building or factory to show that the customer is outside the organization, the symbol used for internal

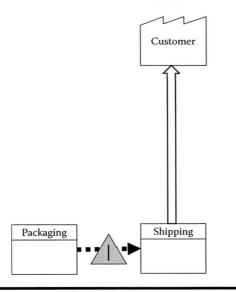

Figure 13.1 Typical alignment of the customer icon.

sources is shaped like a house. This shape is typically used to show that the customer is in-house, which may allow for some limited management of customer demands and customer expectations.

As mentioned, you should place the customer icon in the upper right-hand corner of the map, directly above the last process box in the process flow portion of the value stream, as shown in Figure 13.1. Because product being produced and delivered to the customer is what the customer wants, and should be delivered when the customer wants it, you can connect the customer to the process flow by using a pull arrow.

From this single point, the general flow of overall communication goes right to left on the Value Stream Map. This right-to-left flow essentially completes a looped flow of product and communication going left from the customer through the value stream's organization and the supplier. This flow then enters into the leftmost process step of the product flow and flows left to right on the page, until the customer's needs are fulfilled through delivery of the product to the customer. Figure 13.2 shows this overall flow pattern.

Additionally, by placing a delivery icon on top of the pull arrow, you can show how and when the product arrives at the customer's door. The delivery icon can be a truck, airplane, train, car, forklift, etc. On or beneath this icon, you can place the delivery days and/or times. Figure 13.3 provides an example of a delivery icon, with associated information showing that trucks deliver to the customer two times each day. Although this example in Figure 13.3 uses a truck, you could also use a forklift, train, ship, or even a person or a computer for transaction processes.

If there is a unique customer, this customer's name might be inserted into the customer icon, just as if a single shipping company is responsible for all deliveries, the shipping company name might be added to the delivery icon.

It is possible that there is more than one customer that is served by this value stream. In such occasions, it is not necessary to show a customer icon for each and every customer. For large specific customers, you may choose to place a separate icon on the page for effect. Or in situations where there are multiple classifications of customers (such as retail, industrial, and government), it might be appropriate to show an icon for each classification. Figure 13.4 shows an example of this scenario.

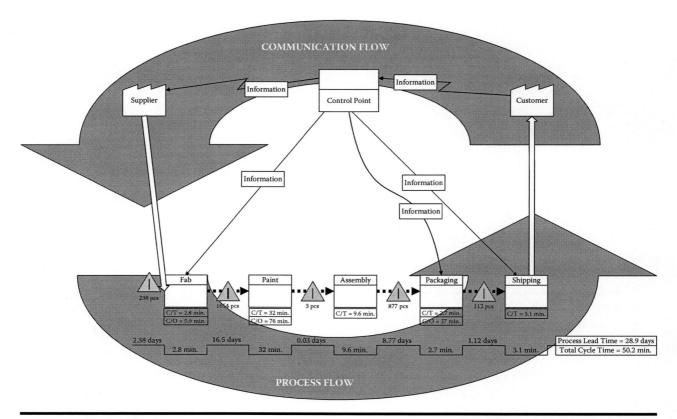

Figure 13.2   Process flows left to right, while the general flow of communication is right to left, closing the loop of the value stream.

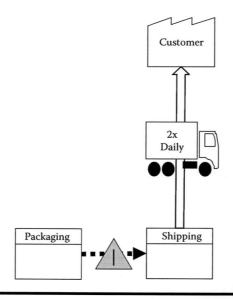

Figure 13.3   Use of the delivery icon, with the delivery schedule summarized on the icon.

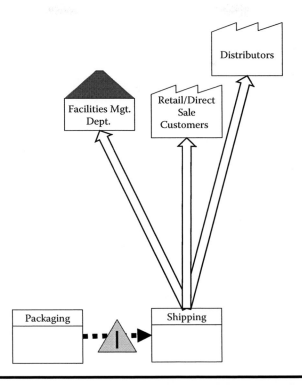

Figure 13.4   Multiple customers, both internal and external, can be shown on your map.

Identify the Supplier

After identifying and placing the customer(s) on the map, you should shift your attention to the left side of the communication equation: the supplier. Just like the customer, you should represent the supplier on the map using an external or internal icon. After identifying the supplier (or suppliers), and understanding whether this supplier is internal or external, draw the icon in the upper left-hand corner of the map directly over the first process box in the process flow portion of the map, as shown in Figure 13.5.

And just as with the customer icon, it is possible to tie it into the process flow using a pull arrow before ever going out into the value stream, because your suppliers deliver to you according to when you request the materials. You can also add a delivery icon here, to disclose the method and timing of material arrival from your suppliers.

Identify the Control Point of Communication

Within every value stream there is a single point that controls the flow and function of the value stream; this is called the *control point*. For most manufacturing operations, this is the production control department or production manager, depending on the size or structure of the company. This single point determines what is

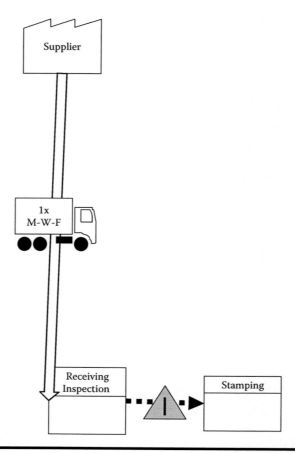

Figure 13.5   Adding the supplier icon to the map, with delivery schedule shown.

produced when, in what quantity, and at what pace. It is the funnel through which all communication concerning the value stream flows. Questions from customers and suppliers alike are routed through this point for answers, explanations, and clarification concerning the production process. Without this control point, the chaos experienced in many traditional manufacturing operations would be so out of control that it would be difficult to ever complete a single order or answer a question about the status of the order for the customer.

The icon for the **control point** is a rectangular box or an oversized process box.

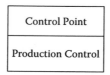

The control point is drawn in the middle of the page at the top in between the customer and the supplier, as shown in Figure 13.6. The name of the department or title of the single person performing this function may be written inside

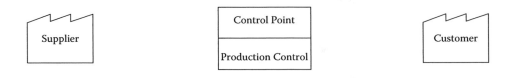

Figure 13.6   Proper placement of the control point in between the supplier and the customer at the top of your map.

the box, as shown above. Once again, this box can be drawn prior to reentering the value stream. You can usually determine what department or person is responsible for this activity during a preliminary meeting, either before or after you have completed the process flow portion of your map.

In the event that multiple persons or departments combine as a committee or council to perform this function (as is often the case in smaller companies), you can divide the bottom portion of the box into multiple sections, and then insert these participating departments or persons' titles to show the council makeup, as shown here.

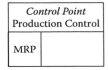

If a computer application, such as an MRP (manufacturing resource planning) or ERP (enterprise resource planning) system is part of this control function, then you can show that in a corner of the control point. Showing this systems support can assist project team members and operators in the value stream alike in their thinking about why certain tasks are completed as they are, and why some information is communicated in a certain format and at certain times.

Capturing Formal Communication

As you walk the process looking for *formal communication*, most of this type of communication will be easily spotted or explained, because formal communication is a documented or required part of the process. Those persons, both supervisors and operators, who are involved in the value stream generally have little difficulty discussing this type of communication. Most, if not all, of this formal communication can be found in paper form throughout the value stream. This type of communication includes, but is not limited to:

- Production schedules
- Work orders
- Sales orders
- Routers

- Purchase orders
- Purchase requisitions
- Forecasts
- Bill of materials (BOMs)
- Parts lists
- Production logs
- Quality reports
- Shipping schedules
- Order confirmations
- Pick tickets
- Bills of lading
- Customer complaint forms

In addition, daily shift-start or shift-end meetings can be formally communicated within the value stream. You should document each and every one of these items on the current state as you identify them.

Control Point		
Purch. Mgr.	Prod. Supvr.	Sales Mgr.

There are different ways to designate different types of communication: manual communication and electronic communication. You should designate communication that is manual in nature (i.e., communication that is not presented and maintained completely in an electronic format) by drawing a line on your map that connects the provider and receiver of the information communicated. You should also attach a label to each piece of communication represented by a line, so that anyone reviewing the map can quickly understand what makes up the communication shown. Use a straight or curved line to show this type of communication, with an arrowhead on the receiver's end pointing in the direction the communication flows, as shown in Figure 13.7.

To document *electronic communication* (i.e., information that is presented and maintained electronically), draw a jagged line and label it appropriately, as shown in Figure 13.8. Electronic communication typically includes drawings, BOMs, work orders, etc., that are maintained on a computer system and that employees within the value stream use computer terminals to look up the necessary information, *and do not print it out.*

How to Document Faxes and Telephone Calls

Inevitably, someone reviewing a Current State Map will want to argue about a piece of communication, even though it is required (i.e., formal communication). The argument is not about whether or not the communication actually exists, but rather whether it is manual or electronic. This argument is used to try and

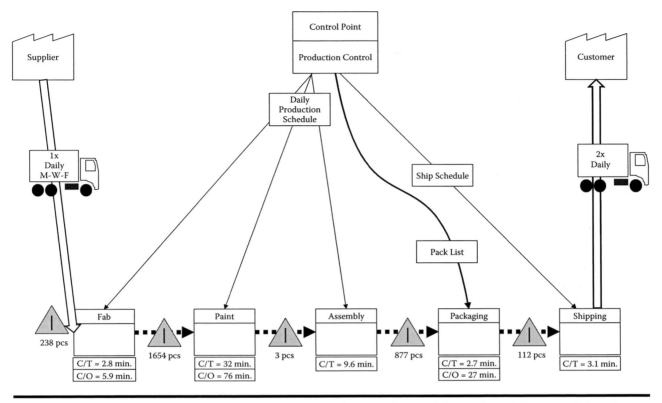

Figure 13.7 Manual or verbal communication can be shown using straight or curved lines, as shown here.

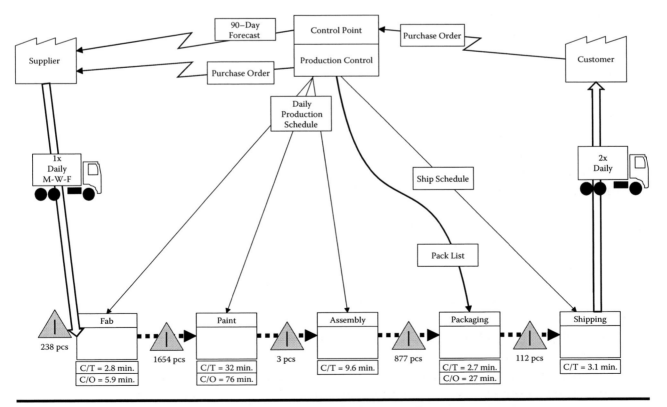

Figure 13.8 Documenting electronic communication using the electronic connector.

confuse the audience or discredit the mapper(s), or is quite possibly nothing more than a smokescreen used to start building roadblocks in front of the project team.

For example, is a fax electronic or manual? Is a telephone call electronic or manual? Is an e-mail electronic or manual? Instead of trying to rationalize e-mail as electronic until it is printed, or faxes as manual because they print a hard-copy (unless they are routed to your e-mail inbox), you should immediately stop this type of discussion. The answer lies within the person asking the question. Therefore, simply ask the person asking the question what he or she thinks. It really does not matter whether or not this type of communication is electronic or manual as long as it is clearly defined for the audience. If the question asker says electronic and it is shown as manual, then change it! Do not get into an argument about something so minor.

Many mappers show faxes and telephone calls as manual lines with a fax machine or telephone drawn above the line. In this manner, you can entirely avoid many of these trivial arguments, and the audience can focus on more critical issues. Figure 13.9 presents an example of how this type of map would look.

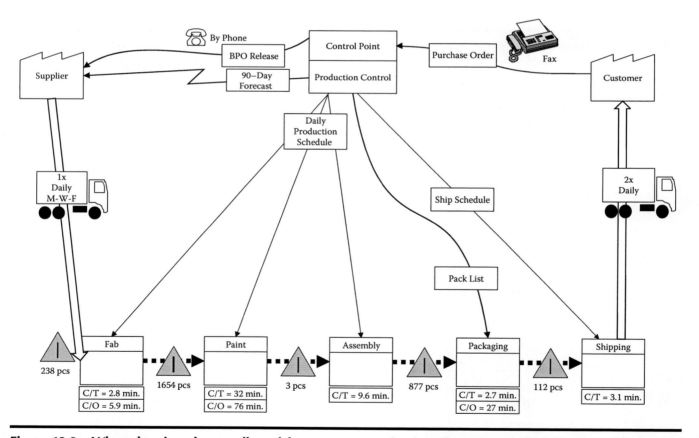

Figure 13.9 When showing phone calls and faxes as communication, draw a symbol of the telecommunications device to avoid unnecessary arguments about the type of communication that is involved.

Capturing Informal Communication

Identifying *informal communication* in a value stream is more difficult than seeing the formal communication within the process. Informal communication includes all of the following:

- Questions and answers that occur all day long within a value stream
- Management's attempt to move expedited orders through the process
- Inquiries from customers and suppliers
- Informal, on-the-fly changes made to schedules
- Ad hoc solutions to problems so an order can be completed

To find this type of communication, you must spend time in the value stream asking questions and observing the normal operating day of the process.

One of the most common forms of informal communication is the informal scheduling that occurs in many manufacturing facilities. This "go see" scheduling mindset occurs where an official schedule is produced, but then management goes out into the value stream to "see" where each process step is production-wise, and then makes ad hoc adjustments to the schedule in an effort to "get more work through the process."

You should draw all of this informal communication on your map in a similar fashion to the way you drew formal communication, using manual and electronic lines. However, when "go see" scheduling or other "go see" activities occur, you may choose to use a special icon to show that this is occurring, because this type of activity can be extremely disruptive to the normal flow of the value stream.

The icon you would use is a set of eyeglasses placed adjacent to the communication line; Figure 13.10 shows how this icon is used.

In many instances, informal communication is a dialog and exchange of ideas and information between two or more people. When this occurs, it is very possible to draw multiple communication lines between those persons involved. Or you might draw a single line between the two parties, and place an arrowhead at each end; Figure 13.11 shows how this might look. Often, one or more of those involved are not working within a process step or the control point, and may not be a customer or supplier. When this occurs, the best way to show this "other" participant is to draw a box in the communication portion of the map, and label it with the department name or job title of the participant. Then draw communication lines between the involved process step, control point, customer,

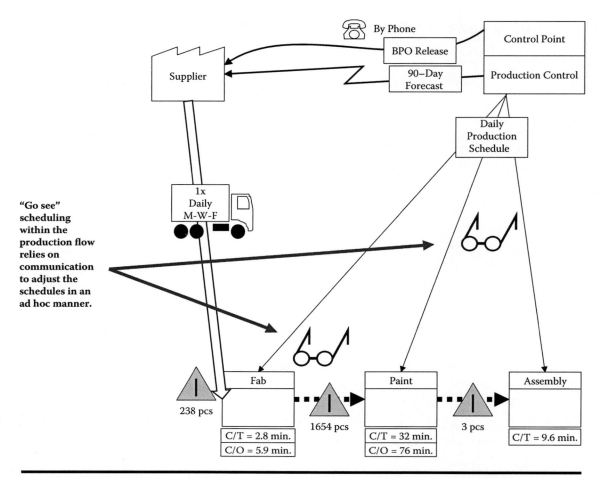

Figure 13.10 A section of a Current State Map showing where "go see" scheduling is occurring.

or supplier and the box representing the other party. Figure 13.11 shows how this concept is used.

Documenting Communication in Remanufacturing and MRO Settings

Although much of what is explained in this chapter has direct application for capturing communication in remanufacturing (i.e., refurbishment) operations and MRO (maintenance, repair, and overhaul) settings, the relationships and impact of customers, the control point, and suppliers can be substantially different from those in a true manufacturing company. Therefore, if you're mapping in a reman-ufacturing or MRO environment, you should be knowledgeable about the facts and techniques in this chapter, but you should also understand the subtle differ-ences in these relationships as they are presented in Chapter 14.

There are many parallelisms between the way customers, suppliers, and the control point relate to the process flow of a value stream in transactional settings

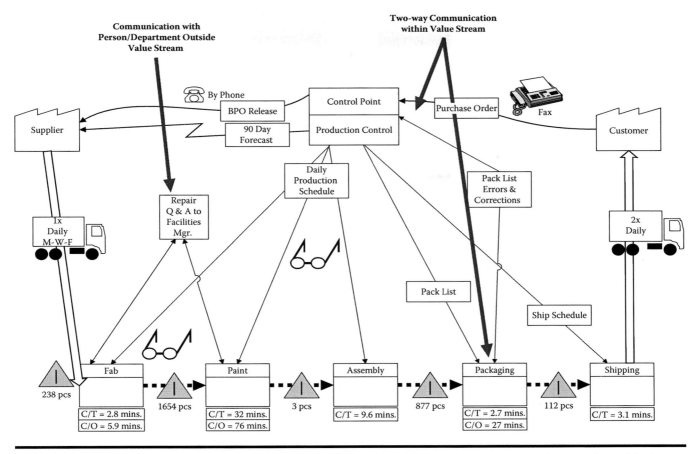

Figure 13.11   Using simple tools such as boxes with labels identifying support persons interacting with the value stream, or two-way arrows, provides powerful information to your audience.

and in the remanufacturing/MRO world. This is one more reason why all Value Stream Mappers should be able to document both production and transactional processes. Sometimes, the subtle differences between process types provide great insight into how to map a unique or "different" value stream.

The More Communication, the Better—Or Is It?

Because the entire purpose of the Current State Map is to portray an accurate and visual representation of how the value stream actually operates, it is important to get all communication on the map. Many mappers have shown a tendency to be somewhat reluctant to do this. However, if the goal is to convince both those employees working within the process and management that chaos exists, then what better way to show the chaos created by excessive communication?

Communication quite often slows down production processes while operators are waiting for replies to questions, directions on what to produce next, or other information. The best way to show this effect on the value stream is to show that a tremendous amount of non-value-added time is used to communicate (or often overcommunicate) information throughout the process. The more lines you draw, the more effective you can be at explaining this lost production time. This is a waste! So don't be afraid to show it.

Chapter 14 will take these concepts into transactional processes.

Chapter 14

Capturing Communication Flow in a Transactional Environment

The worst thing about the miracle of modern communications
is the Pavlovian pressure it places upon everyone
to communicate whenever a bell rings.

Russell Baker

Introduction

Capturing communication in a value stream is no different in a transactional world than it is in a manufacturing setting. As a matter of fact, many value streams found in a "transactional" company or organization are in fact production processes, and mapping these value streams should be done using the tools and techniques described throughout this book to document manufacturing (i.e., production) value streams.

Yet many people continue to believe that mapping transactional value streams is a different tool altogether. Earlier chapters have already discussed the similarities and differences in capturing the process flow in each of these two worlds. The purpose of this chapter is to address the similarities and differences specifically in the *communication* aspect of the mapping process.

In some respects, documenting communication in a transactional value stream is more difficult than documenting communication in a manufacturing value stream. This higher level of difficulty is simply due to the challenge faced by the mapper in separating *communication* from *process*. But once you have identified this differentiation, the course of action you use to capture the communication flow is identical, regardless of the setting. Therefore, let's look at that problem first.

Separating Communication Flow from Process Flow

Before you even delve into the communication portion of a Current State Map, there's a very helpful exercise you can conduct that can help provide the proper focus on communication. First, review the process flow in a transactional value stream so that you understand what the product or service is that is moving through the process, and then separate out the data that is associated with this movement. Doing this can provide some much-needed clarity to the task at hand. If you don't understand what the process flow focuses on, and what data is used strictly as necessary inputs into creating the finished product or service, it can be extremely difficult for you (and your mapping team) to keep the communication and process flows separate, as you are mapping out not only the communication portion of the map, but the map as a whole.

As you begin to filter out these pieces, list on a sheet of paper or whiteboard what the focus of the process flow is. Underneath this label, list any and all data that the project team can identify as a part of a task or process step in the process flow. List data regardless of whether or not it appears to be value added. Finally, next to each data point listed, write down how each piece of data arrives at the process step where it is used. This description should be fairly basic and simple—for example:

- "It is already provided in hard copy."
- "It automatically arrives electronically."
- "The employee performing the task must query a system."
- "The employee must ask another person for it."

Communication exists where interaction occurs between the employee(s) within the process step and another person (or persons) to gain or transfer information or knowledge about the process. It also occurs where interaction takes place with a computer system, network, or other equipment to gain or transfer information or knowledge. If the data already exists at the point it is used without an inquiry, query, or a verbal or written exchange, it should not be mistaken for communication. Figure 14.1 is a quick summary of the exercise of separating communication from process.

Similarities of Transactional Communication to Communication in Manufacturing

Communication in transactional value streams is essentially the same as in a manufacturing setting. As you explore what is actually occurring in various "transactional" value streams, it becomes clear that many of these are, in fact, production value streams within a transactional world. As discussed in earlier chapters, in-house print shops, claims payment departments, mortgage processing companies, and various other departments and companies contain many

```
┌─────────────────────────────────────────────┐
│  Separating Communication from Process        │
├─────────────────────────────────────────────┤
│                                               │
│  (1) Identify the focus of the process flow   │
│                                               │
│  (2) List all data associated with the process│
│                                               │
│  (3) For each data point, show how this data  │
│       arrives at the process step where it is │
│       used                                    │
│                                               │
│  (4) Data is part of communication when       │
│       interaction occurs between employees    │
│       and/or systems to gain or transfer      │
│       knowledge                               │
│                                               │
└─────────────────────────────────────────────┘
```

Figure 14.1   How to separate communication from process before documenting communication in a transactional environment.

production value streams. With this knowledge in hand, it should be relatively easy to capture the communication throughout the process.

Some mappers actually believe it is easier to see the communication in a transactional world due to the functions performed by employees in office settings. Because a larger percentage of these employees communicate verbally with "outsiders" as a normal part of their jobs, it is easier for mappers to discuss what these employees talk about, with whom, and how often—much easier than trying to find the same information on a manufacturing floor. And because, in many cases, there is much more communication going on, it is easier to capture and document chaos on your Current State Map, as shown in Figure 14.2.

But regardless of the type of value stream you encounter in a transactional setting, the end result is the same. Employees within the value stream communicate with each other about a wide variety of things. They communicate with supervisors and managers about defects, instructions and the lack thereof, as well as the priority of work before them. These employees also communicate with people and systems outside of the value stream on a regular basis in order to complete their work. These employees often work according to a schedule and have the work "rescheduled" in exactly the same way that operators on a manufacturing floor do; "hot orders" exist even in a transactional world.

Differences in Transactional Communication

Even though you must understand that communication is just communication—regardless of the setting, industry, or functional area of the organization—you must also understand that subtle differences do exist. The major difference was discussed in the opening paragraphs of this chapter: knowing how to separate *process* from *communication* is an essential ingredient in portraying a value stream in such a way that the audience is convinced that a fair and accurate depiction of their world has been presented. Without this buy-in from the

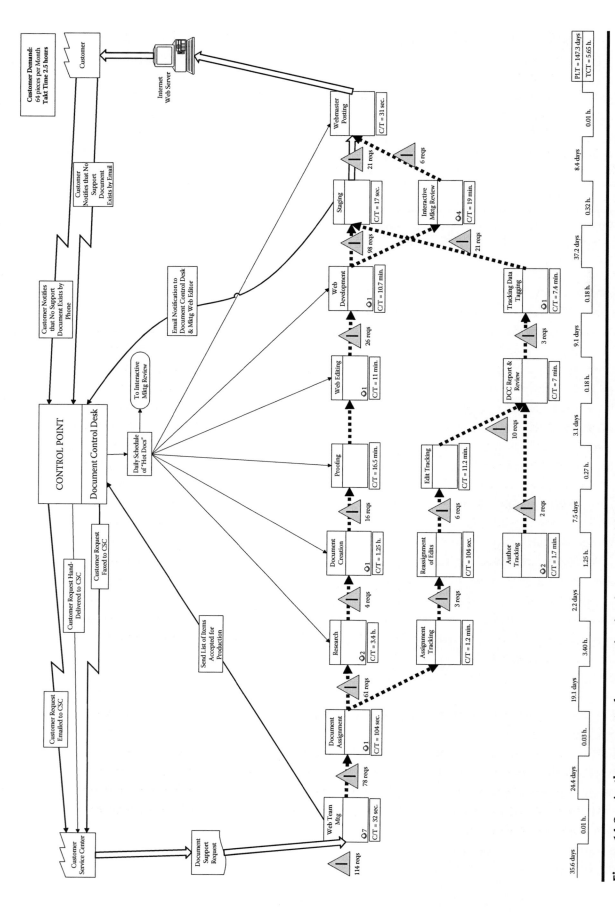

Figure 14.2 As the amount of communication increases within a value stream, chaos increases as well. This Current State Map appears to be "under control" when reviewing the communication. However, as more communication is identified and added to the drawing, it is easy to understand why chaos occurs.

workforce, it can be extremely difficult to engage the employees in making positive change.

By separating out process and data (which are synonymous with material or parts in a manufacturing setting) from communication, you can clear this first hurdle when mapping a transactional value stream. Many employees do not understand that they even have a process, but they do understand that they communicate all day long. By getting this piece correct, and documenting it on the map in a manner that accurately depicts the situation (even if this means showing absolute chaos), you can quickly begin to gain acceptance from the employees in the value stream.

Mapping Customers Who Also Function as Suppliers and Control Points

When mapping some transactional value streams (as well most remanufacturing or maintenance, repair, and overhaul, or MRO value streams), it is possible to quickly get confused about who is the customer and who is the supplier if you try and use the basic mapping technique described in Chapter 13. The concepts of "customer" and "supplier" are fairly straightforward in manufacturing, but the lines begin to blur when you leave basic manufacturing and begin to focus on other value streams.

In a transactional world (as well as in MRO and remanufacturing), it is possible that your customer is *also* your supplier. It is a very common situation to find transactional processes where the customer submits work into the value stream to be processed (i.e., to have value added) and returned to the customer. In scenarios such as this, the customer is the supplier. (This concept was first introduced in *Value Stream Management for the Lean Office,* by Tom Shuker and Don Tapping, Productivity Press, 2003.)

Whereas it is possible to simply show the customer icon and the supplier icon (as described in Chapter 13), you can also show them as a single icon on one side of the map or the other, and show that this single source is both feeding the process flow and receiving the finished product or service at the end of the process flow. An example of this is shown in Figure 14.3.

It is also possible that a customer could be the supplier *and* the control point. In many situations, a customer provides materials, products, or forms to the first step in the process flow. This customer, who is now acting as the supplier, may retain ownership of what was submitted and inform the process flow as to where in the work schedule the item submitted is to be handled. Questions, inquiries, etc., from within the process flow are directed to the customer for explanation and determination. In situations such as this, the customer fulfills all three roles, as shown in Figure 14.4.

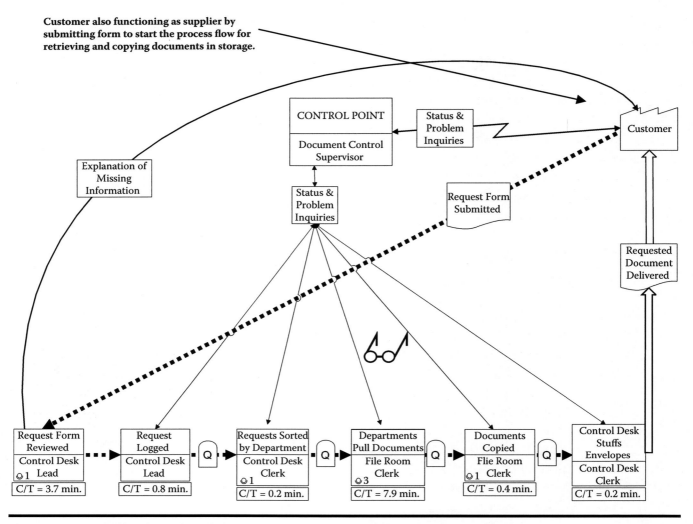

Figure 14.3 How to show that the customer is also the supplier.

Mapping Multiple Control Points and Informal Control Points

It is even possible to encounter value streams where multiple control points, or no control point, exist. In situations like these, you should draw exactly what you find.

Mapping Multiple Control Points

If you or your mapping team are told by employees and/or management in the value stream that two or more control points exist, as you are asking questions and observing the value stream in operation, then you should draw the value stream this way. Show the multiple control points as separate boxes on the top of the page, as illustrated in Figure 14.5, and include all communication identified. When you map these types of value streams, they look much more chaotic than maps with a single control point. The reason is simple: they are!

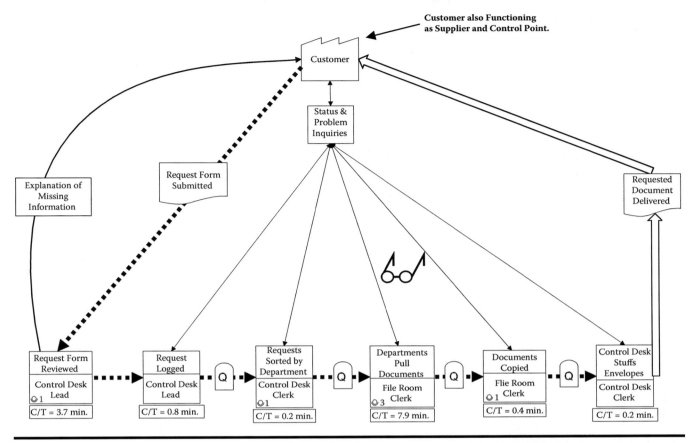

Figure 14.4 In transactional and even in some production environments, it is possible that the customer may also be the supplier and the control point.

Mapping What Seem Like No Control Points but Are Informal Control Points

A unique situation that can occur is the value stream with no control point at all. When you map a value stream with such a condition, it can become very difficult to show exactly what is happening. The customer may or may not also be the supplier; it really does not matter. It is a challenge to accurately show such a situation without confusing the educated value-stream audience. If your audience has seen Current State Maps before, they will begin to ask questions about the missing control point. If you place the customer or supplier icon too close to the middle, it may be misinterpreted as the control point. Therefore, these maps, like the one shown in Figure 14.6, require a great deal of explanation from the mapper. When value streams like this exist, the natural inclination of the employees working in the process will almost always be an absolute certainty that there is nothing controlling the process. They believe that the value stream just operates on its own with no one in control.

The reality of the situation, however, is that there are actually *multiple informal control points* throughout the value stream. These informal control points may be employees, groups, or departments within the process flow. They might also be

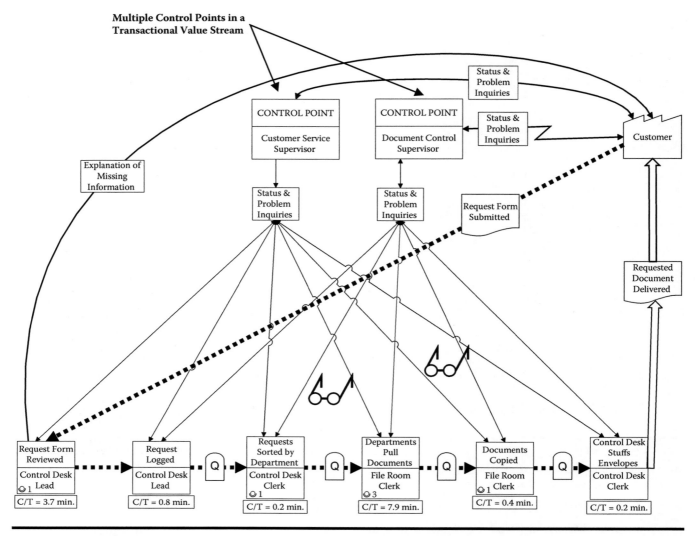

Figure 14.5   Mapping multiple control points in a transactional value stream.

supervisory or management-level employees, or offices that are not in the process flow but that are still heavily involved in the communication portion of the map.

For example, looking within the communication portion of Figure 14.6, it is possible to find at least four separate employees that are functioning as multiple informal control points. As you can see by the large number of communication lines on the map, the amount of chaos present can be easily seen by the audience.

Remember to Map What You See

Regardless of what type of situation you encounter, you should stick to the single most important rule of Value Stream Mapping: *you should map what you see.* It may seem completely unreasonable and illogical at the time, but mapping what is actually occurring is the goal. When you review your map with selected employees working within the value stream, you will quickly identify any corrections

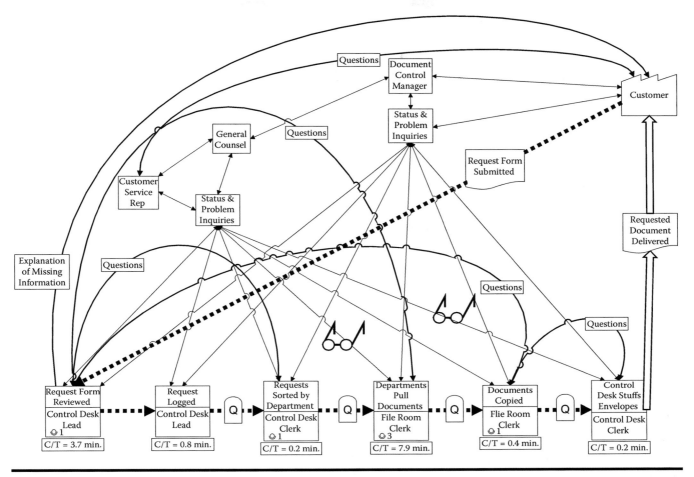

Figure 14.6   Mapping a transactional value stream with no control points.

that you need to make. But most important, these employees will provide the validation of what you have drawn. Once you achieve this validation, the process of gaining buy-in from all employees can begin.

Case Study in a Transactional Environment

Current State Map

Case Study: Path Links Pathology Services

Health care organization—histology laboratory

The Current State Map shown in Figure 14.7 is from Path Links Pathology Services in Lincolnshire, England, as mapped by a Lean team during Value Stream Mapping training. During a two-day workshop, the team was able to identify numerous instances of waiting, excess motion, and excess travel. As the team members mapped, they also identified that excessive amounts of communication existed, which routinely added to the time required to process specimens through this histology laboratory.

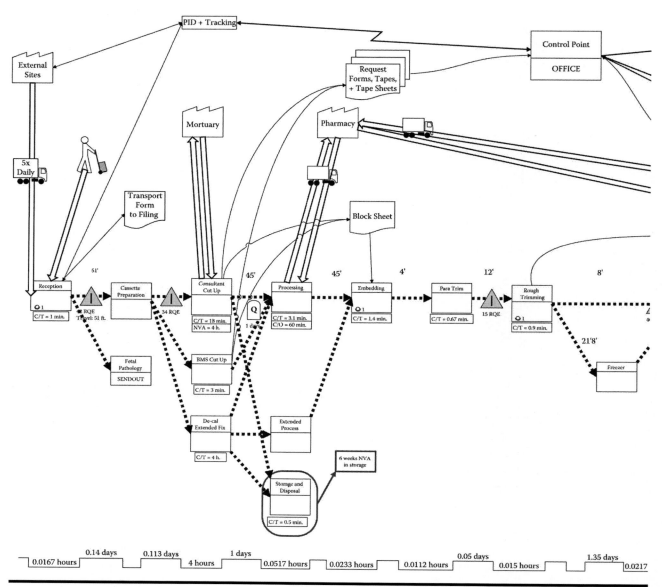

Figure 14.7 Current State Map, Path Links Pathology Services (health care organization—histology laboratory).

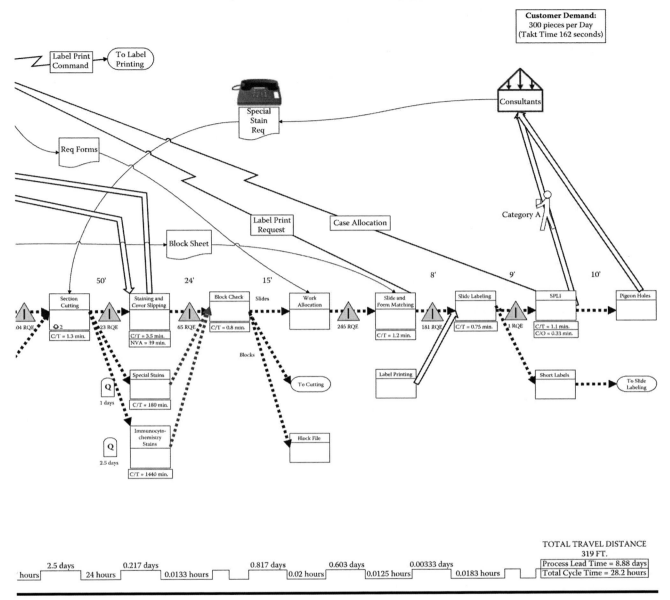

Figure 14.7 (Continued).

Although much of the work conducted within this setting is heavily regulated by the government, the team found that the majority of non-value-added activity within the value stream was well within the laboratory staff's span of control.

The outcomes from the complete mapping exercise and associated kaizen events are discussed at the conclusion of Chapter 17.

After you have completed your Current State Map, Chapter 15 will prepare you for presenting it to your organization.

Chapter 15

Presenting the Current State Map to the Employees Involved

Our own reality may be difficult for us to face with honesty,
but it is the only reliable and reasonable place to begin.

Donald DeMarco

Introduction

Once you have drawn the Current State Map, the real work begins. You must understand very early on that the Current State Mapping process never ends. Just like all other continuous improvement concepts, this is a *continuous cycle*. Every time the map is presented, every time someone reviews the map, and every time a group meets to discuss the value stream (and therefore the Value Stream Map), there is a very strong probability that someone will recognize the need to update the map. *And they should!* Informal additions to posted maps by penciling in suggestions and thoughts is a common way of bringing issues and ideas to the mapper and/or project team. However, official maps should not be *formally* updated without discussion by the team, and updating should be done only within boundaries established by the Executive Council.

Presenting the Current State Map is powerful. This is the single most compelling argument a project team has to expose the problems, issues, and opportunities associated with a value stream. By first presenting the map to the employees working within the value stream, you can quickly address any obvious errors, omissions, and corrections; in fact, you can address them on the spot by drawing directly on the map you're presenting. This fast action can create a strong sense of openness and inclusion for employees.

Getting this buy-in from the workforce goes a long ways toward winning the immediate battle faced by any project team: acceptance on the part of employees concerning the need to change. With employee buy-in comes faster approval of the ideas presented to management. Although the greatest roadblocks often occur from midlevel managers, if the frontline employees and upper management all agree on the opportunities, the battle at the roadblocks is much easier to win.

It is possible, though, to knock down many of these roadblocks during the mapping process if supervisors and midlevel managers can also believe that their concerns are adequately addressed. Listening to these segments of the workforce and ensuring that the issues they bring up are included, or at least discussed, will simplify the work required to overcome these barriers. And while it is extremely important to listen to everyone during the mapping process, it may be even more important to present the Current State Map in a manner that is open and honest, that invites comment, and that allows for changes to be made to the map "on-the-fly." Understanding how to present the map in an effective manner can make your job and the project team's job much easier.

The Purpose of Presenting the Map

Presenting the completed Current State Map is not an exercise to merely allow the mapper and project team to review their work one last time prior to working on the future state. The sole purpose of this presentation is to create acceptance and agreement from employees and management working within the value stream. Therefore, you should listen carefully to the questions, concerns, and feedback provided during this presentation.

Listening to the audience, making adjustments to the map as necessary, and responding to the questions and inquiries can greatly simplify the task of gaining acceptance. There is no better way to gain employees' trust than to show them that their input is valued—in other words, that their ideas and concerns are legitimate. The goal of creating the map is to document the reality of the current state, to develop a starting point for change. But, as shown in Figure 15.1, the objective of *presenting* the map is to *create a single team* of employees and managers alike within the value stream who are *dedicated to improving the process.*

It is nearly impossible to get unanimous buy-in from large groups of employees, or from employees and managers who have existed in a poor work environment

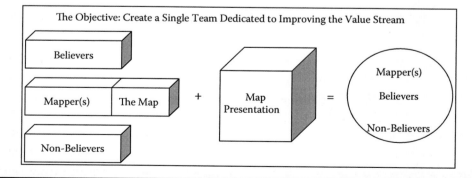

Figure 15.1   The objective of presenting the Current State Map to the employees in the value stream is to create a single team dedicated to improving the process.

for an extended period of time. Because of this reality in dealing with people, mappers and project teams must accept the fact that they may not be able to sway every person in the audience.

You should never compromise your integrity by blindly changing the map just to try and convince the one holdout. But, making legitimate corrections and additions sends a powerful message. And in return for this willingness to include the workforce in an attempt to "get it right" through this presentation, project teams will see faster and stronger buy-in from the majority of the workforce.

To this end, the team may want to conduct one final brainstorming session on the current state before presenting it to the workforce. Using the same methodology as presented in Chapter 3, the team should review the Current State Map and allow all team members to brainstorm the perceived pain, problems, and issues. This exercise will now provide a forum for identifying any perceived problems or pain that might have been overlooked during the actual mapping, and these issues will once again come to the surface, allowing discussion to help the team determine what should be reviewed once more.

As stated in Chapter 3, you should not stop with this brainstorming list and discussion. Conduct a follow-up exercise by having each team member independently work through the brainstorming list to categorize each problem into the eight wastes of Lean (see Quality Glossary at the end of the book). Each team member should write down which of the eight wastes apply to each problem listed. More than one waste can be assigned to a problem.

Once everyone has had the opportunity to assign waste, you can then total up the number of times each Lean waste appears, as well as the number of total wastes that appear for each problem. From this exercise, you can not only eliminate preconceived ideas from the mapping team's collective mind and focus on what the team as a whole believes is the biggest problem (based upon the number of wastes listed next to each problem), but you can also prepare yourself for many of the issues that will be brought forth by the employees working within the value stream when the Current State Map is presented to them.

How to Present the Map: Keep an Open Mind

Because the goal of Current State Mapping is to document how the value stream actually operates, and the objective of the presentation is to obtain agreement on this reality, you must go into the presentation phase with an open mind. It is very likely that the world will change quickly once all employees in an area have an opportunity to express their ideas, opinions, and concerns.

Hidden issues may surface during this meeting. It is not uncommon that painful issues—such as difficult changeovers or interpretation of customer information—were not observed or captured during the initial mapping exercise. Distractions and demands on employees' time during the mapping may have allowed some items, such as these, to slip through the cracks. Therefore, this presentation is the perfect time to either add the information or to schedule time to go back into the value stream and observe it firsthand after the meeting for verification and accuracy.

Not everyone in the room will agree with the map. For that matter, not everyone in the room will agree with each other on a wide variety of topics related to the Current State Map. Accept this fact. Make a strong attempt to listen to all points of view. This does not mean that you need to include everyone's thoughts in the map. Sometimes, the position held by an individual is clearly off base. This position may be self-serving; or it might be a defensive mechanism driven by fear; or it might be a simple lack of understanding.

Be prepared to change the map. This is not a sign of weakness or failure. Change is part of the process. Subscribing to the underlying theory of Lean, it is continuous improvement. Each and every time the map is reviewed, additional information or errors may be identified.

Make Sure Your Audience Understands the Map

Because the objective of presenting the map to the employees working within the value stream is to gain the audience's acceptance of the facts and obtain their agreement with the decision to pursue positive change, it is imperative that the audience understand what is being presented. All too often in process improvement projects, reports or presentations are given to management or the workforce without regard to the impact on these employees. In such situations, a mandate has been given to change the process, and therefore, in the project team's collective mind, it does not matter what employees within the process think. This unfortunately creates a situation where, as presentations are made, either no input from the workforce is allowed, or the input that is offered is totally ignored.

To be successful, the audience must understand what the map says and be allowed to offer corrections or additions. Without your audience's understanding, you might as well be talking a foreign language when explaining what happens next. When the audience does not understand the map, their minds will shut down to what you are saying, and there will be no acceptance or agreement on the issues represented on the map.

Keep Your Presentation Brief and Focused

To this end, it is important to consistently follow a set of presentation rules, which are intended to simplify the learning in a relatively short meeting. By design, these Current State Map presentations should last no more than 30 min. By keeping the meeting moving and focused, you can help the audience stay tuned in and on task. This may require a tremendous amount of effort from the mapper presenting at the meeting, because there is always at least one person in the audience who wants to either solve the problem "right now" or wants to debate each and every step of the map in great detail. *Keep it short and focused.*

Make Sure Your Audience Can Read the Map

To prepare for the presentation meeting, there is a basic set of aids that you should have in hand to assist you with your audience's learning. The following paragraphs describe a few of these options.

Individual Maps versus One Large Display Map

When presenting, make sure that each member of the audience has a legible copy of the map to help them in following along with the discussion; otherwise, you should display, in a central location, a single map that is large enough for everyone to see. The format of this Current State Map largely depends on the environment and the expectations of the project team, upper management, the Executive Council (or continuous improvement steering committee), and the employees within the value stream.

Many times, a single map is drawn on a whiteboard, a large roll of paper, or flipchart paper and is displayed on the wall. From these large wall-based maps, it is possible to have the audience stand in a semicircle at the map as the presentation is made. Standing in a meeting such as this also assists with keeping to a timeline to end the meeting as scheduled. In some instances, the mapping team may choose to take a digital photo of the map and print individual copies for each person in attendance.

Digital Photos

It is easy to see from Figure 15.2 the difficulty in using digital photos taken of a whiteboard for this purpose. The clarity of the photo is often less than perfect, and glare from lights can distort or completely hide text from the map. However, for smaller maps, this method works well.

Digital Maps Created with Software

For presentation purposes (and for long-term preservation of the map), it has become commonplace to take the initial efforts of the mapping team and merge them into a single map through the use of software, as shown in Figure 15.3. This digital version can then be printed out as individual maps (assuming the maps are not too long or too detailed) or can be plotted to an appropriate size and displayed on the wall.

Slide Presentations

Another way to display the map is as part of a slide presentation. This method is quite acceptable, assuming that the audience can read the map. Unfortunately, this presentation style, similar to the problems with digital photos, often results in illegible or hard-to-follow maps. If the map is too long or detailed, the type may be so small that the audience cannot read it. Or, if the process flow is long,

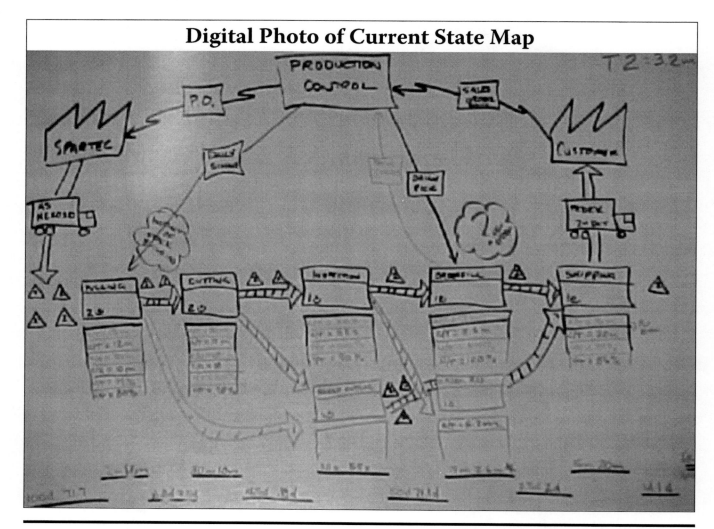

Figure 15.2   While digital photos of Value Stream Maps are a very efficient way to capture the map, this form of documentation can also be difficult to read.

the text can be made readable only by displaying it in sections, and a screen scroll or subsequent page must be shown. This presentation style can actually hinder the learning process, because the audience cannot visualize and absorb the map as a whole. Regardless of the format you choose, *ensure that the map is visible and legible* to all in attendance.

Explain the Icons You Used in Creating the Map

Start out the presentation with an explanation and perhaps a legend or key of the icons used in the map. Many mappers prefer to show a legend on a wall or as a slide in a presentation projected on a screen, as seen in Figure 15.4. For Current State Map presentations, we recommend that you display and explain only those icons you used on the map itself. This can greatly simplify the presentation and keep the focus on the map at hand. Showing a legend of the icons used in the map prior to explaining the map enhances and speeds up the learning process.

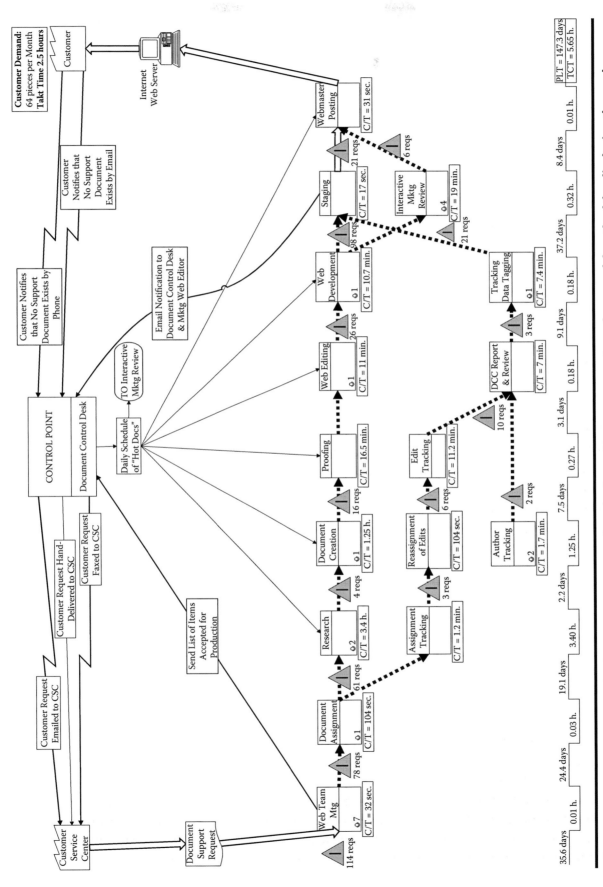

Figure 15.3 Digital versions of Value Stream Maps produced using software are an extremely powerful method for displaying the work completed by you or your mapping team.

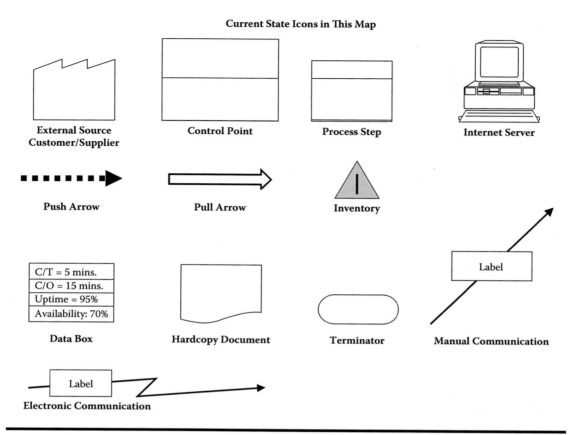

Current State Icons in This Map

External Source Customer/Supplier

Control Point

Process Step

Internet Server

Push Arrow

Pull Arrow

Inventory

C/T = 5 mins.
C/O = 15 mins.
Uptime = 95%
Availability: 70%

Data Box

Hardcopy Document

Terminator

Label

Manual Communication

Label

Electronic Communication

Figure 15.4   An example of a legend of Current State Map icons used to educate the workforce.

Answer All Questions and Comments While You're Presenting

Take time to explain the current state in as much detail as necessary. Do not ignore any question or comment. Pay close attention to the audience's reactions as you present the map. If anyone appears to be confused or upset, include that person in the conversation to determine the cause of his or her reaction. If the individual still doesn't understand something, drill down into more detail, and use the project team and other audience members to help that individual understand. For those people who become upset or defensive about something in the Current State Map, encourage other audience members who are obviously in agreement to assist in breaking down this issue.

Change the Map as You Present It

As you present the map, there will be instances when someone in attendance will identify a correction or missing information. When this occurs, do not gloss over, ignore, or defer until later making the change. To gain further acceptance of the map, you should invite the person who brought the item up in discussion to come forward and *make proposed changes directly on the face of the map* with a colored

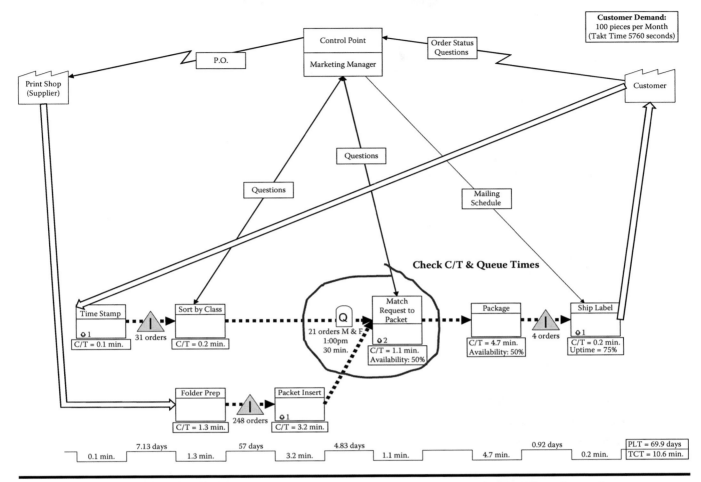

Figure 15.5 When presenting the map to an audience, invite participants to write directly on the map as they bring up issues that may not have been observed or addressed earlier.

pencil or marker, as shown in Figure 15.5. The mapper or a project team member can assist as necessary to ensure that the correct icons and symbols are used.

Once again, this technique helps you gain acceptance and understanding of the map and recognition of the issues and opportunities that exist within the value stream. If a suggested change is lacking data to support the recommendation, there may not be a correct answer available when the issue is discussed. This should not stop the task of temporarily updating the map during the presentation. Simply circle or highlight the incorrect data, or write in the data label (such as C/T, C/O, Avail, etc.) with a colored pencil or marker so that the mapping team can go back into the value stream after the presentation and collect accurate data for validation.

Setting the stage with the Current State Map may determine the level of success experienced by the project team during implementation. If the employees working within the value stream understand the map and accept the reality of this current condition, the project team can implement improvement with confidence that the workforce as a whole is accepting of the need to change.

Current State Map Presentation Tips

1. Present the map with an open mind
2. Be prepared to change the map
3. Keep in mind that your audience needs to understand
4. Keep your presentation short and focused
5. Ensure that the map is visible and legible
6. Show a legend of icons you used to create the map, before you explain the map
7. Make changes directly on the face of the map

Figure 15.6   Summary of tips for presenting a Current State Map to employees.

In contrast, if you do not communicate your message effectively, and if multiple persons show resistance to change or do not understand the issues, the team can expect to experience numerous challenges along the implementation path. Figure 15.6 summarizes these presentation tips.

Document Opportunities for Additional Improvement Projects

When you're presenting a Current State Map, you should take advantage of this opportunity of meeting with your audience to listen for additional project opportunities. Listening to employees' concerns about other value streams can create buy-in by showing that the efforts of the project team and overall improvement initiatives are not limited to one specific area. Just giving some employees the opportunity to speak goes a long way toward gaining their acceptance. As discussions start to identify new opportunities elsewhere within the organization, make sure that a mapper or a member of the project team is capturing this valuable information. Write down all such ideas, concerns, and opportunities on a whiteboard, flipchart, or even a piece of paper, if that's all that is available.

If time allows, move this discussion into a brainstorming session, first on the value stream presented in the Current State Map, and then on other value streams (again, as time allows). Remember, however, to stick to the time frame originally established, because it is very easy for these types of brainstorming sessions to quickly get out of control and go on too long.

Actively involving workers within the value stream in a brainstorming session creates ownership in the continuous improvement effort. Allowing employees to voice their perception of problems, issues, and opportunities is the perfect situation to start the process of cultural change. This exchange of ideas and concerns eliminates many barriers between the workforce and those who are assigned to a project team. As employees lay their concerns on the table, the amount of ownership they have in the value stream begins to grow. If employees truly believe that they are being included in the process of change, it is much easier to implement change.

Employees can easily recognize that mappers and team members alike are proactively listening when Current State Map presentations evolve into a brainstorming session on problems. Although this alone is extremely powerful, it is not the sole purpose of the session. Many beneficial observations come out of these sessions. Perhaps the most important outcome is not what is *said,* but what is *observed.* When you begin to watch the participants in a brainstorming session, other opportunities present themselves. This is the perfect time to start identifying future project team members. The intensity and passion that some employees exhibit during these sessions allows you to scout out future project team members and perhaps even future Value Stream Mappers.

Once the Current State Map has been finalized, move on to Chapter 16 to learn how to create a manufacturing process Future State Map.

FUTURE STATE: DESIGNING AND MAPPING YOUR NEW (OR DESIRED) PROCESS

Chapter 16

Creating a Future State Map in a Manufacturing Environment

There's a way to do it better—find it.

Thomas A. Edison

Introduction

Once you have presented the Current State Map, you and the project team can begin the real work associated with Value Stream Mapping (VSM). The team can now create a Future State Map of the value stream to guide positive change in the days and weeks ahead. Whereas the Current State Map provides the insight into the problems that exist in the value stream, it is the *future* state that determines the goal for the team.

Future State Maps are what each and every mapper wants to complete. This Future State Map is the basis for action in a continuous improvement project. Lean practitioners rely on this map as the tool from which action plans are developed by project teams.

Perhaps the most interesting thing about Future State Maps is that it is rare that the value stream ever actually turns out exactly as the future state was drawn. This map is the goal. It is the inspiration. But every mapper needs to recognize that as each of the action items (which are outcomes of the Future State Map) are implemented, the value stream begins to change, because new issues and opportunities are discovered. The value stream itself is morphing, and as a result, the eventual outcome in terms of change will come close to that expressed on the map, but it will not be exactly as shown on the map.

Some things will take too long, or are too expensive, or cannot be accomplished due to other business considerations. This should not stop the mapper and the project team from moving forward with the Future State Mapping exercise, or the implementation that follows development of this map.

As stated previously, the intent of this book is not to teach you about Lean concepts and principles. Instead, the purpose of this book is to teach you about Value Stream Mapping. We assume that you already have a general knowledge of Lean principles and concepts. If not, you may need to learn more about pull systems, supermarkets, kanbans, continuous flow, and setup reduction. Additionally, if you haven't already learned how cycle times, availability, uptime reliability, and staffing affect process throughput and flow, now would be a good time to become educated on these topics as well.

Using Future State Icons

When drawing a Future State Map, there are additional icons available to help you clearly represent how an efficient value stream should look and operate. The additional icons contained in this book are by all means not every symbol available to you. As we stated during our discussion of the current state, you can and should use whatever icon is required to get the message across to your audience. Figure 16.1 contains the most commonly used icons for Future State Maps. These icons should be used in conjunction with any and all current-state icons to create the Future State Map.

Just as the Current State Map is a visual representation of the process as it actually operates today, the Future State Map is intended to be just as visual a picture of how the value stream should operate as an efficient process. One of the more challenging issues for a mapper is to keep control of the project team and not let their ideas for the future state become too large or futuristic. It is

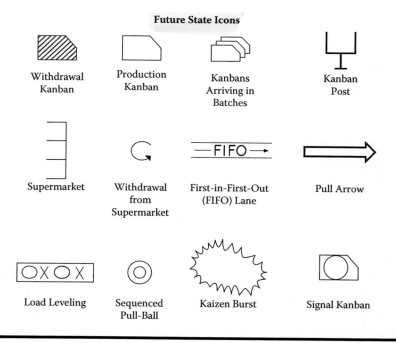

Figure 16.1   The basic Future State Mapping icon set.

recommended, especially on the first pass, that the Future State Map be a visual picture of what improvements the team thinks can be accomplished in 6 to 12 months. If the team, or management, believes that the perfect process should be drawn now, regardless of cost or effort, then it may be wise to draw an *Ideal State* Map in addition to the Future State Map.

The Future State Map Is a Blueprint for Change

The Future State Map is a blueprint for change. It is the guiding document for project teams, the goal for positive process improvement. And the organization should use and treat this exactly as a blueprint is used to build a house or building. Nothing is perfect. We should always be evolving in a state of change, and this is no different.

As project teams work on implementing change within the value stream, they will encounter situations that require deviation from what is on the Future State Map. The deviation will result in a better process and should be implemented. Just as contractors in the construction industry do, so should the mapper with the Future State Map. The team should make redline changes directly to the face of the map to show the deviation made. There is absolutely nothing wrong with making positive changes on-the-fly. The key is to *document it*, and there is no better way than to mark up the existing Future State Map. You can go back later and produce a new revised copy of the map for the team's use. Like the Current State Map, the Future State Map becomes a living, evolving document.

Brainstorm Using the Current State Map

To start the Future State Mapping process properly, you should engage the project team assigned to improve the value stream. Beginning with a simple brainstorming session, teams can jump-start the entire process of envisioning the future state.

Gather the team around a copy of the Current State Map to begin this session. It is important that the team *use a "copy" of the Current State Map* (retaining the original for future reference). Before the session is over, this copy of the map will not look anything like it did when the team started.

Allow each team member to suggest possible solutions to the identified problems and opportunities on the Current State Map. To truly use the concept of brainstorming, do not set any ground rules other than that ideas must be focused on the Current State Map at hand. As possible solutions are stated, first document them on a flipchart or whiteboard. To this end, it may be beneficial to assign the duty of scribe to one team member. If a scribe is assigned, ensure that the chosen person understands that any idea that he or she thinks of can also be written on the list.

As these potential solutions are being documented, another team member should be using a colored pencil or marker to mark up the Current State Map with the ideas presented. In doing so, the person assigned to mark up the map should *draw directly on the Current State Map*, on top of the existing icons, to show how/what the changes look like. Only after all team members agree with the item should it be added to the map. Figure 16.2 shows an example of this type of markup.

Use the **kaizen burst** icon to show what must be done to make the change a reality.

This symbol, often called a *kaizen lightning burst*, shows the viewing audience what must be done, preferably at the speed of lightning, to make the change happen. Even though you may be scratching out communication lines or merging process steps in a visual manner on the map, you must still use kaizen bursts to document the actual change.

As the brainstorming session continues, there will be potential solutions presented that are met with resistance. When this occurs, stop and discuss the idea as a team. The role of the mapper(s) and the project facilitator or project manager should be to work through issues such as these, looking for consensus. *You do not need to have unanimous agreement on solutions.* If there is a split vote, the team may want to look at trying several different solutions to find the best method. If this is the case, simply show the solution with the most votes on the map and use a kaizen burst to document the alternate solution.

Because Value Stream Mapping is a tool commonly used with fast-paced continuous improvement methodologies, it is recommended that you limit the duration of the brainstorming sessions. The number of potential solutions presented can be used as a benchmark on how long to run a session, but it is recommended that these brainstorming meetings last no longer than 30 to 45 min.

Know When to Start Fresh

As the brainstorming session progresses, the amount of information drawn on the Current State Map may become excessively cluttered or confusing. This is the time to start fresh with a clean sheet of paper, and transfer the knowledge from the cluttered map. Start out by redrawing all icons and information from the Current State Map that have not been altered or deleted. Redraw them in approximately the same location on the new mapping sheet that they occupied on the old map. Figures 16.3 and 16.4 show what this looks like: Figure 16.3 shows how messy the old map can get, and Figure 16.4 is the start of the new map, after the icons from the old sheet have been drawn on the new sheet.

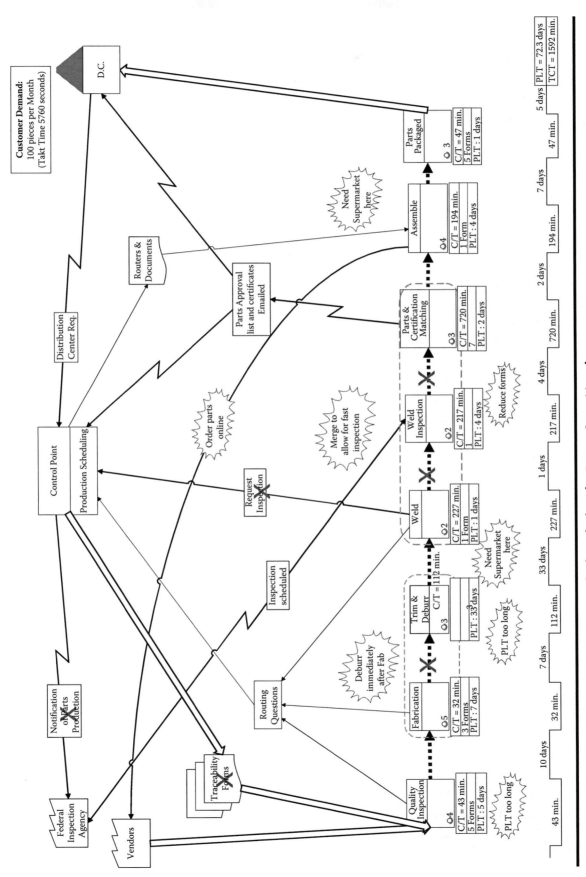

Figure 16.2   Example of Current State Map marked up during the Future State Mapping process.

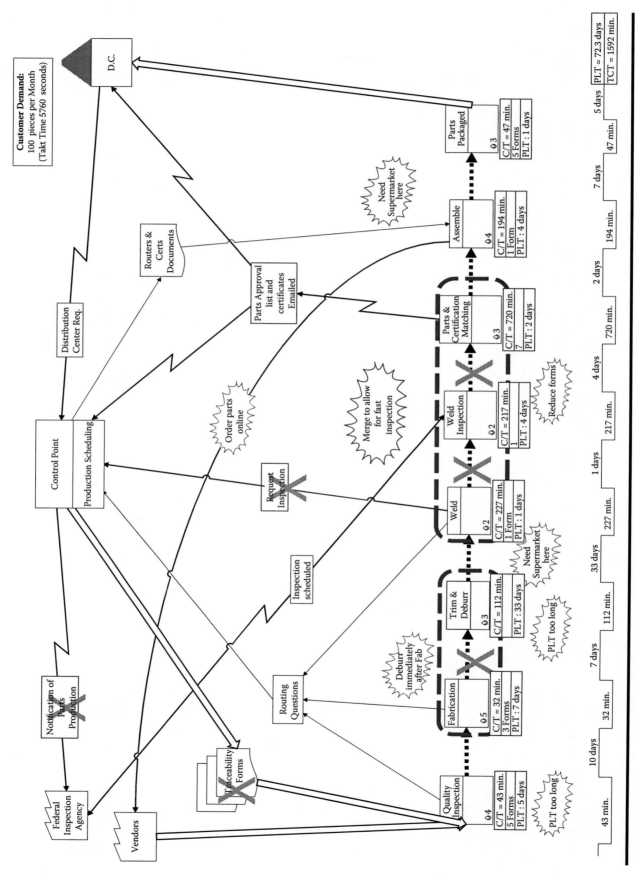

Figure 16.3   The Current State Map prior to starting over on a clean sheet of paper.

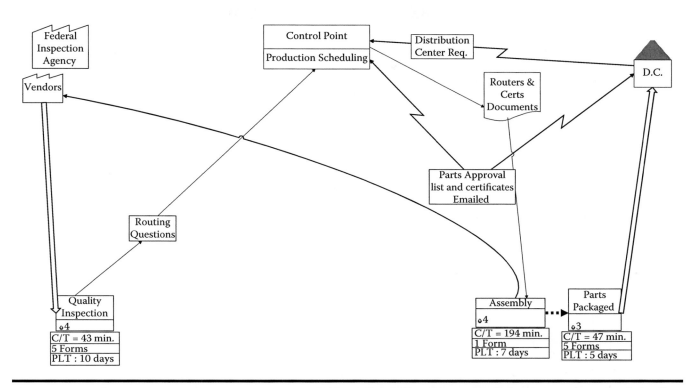

Figure 16.4 The "in progress" Future State Map, taking all unaffected pieces of the current state and duplicating them on a clean sheet of paper prior to adding the remainder of the future state.

Occasionally, as you brainstorm ideas for the future, you or the project team will determine that there is nothing worth saving on the Current State Map and decide that it is a better decision to simply start from scratch on a new sheet. When situations like this occur, you must ensure that the Current State Map remains visible and that the focus continues to be centered on reviewing the opportunities and issues in the current state and identifying potential solutions for improvement. Sticking to this basic rule will produce cleaner, faster, better-focused Future State Maps to guide implementation efforts.

Draw the Future State Using the VSM Icons

At this point, it may seem unnecessary to say, "Use the VSM icons to draw your map," but as you are learning the technique and trying to manage the sometimes rapid-fire list of ideas and team member behavior, it is not uncommon for mappers or even entire teams to default back to using traditional flowcharting to draw the future state. *Do not let this happen.*

It is better to slow down the pace of the exercise by having a team member draw the ideas on the map instead of doing it yourself. This alone will slow down the process, because the use of a less-skilled person to draw the map will start a dialogue centered around which icons to use and how to place them on

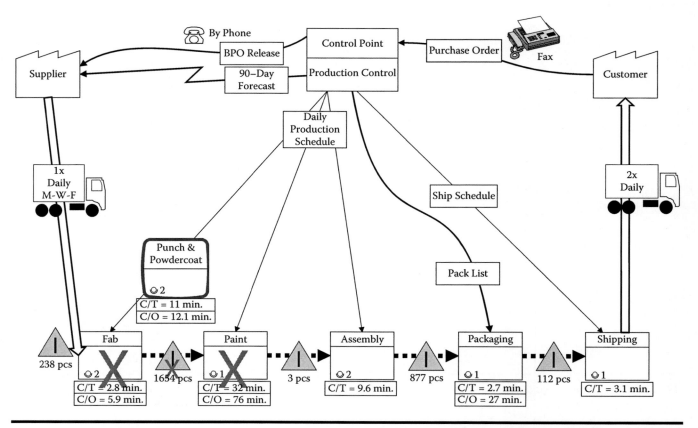

Figure 16.5   Drawing in a replacement process step where flow is continuous directly on the Current State Map is the easiest way to document an idea.

the map. Another approach to utilize when the ideas are coming too fast is to simply capture these potential solutions in a list written on a whiteboard or flip-chart. Once the ideas have stopped, or the meeting time expires, you can then take the list, mark up the Current State Map, and then redraw to a clean sheet at a more controlled pace.

When reviewing the Current State Map, the first thing that you and/or the project team should be looking for is simple, basic, non-value-added activities and communication that can be eliminated. When a process step or a piece of communication can be eliminated, the simple way to show this on the first cut (using the Current State Map) is to "X" out the step or communication line, as shown in Figure 16.5.

The team may recognize that several steps can be eliminated and replaced by a single totally different task. When this occurs, "X" out the old and draw a new process box above (or below) and centered on the old boxes. Write in the name of the new task and assign any known data in the data box. Figure 16.5 shows an example of this type of situation.

If the decision is made to create flow by merging multiple steps, you can show this on the first markup by using dotted lines to connect the process boxes, as shown in Figure 16.6. However, when you transfer this information to a new

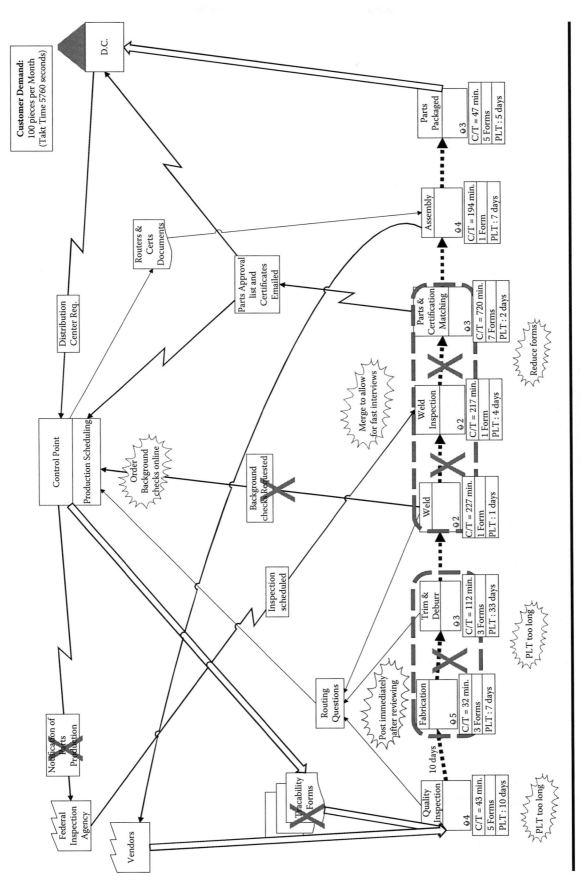

Figure 16.6 Initial documentation of process steps to be merged in the production flow.

sheet, *do not show this merged process box as one big long box.* Instead, use the same size process-box icon to represent the new merged and flowing task. This not only makes it easier to align cycle times and inventory times on the timelines, but it also looks much cleaner to the viewing audience, as shown in Figure 16.7.

The Supermarket Icon

As the team works to create flow and the use of "pull" concepts can be implemented, the team (either on its own or forced by the mapper) will undoubtedly discuss the use of *supermarkets* to control work and inventory where continuous flow is not possible. *Supermarkets* are a controlled inventory where maximum levels are established and replenishment is signaled through the use of kanbans. Kanbans (also called *replenishment signals*) are visual aids designed to inform employees within the value stream that additional work-in-process (WIP) or inventory is now required. These signals can be in the form of cards, lights, marked totes, racks, or bins, as well as painted lines on the floor or shelf.

The supermarket may manage only a few items or more than 100 items. The amount of work managed through supermarkets can be determined by the project team making improvements, but this number is quite often established by using the 80/20 rule, which analyzes the items flowing through the value stream. The 80/20 rule (also known as the *Pareto Principle*), establishes the fact that a small number of items (approximately 20%) account for the majority of what matters (approximately 80%).

When drawing a supermarket, it is advisable to simply draw the icon as it is shown below. The number of slots available on the icon does not have to match the number of items in the supermarket.

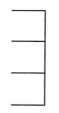

If the project team (or any member of the viewing audience) is interested in what is in the supermarket, the items might be listed above the icon, as shown in Figure 16.8. When you use this symbol, you and the project team should establish the number of days of inventory you want maintained in the supermarket and write it in below the icon.

As you add supermarkets to the Future State Map, you need to identify where in this process they should be located and how withdrawal from the supermarket is conducted, and then place an icon at the appropriate location, as shown in Figure 16.8. You should also make sure that adequate discussion covers the topics of kanbans.

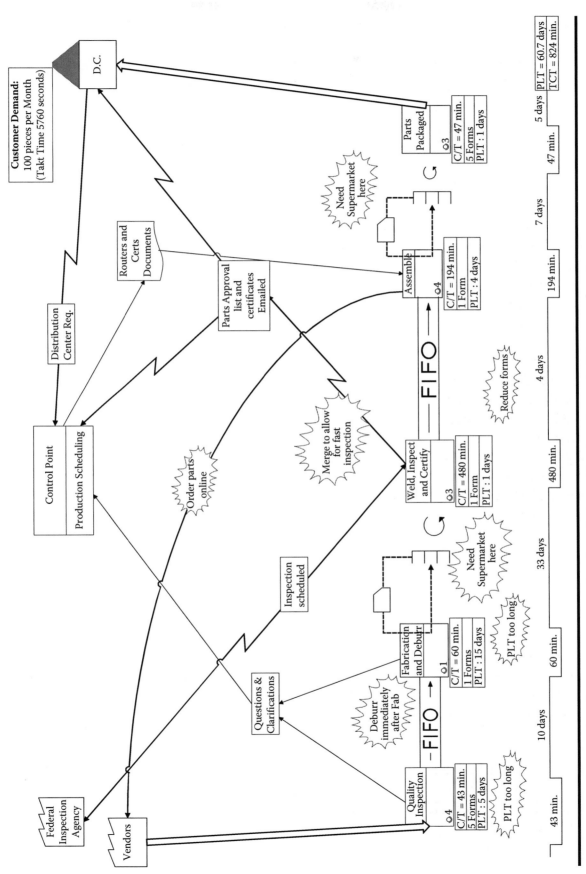

Figure 16.7 The completed Future State Map showing what must be done to create this new value stream.

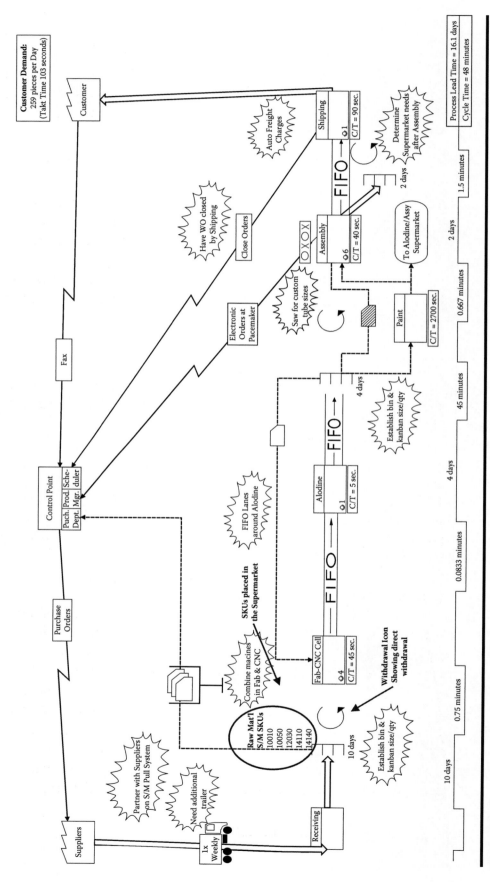

Figure 16.8   You can show what parts or products will be stored in the supermarket by listing their SKUs (stock-keeping units) over an icon. The withdrawal icon signifies that product will be withdrawn from the supermarket and moved to the next process step.

The Withdrawal Kanban Icon

Replenishment signals (aka kanbans) are used to visually inform workers within the process when replenishment is required. A **withdrawal kanban** is used to inform an employee that raw material, WIP (work-in-process), or finished goods should be pulled from a supermarket and returned to the next step of the value stream to have value added.

This situation typically occurs when the supermarket is not located immediately adjacent to the process step immediately downstream. To show this on the map, draw the icon above and between the supermarket and the process step that is withdrawing the work. A dashed line, called the *kanban path*, shows where the kanban originates, where it delivers the signal, and where the withdrawn WIP and the kanban are returned. (Figure 16.9 shows an example of this use of a withdrawal kanban.)

The Production Kanban Icon

Production kanbans are replenishment signals sent from a downstream supermarket back upstream, informing a process step to produce additional product or parts and move it into the supermarket.

Production kanbans travel upstream from the supermarket when additional product is necessary to replenish the supermarket. They are typically drawn between the supermarket and the process step where the value-added tasks are performed to complete the work required to fulfill the supermarket needs.

In a pure pull-system environment, these kanbans typically go to the process step immediately preceding the supermarket. Just like withdrawal kanbans, a production kanban path is drawn as a dashed line starting at the supermarket traveling to the process step, which receives the replenishment signal; then it returns to the supermarket, as shown in Figure 16.9.

However, it is possible that the kanban might travel further upstream and that the starting point for replenishing the supermarket is not the process step immediately next to the supermarket. It is also possible for the kanban to travel outside the process flow and inform the purchasing department as shown in Figure 16.10, or it may even travel directly to a supplier. In the example shown, these kanbans traveling to the purchasing department are collected at a central point, called a **kanban post**, and then returned in batches to purchasing.

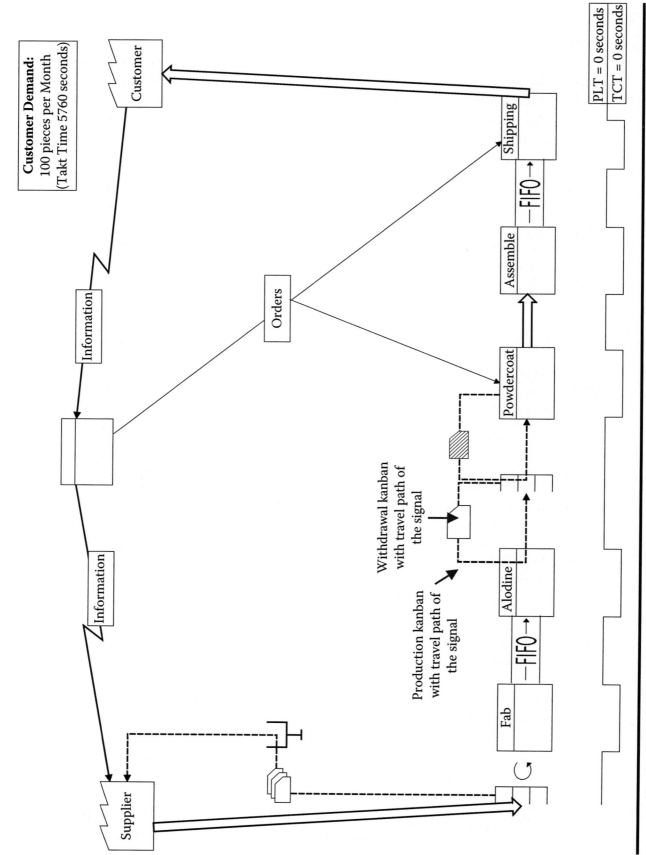

Figure 16.9 Example of how both production and withdrawal kanbans are used on a Future State Map.

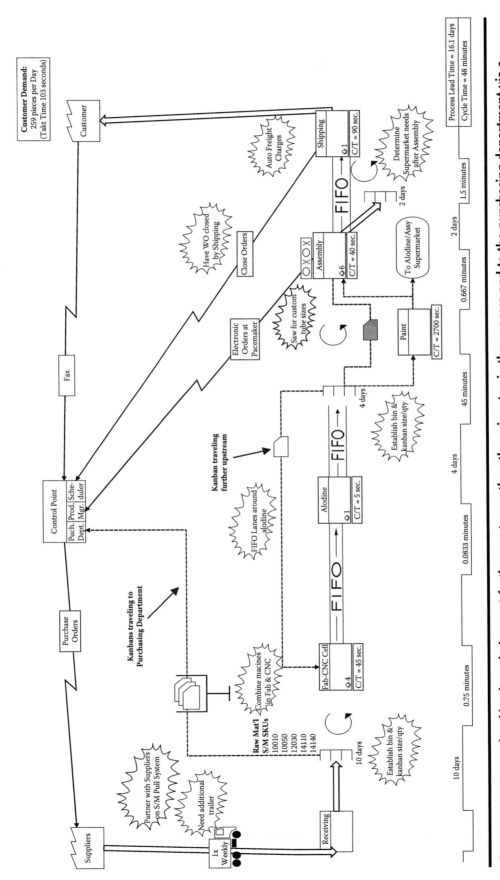

Figure 16.10 Example of kanbans being sent further upstream than the prior step in the process and to the purchasing department via a kanban post.

The Sequenced Pull Ball Icon

There are also several unique types of kanbans that may be used in production settings. *Sequenced pull balls* are kanbans that are used without supermarkets, in most cases. When the replenishment time is extremely short and the upstream process step can quickly add value and move the work on to the next step, a **sequenced pull ball** may be the answer.

This type of kanban is a colored ball that is rolled through a tube or track from one process step to another. The color and order of arrival is what tells the reacting process step what to make when.

The Signal Kanban Icon

Signal kanbans are replenishment signals used to inform the upstream process that more than one bin, tray, or carton is required. This icon being drawn as a kanban card with a circle in it is merely done so as a matter of consistency with the other two types of kanban icons.

These are typically found where the project team has not been able to get the system down to a two-bin system: one bin, box, etc., of parts at the workstation and one getting replenished upstream.

Another icon often used to show these signal kanbans is an inverted triangle.

The problem encountered by many mappers and project teams alike with the inverted triangle is the confusion between this symbol and the inventory icon used in Value Stream Mapping: as you recall, the inventory icon is also a triangle, although not inverted. On more than one occasion, the signal kanban has been drawn upside down, which causes people to try and understand why inventory is being placed at that location. Therefore, it is becoming more and more common to simply use the standard withdrawal and production kanban icons and reduce the confusion associated with this concept.

Using a Pacemaker to Determine Process Speed

The single process step in the value stream that determines the speed of the process is known as the *pacemaker*. In a perfectly balanced and flowing value stream, whatever speed the pacemaker performs at is the speed that all other steps in the value stream perform at. As a part of the solution brainstorming process, you or the project team may want to review the cycle times of all process steps in order to look for ways to manage the flow. This analysis—combined with the use of supermarkets, kanbans, and FIFO (first in, first out) lanes—can make for much stronger solutions than just attempting to use each tool individually.

Using Line-Balancing Charts to Determine if Flow Is Balanced

By using a simple line-balancing chart to list the cycle time for each process step in the current state, you can quickly determine if the current-state flow is balanced. This technique has long been used by industrial engineers to balance workflow and create more efficient processes, and the technique has been enhanced through the use of Lean concepts. In Value Stream Mapping, the addition of the Takt time to these charts provides for quick analysis of value stream capability.

Figure 16.11 shows an example of pulling each listed cycle time for all process steps in the value stream into a line-balancing chart. By including the Takt time for the value stream, it is very easy to see two critical pieces of information:

Is the value stream capable of meeting customer demand?
Is the value stream balanced?

As shown in Figure 16.11, it is obvious that neither condition has been met. The brush finish and shipping process both exceed the Takt time, which tells the team that this value stream is incapable of meeting customer demand as it was observed operating during Current State Mapping. Additionally, the extreme fluctuations of cycle time—from 0.0167 to 1.5 min. (as shown through the size of the bars and documented times)—visually show how out of balance this value stream has become.

The goal of balancing and pacing the flow of the value stream is to have all process steps' cycle times less than the Takt time and as close to the same as possible. Understanding that it is nearly impossible to have each cycle time identical will save much angst for both you and the project team. In reality, you may never see a value stream perfectly balanced. Therefore, the team should do its best to balance the flow and continue to look for ways to further balance it in the future.

In Figure 16.12, you can see the effects of line balancing and how to use supermarkets to assist with managing the work. The line-balancing chart confirms that the value stream is capable of meeting customer demand, because all cycle times are less than the Takt time. However, you will notice that there is still a wide range in cycle times. To control these swings, supermarkets have been placed after receiving, where the cycle time is extremely short. Supermarkets

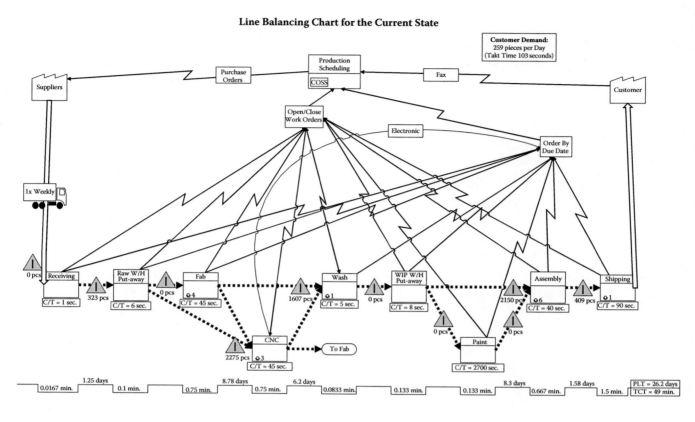

Line Balancing Chart for the Current State

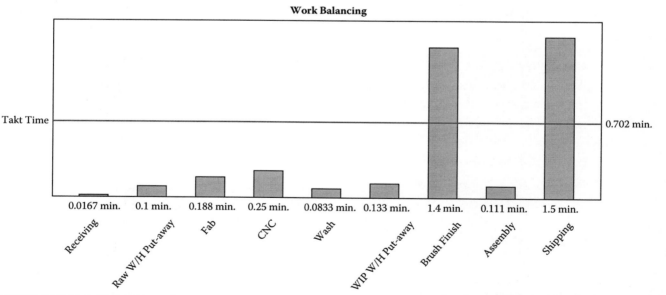

Work Balancing

Figure 16.11   Line-balancing chart aligned underneath the Current State Map to assist in determining what process steps must be adjusted in the future state.

have also been placed in front of the brush finish and shipping process, as a way to provide adequate buffers and inventory to ensure that work can continue to flow, because these two steps react much faster than the remainder of the value stream.

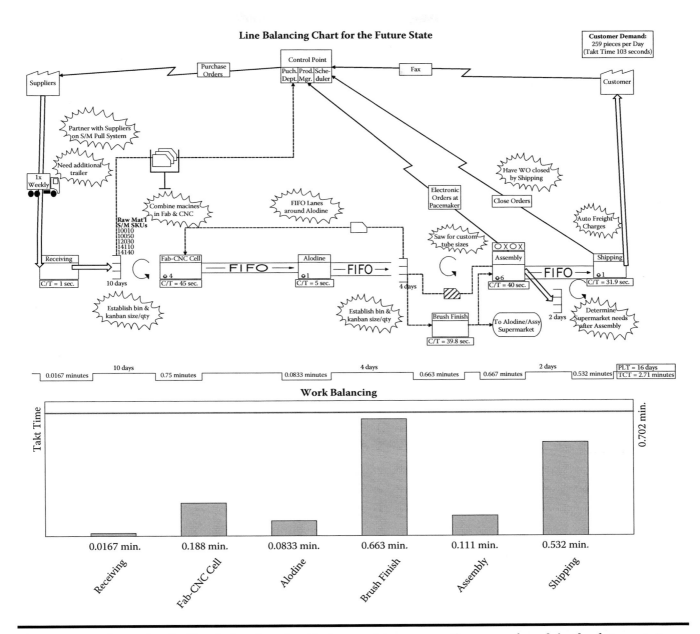

Figure 16.12   Example of a line-balancing chart being used to manage the pace of work in the future state.

Using FIFO Lanes to Manage the Flow of the Value Stream

Another useful concept in managing the flow of the value stream is **FIFO lanes**. FIFO (first in, first out) lanes are designed to manage work through a process step, ensuring that the oldest work flowing into the area is the first work to receive value-added activity and be completed, before working on any other WIP waiting.

$$-\text{FIFO} \rightarrow$$

Figure 16.13 shows an example of a FIFO lane being used to control the flow. This example shows that the first FIFO lane is very basic, and whatever flows

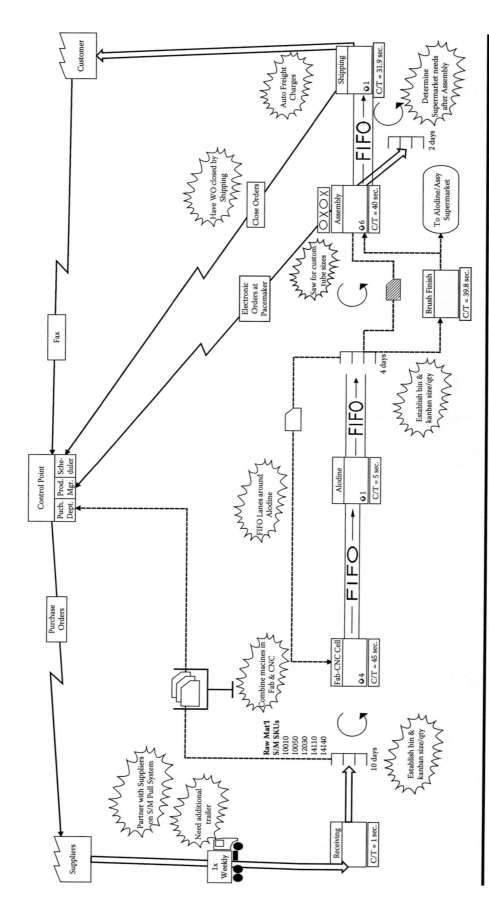

Figure 16.13 FIFO lanes being used to control the flow of product through the value stream.

into the lane will be worked FIFO at the Alodine station and then will be moved into the supermarket FIFO as well.

In many situations, the project team will want to limit the amount of work that can sit in the FIFO lane at any given moment in time. When this occurs, you should write the maximum number of units of work, or WIP, that is allowed; write this number above the FIFO icon, as shown here.

Max. 5 Trays
— FIFO →

In this way, the employees working within the improved value stream know the limit on work in the lane and can use this limit as a signal for potential problems. If the maximum is reached, and the amount of work sitting in the lane does not reduce in a reasonable amount of time, it should be taken as a signal that there may be problems downstream. Employees can then investigate what is occurring downstream and react to problems, other than reduced customer demand, if and when they exist.

Another situation you must be aware of is the need to bypass supermarkets in mixed settings. Reality should trigger some common sense for many people working with these tools. There are times when the majority of work flowing through a value stream is the standard run-of-the-mill work that fits nicely in a supermarket. But if you have used the 80/20 rule to determine what goes into a supermarket, or if you have a mix of high-volume product with some customized products, then there is a need to show how to handle such scenarios where you must move the inventory past the supermarket.

Figure 16.14 shows such a situation drawn out on the Future State Map. Above the supermarket is a FIFO lane. This allows for customized product, or for the very occasional product not supermarketed, to bypass this controlled point in the value stream and be handled "next up." The FIFO lane can be placed above the supermarket if it is a higher priority than supermarket work, or beneath the supermarket if it is more important to respond to the supermarket first.

To successfully use the pacemaker to regulate flow, it is important to understand not only how to use these concepts, but also how to visually represent them on a Future State Map. If the employees working within the value stream and management are expected to understand the ideas for positive change, then the project team must be able to visually show each and every person involved how the work is going to flow.

Using Load Leveling to Manage Mix

The final piece of flow management required to ensure successful implementation of a pacemaker is **load leveling**.

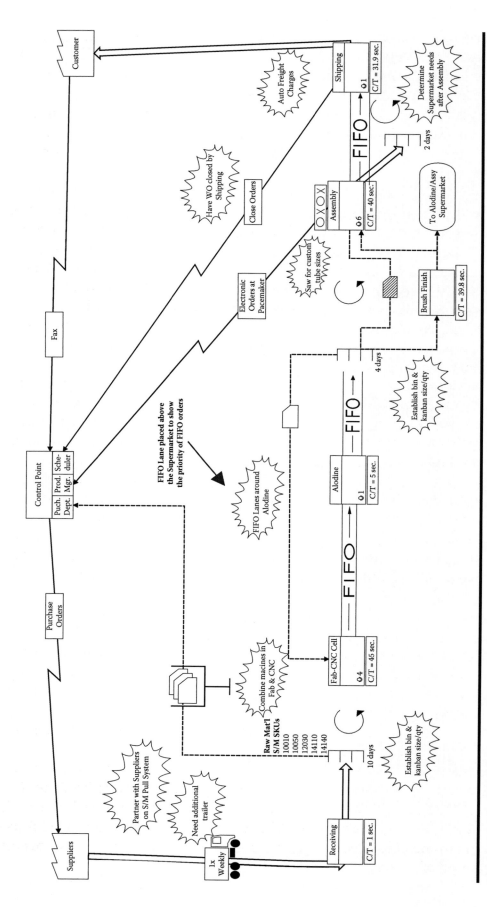

Figure 16.14 FIFO lanes can be used in conjunction with supermarkets when the company needs a way to bypass the supermarket for custom orders.

This concept is used to manage the mix of work being performed. When multiple products or services are being provided in a value stream, there must be a method for making sure that the right thing is being worked on at the right time.

The icon is drawn above the process step where the leveling takes place, as shown in Figure 16.15. By acknowledging the fact that prioritization of work must be determined in many situations, it is much easier for employees to accept the changes being made to the value stream. A note may be added above or below the load-leveling symbol to assist in the prioritization strategy. Oftentimes, when customized or low-volume work is mixed with high-priority supermarket items, the same note from the Future State Map may be posted at the workstation as a visual reminder of the prioritization.

With all of these flow management tools in place, the project team has the ability to review the value stream's process flow and determine where the pacemaker should be located. For pure pull-system value streams, you should place this pacemaker as close to the very end of the process flow as possible. All other process steps and signals will be based on the speed and duration of the pacemaker. This is what keeps the flow controlled.

In mixed and/or customized production settings, the pacemaker is often found much farther upstream. The usual positioning of the pacemaker in these value streams is at the last point of commonality. This concept is what makes Value Stream Mapping and many Lean concepts applicable in any production setting, i.e., high-volume/low-mix as well as job shops.

Once the pacemaker has been identified, the project team members can then review their solutions and work toward creating and controlling flow from the pacemaker. If the pacemaker is at the end of the process, adequate signals must be in place to start and stop the flow at all process steps upstream when appropriate. When the pacemaker occurs early in the value stream, the challenge becomes ensuring that flow will continue uninterrupted downstream.

The Importance of Using Kaizen Bursts

As the Future State Map is being created, it is extremely important to make sure that all kaizen bursts that were initially drawn on the map are included in the final product, if they are to be a part of the change process. Place the bursts as close to the location of the change in the value stream as possible. In this way, it is much easier to identify at what point or points in the value stream that effort will have to be applied to make change happen.

As ideas are agreed on, make sure the kaizen bursts are added to the map. The more bursts that appear on the map, the more work needs to be done. If the number of bursts becomes too great, it may be necessary to break the work down into multiple projects or events. This visualization alone is a powerful tool in explaining to the employees in the value stream how much work is necessary to create the future state.

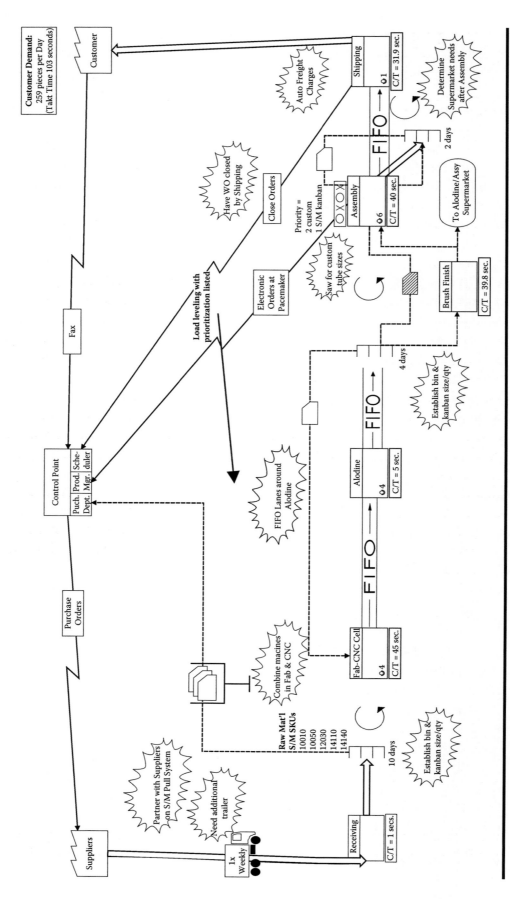

Figure 16.15   An example of how to use the load-leveling icon to show this adjustment of work in the value stream.

Case Study in a Manufacturing Environment

Future State Map
Case Study: Pelco Products, Inc.
Manufacturing company

The Future State Map in Figure 16.16 depicts the short-term goal state that the Pelco Products Lean team designed to address excess inventory, waiting, excess motion, unnecessary processing, and excess travel in the value stream. The Current State Map presented at the conclusion of Chapter 7 (Figure 7.8) provides great insight into the starting point for the series of Lean improvement events focused on this map.

Major results through the first 15 days of the implementation effort included increasing inventory turns for the mapped product family from 9.9 turns per year to 16.1 turns per year. Total cycle time for assembling the finished components (*assembly cell* portion of the Current State Map) was reduced by 50.0%, from an average of 40.0 to 20.0 sec. per unit. Additionally, the travel distance for the product through the fabrication and assembly path was reduced from 2.75 miles to 0.3 miles.

Subsequent kaizen events that were focused on moving the look and feel of the value stream closer to the Future State Map produced even larger results. While the estimated change in process lead time on the Future State Map was set at a reduction of 10.1 days, the actual process lead time was reduced from 26.2 days to 11.0 days, equivalent to 23.6 inventory turns per year.

In addition to the very visible results presented here, Pelco has used these improvements to establish a Lean transformation model for the entire organization. Employees working in the assembly cell, as well as those assigned to the fabrication/CNC (computer numeric control) cell, are now empowered to initiate production in response to visual signals as well as the demands of both custom orders staged in the build-to-order lane and of kanbans requesting replenishment downstream.

Presenting the Future State Map

Once you and the project team have agreed on the Future State Map, you *must* present it to the employees within the value stream. It is *not* recommended that change be initiated without a future-state meeting with the employees and management. Because Value Stream Mapping depends so much on the involvement of the employees, through their input and ownership of the value stream, it is critical to include them in the vision of the future.

This meeting is very similar in nature to the current-state brainstorming meeting. It should be direct and short. A full explanation of any new icons used is

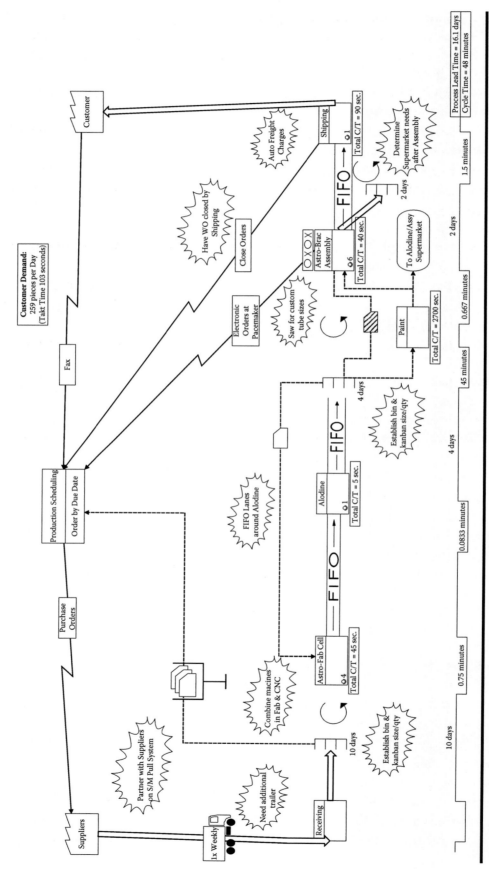

Figure 16.16 *Actual* Future State Map from Pelco Products, Inc. (manufacturing company).

imperative. Make sure that the viewing audience understands the symbols on the map, and take the necessary time to explain new concepts being introduced.

In the event that any additional ideas or solutions are presented, add these to the map or list them on a flipchart or whiteboard for further review. Do not make the mistake, however, of allowing people to bring up new issues or problems. If this occurs, explain that Value Stream Mapping is a continuous improvement tool. Have them write down their issues and opportunities on a piece of paper and submit them to the team after the meeting. Explain that they will be incorporated into the *next* round of change. The Current State Map can be updated at that time to show these new issues, assuming that they still exist after the changes have been made.

In the event that an Ideal State Map has been created, it should also be presented, but in much less detail. This will allow employees to have a glimpse of the long-term future envisioned by the project team or mapper(s).

Once this meeting has been completed, the project team can regroup and review the map one last time. Any new ideas or changes required can be added. Then the team is ready to begin the change process.

Chapter 17 will demonstrate how to create the Future State Map in the transactional environment.

Chapter 17

Creating a Future State Map in a Transactional Environment

The visionary is the only true realist.

Federico Fellini

Introduction

Much has been written about Value Stream Mapping in transactional settings; in fact, entire books have been written on this subject. Each book has brought insight into the struggles and unique characteristics mappers encounter when mapping this type of value stream. But each and every mapper must remember that *there is much more in common between these two types than there is new and unique.*

Chapter 9 discussed the similarities between the current state in manufacturing and transactional value streams. These same similarities exist with the future state. If, for any reason, you bypassed Chapter 16, which addressed Future State Mapping (FSM) in a manufacturing world, now is the time to stop, go back, and read that critical chapter. Many, if not all, of the lessons learned are applicable to the transactional value stream. There are subtle differences, but it is not possible to capture a transactional future state without knowing how to map a production process.

Getting Started: Four Points to Keep in Mind

When mapping the future state in a transactional environment, there are several important things to remember:

Understand the similarities and differences between production and transactional value streams, thereby establishing a strong foundation for creating the Future State Map.

Recognize that many value streams in transactional environments are actually production value streams.

Address employees' concerns early.

Accept that continuous flow may be difficult to achieve in occasional on-demand value streams.

The next sections describe each of these points in more detail.

Understand the Similarities and Differences between Production and Transactional Value Streams

Each and every single concept that is used in mapping manufacturing (aka production) value streams can be used in the transactional world. Recognizing this basic and somewhat obvious fact makes it much easier to improve transactional value streams at the same speed as production value streams. If you step back and think about what actually happens in the transactional world, it will be easy for you to see the similarities. Also, the comparison is sometimes easier to understand if you use customized job-shop manufacturing processes as the benchmark.

Recognizing the differences between production and transactional value streams can be challenging. As discussed in Chapter 9, separating communication from the process flow can be difficult, because many transactional processes involve the capture and use of data. Understanding what is data being used in the process flow and what is communication can be difficult for even the most experienced mappers. Yet, proceeding into a future-state brainstorming session with this issue resolved will greatly simplify the task of identifying solutions.

Perhaps the most important difference is the people. You must recognize that employees in a transactional value stream can play a much different and influential role than in a production setting. Understanding how much of an impact the employee actually has on how and when a value stream operates is critical to successfully mapping the future state.

Recognize That Many Production Value Streams Appear in the Transactional World

As discussed previously, many value streams encountered in the transactional world are nothing more than production value streams. They truly are identical to manufacturing value streams and, therefore, you should analyze and treat them as such when developing a future state. Some examples of these production value streams in a transactional world include (but are not limited to) many print shop operations, accounts payable, and purchasing processes.

When working with these production processes, you and the project team should be looking for the opportunity to create continuous flow, establish supermarkets with kanbans, and use FIFO lanes where flow must stop. The exact same techniques should be considered for scheduling work: from order boards to Heijunka boxes (a box divided into multiple sections where work assignments are notated and used to regulate both time and quantity of work) to staging orders with all parts and materials in a FIFO lane.

Address Employees' Concerns Early

It is critical to remember that employee buy-in is essential to success in a transaction value stream. Employee buy-in is important to gaining agreement and acceptance of the current state, and it is vital to the Future State Mapping exercise if the change process is to move forward.

Employees not only want to be a part of the process and have input into what is being reported out, but they also want to know that the issues important to them are being addressed. By including many of these employee concerns early in future-state development, you and the project team can show employees that you are in tune with the "pain" felt working within the value stream.

Accept That Continuous Flow May Be Difficult to Achieve

For those values that are not production processes, achieving continuous flow may be difficult, if not impossible and impractical. Accept this and move on. Not every value stream (even on the manufacturing floor) will be capable of achieving continuous flow. So stop trying, and focus instead on creating a future state that eliminates as much waste as possible without this feature.

Look for opportunities to use as many Lean concepts as possible, including the use of synchronous flow in its most basic form, i.e., flowing the product or service from start to finish without interruption. It does not have to "always" be operating to flow. Many times, you hear Lean practitioners say, "When the process operates, it flows." Using the right tool to eliminate waste is much more important than trying to achieve the unachievable.

Employees Have Answers

They just don't always know it. When you developed the Current State Map, it was critically important to bring the workforce into the observation and documentation process of the map. It is no less so with the future state. As the Current State Map was produced, employees were sought out to bring their pain and frustration to the exercise. Without this input, mapping the current state would have taken considerably longer. Use this same methodology to develop the future state.

By including employees from within the value stream on the project team, you bring an incredible resource to your fingertips for finding solutions. The secret is in getting these team members to open up. They must be willing to give suggestions, and they must be willing to provide feedback on various ideas presented by other team members.

Ask Leading Questions

When searching for solutions to place on the Future State Map, ask team members who work within the value stream leading questions. By asking, "What would you do to fix the problem?" or, "If you had a magic wand and could change one thing about the value stream, what would it be?" the team can quickly understand what is important to the employees. With a good understanding of the current state and some basic knowledge about the concepts of Lean and waste elimination, employees can provide some very insightful solutions. They may not know how to implement, but they have ideas that may be transformed into excellent solutions. They are not only assisting the team in finding the solution, but they are also gaining ownership of the value stream.

This format for finding solutions is not new. The concept of brainstorming as a continuous improvement tool is rooted in using the employees who are experiencing the pain to pinpoint the problem(s) and finding all possible solutions in a rapid-fire setting. Figure 17.1 lays out this concept in a SIPOC chart (supplier-input-process-output-customer). The power of this chart is that the supplier of the solutions is focused on the needs of the customer, because they are one and the same. This can create nearly instantaneous ownership in the changes to be implemented.

It may also be of some use to repeat this exact same exercise with other employees working within the value stream that are not on the project team.

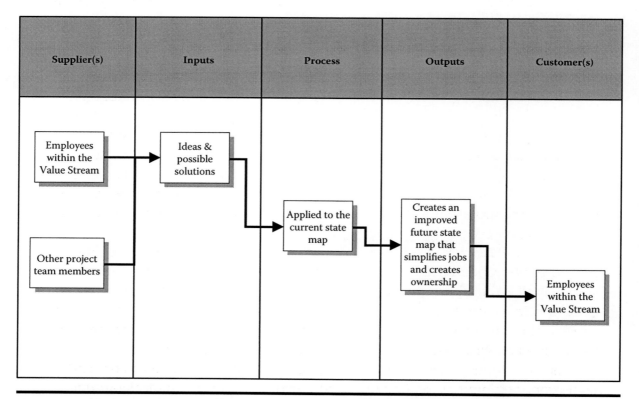

Figure 17.1   SIPOC chart showing the Future State Map development process.

By proactively widening the input base for solutions, you can gain more acceptance and ownership faster, instead of waiting on a presentation meeting to start achieving this critical buy-in.

Reinforce That There Is a Process to the Work Being Done

As the team works to find solutions for transactional value streams, they will encounter resistance from those who do not believe that the problems can be resolved. These roadblockers may actually accept the Current State Map as an accurate depiction of the value stream, but they may continue to argue that "there is no process." As discussed in Chapter 9, it is unfortunate that many people working within transactional value streams, and more specifically in office settings, do not think that the job they do on a daily basis consists of a series of processes. This presents a challenge to the team—not an insurmountable challenge, but one that requires extra attention to the roadblocker(s) and a strong dose of creating and documenting standardized work.

The easiest method for addressing this issue is to convince the resistant employee to separate out all other duties and tasks that do not pertain to the value stream. Focus only on those tasks (notice we are not calling them "process steps" to avoid the conflict) that are being reviewed. Walk through the current state step by step, and get acknowledgment on the non-value-added (NVA) activity. Ask the roadblocker how he or she would do the job if this NVA was not present. Then ask how he or she would do the job exactly the same way repeatedly from this point forward without the NVA.

Document what the employee says. Use a flipchart or whiteboard at first to capture bullet statements of the ideas. Invite other team members to strengthen the ideas as you progress. However, do not allow the other team members to greatly alter the resistant employee's ideas. If the goal is to get buy-in and overcome the "no process" problem, the resistant employee must lead the charge.

Once you have completed compiling the suggested list of tasks, work with the entire team to transfer this knowledge onto the face of the Current State Map. Include the roadblocker(s) in this activity to further their understanding that processes exist. As explained in Chapter 16, if the map begins to get excessively cluttered, redraw the untouched icons onto a new sheet of paper and then start drawing in what the marked-up work represents.

This provides an excellent starting point for the future state. However, it does not close the matter with the resistant employee(s). As you draw the Future State Map, remember to include kaizen bursts that remind the project team to develop, train, and implement standard operating procedures (SOP) throughout the value stream. The documented tasks can become the actual SOP, or they can be used as the basis for *quality-at-the-source checklists* for use in the process.

Most employees understand what SOPs or policies are intended to do, and with proper training, most employees will follow them. *Quality-at-the-source* checklists are quick-hitting bulleted lists that are intended to provide guidance

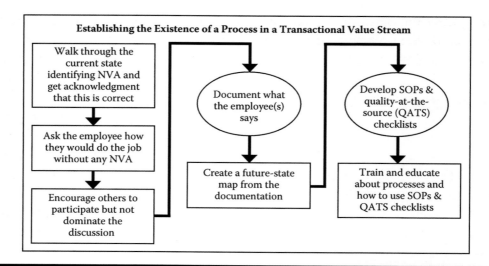

Figure 17.2 This flowchart outlines the process often used to break the cultural barrier that denies the existence of processes in transactional settings.

and reference to ensure that the process is followed and that quality work is produced. With the creation of either SOPs or these checklists, the project team can then start the education piece with these resistant employees to convince them that a process exists. It may be helpful to have the definition of "process" at hand for these educational sessions, i.e.,

A process is a series of actions or operations conducing to an end.

Figure 17.2 summarizes the activities surrounding this issue. By addressing this cultural mindset early in the game, you can move the future-state development activities forward at a much faster pace.

How to Address the Problem of Availability of Personnel

Availability of personnel (AOP) provides the answer that many transactional employees seek when the concept of Value Stream Mapping is introduced into their world. As discussed in Chapter 10, one of the biggest challenges to overcome is how to show the reality of multitasking in an office setting. Early in the Future State Map development cycle, you must address multitasking with the project team and personnel who work within the value stream every day. By doing this, you can gain acceptance of the future state much faster.

A review of AOP data in the process flow of the Current State Map is the starting point for addressing availability. As you and the project team conduct this exercise, you should focus your thoughts on situations where AOP is low or where bottlenecks exist immediately in front of the process step. The final component of this review should be a discussion of the number of employees who work within the process step.

When AOP is low, when bottlenecks exist, and/or when multiple personnel operate the process step in question, you and the project team can redesign the step by consolidating duties. This may require off-loading some duties to other employees to free up more time (AOP) to work the process step. When multiple employees are involved, you and the team should look for ways to consolidate duties and tasks in such a way as to reduce the number of employees involved in the process step and increase the AOP.

You and the team can also address the argument of needing multiskilled employees that know how to do the task in question for coverage due to vacations, illness, meetings, etc. The Future State Map should include a kaizen burst, or bursts, that create a system for cross-training personnel on all duties/tasks within the value stream. Additionally, regular rotation of jobs should be included so that all employees working within the value stream are capable of working these tasks/duties on an ongoing basis. Figure 17.3 shows an example of how this future-state change might look on a marked Current State Map.

Showing employees within the value stream that the challenges and frustrations of multitasking can be reduced or eliminated is critical to success with transactional value streams. If you can demonstrate early on how to solve these problems, you can generate excitement and create buy-in, as well as produce more input from the personnel working within the value stream.

How to Address the Problem of Lack of Flow

One misconception that continues to exist about Lean enterprise is the notion that you must create one-piece flow. James Womack and Daniel Jones did not say this in their book *Lean Thinking*, in explaining the concepts of the Toyota production system; in fact, they have never stated this, yet the idea continues to be pushed by many people.

For example, when Lean first became seen as a viable tool in the health care sector, there were actually consulting firms telling hospital and reference laboratories that they must create one-piece flow. This same concept was pushed hard in many service-sector settings. Yet it is not true; it never has been, and it never will be. Lean is about identifying and eliminating waste. How an organization addresses this waste can vary greatly.

The reality of actual processes in the world should be acknowledged by everyone. You may never eliminate all non-value-added activity. You do the best you can do with what resources you have available at the moment. It is called *continuous* improvement for a reason; you can revisit the value stream at any time to eliminate additional waste as resources and situations change.

In the event that you cannot create continuous flow, do not struggle with the concept. Acknowledge the situation publicly and then create the best possible value stream in your Future State Map. Make sure that all employees within the value stream, as well as management, are aware of this lack of flow. It should not be a point of conflict for those human roadblockers who don't want to change. Put the facts on the table quickly, and then work with the team to create flow where and when possible.

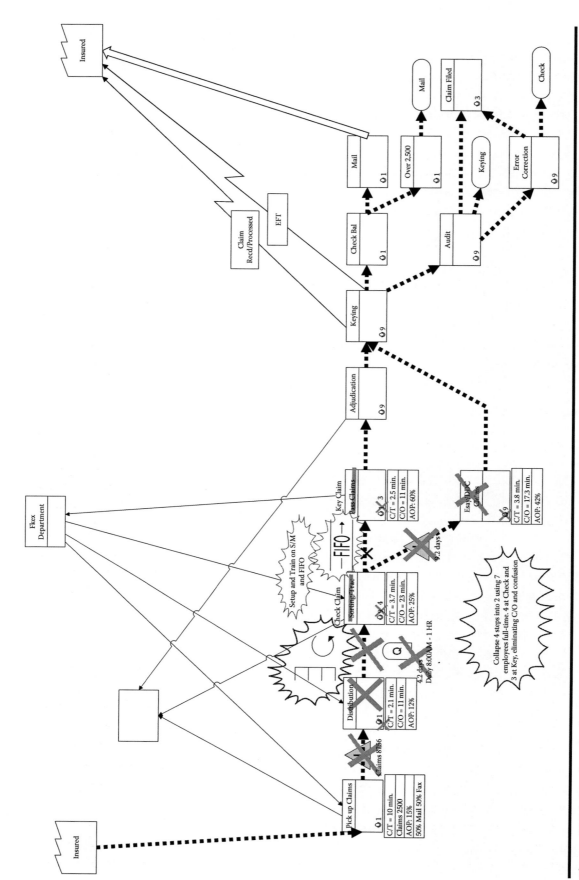

Figure 17.3 Starting the future-state development requires writing directly on the face of the Current State Map with a colored pencil or marker.

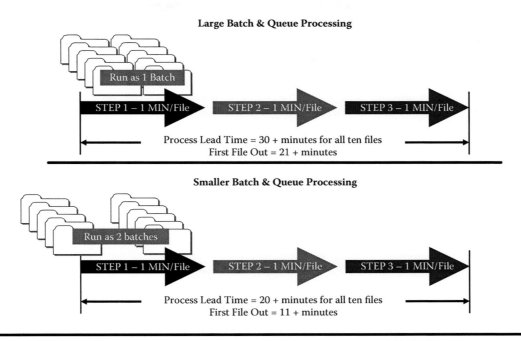

Figure 17.4   Example of batch-size reduction when processing files. (Source: Concept developed from NIST/MEP *Principles of Live Manufacturing with Live Simulation.*

Where high-volume value streams exist with irregular or indeterminate arrival or demand patterns (such as health care laboratories often see), the answer is to look for ways to reduce the batch size to the optimal point so that work can flow whenever possible. When flow ceases, the work can be managed and controlled in smaller batches. Smaller batches mean faster turnaround times, which in turn relates to faster throughput and higher levels of productivity for the organization.

As you can see in Figure 17.4, cutting the batch size in half reduces the time it takes to get the first unit of work out the door by 33.3%. If this is the best that can be achieved, take advantage of it. Put it on the Future State Map and move forward.

For seldom-used, on-demand-type value streams that operate almost randomly in a low-volume setting, there is little chance for creating continuous flow. Because many of these low-volume value streams are operated by a single person from start to finish, it is also impossible to use the concept of one-piece flow as it is used in high-volume production settings. But not being able to use the concepts as presented in high-volume production environments does not mean you cannot create flow. It merely means that the way you set up the future state may require thinking outside the box. If the current-state batches work throughout the process in an attempt to "take advantage of employees' time," there are simple ways to create flow—not continuous, but at least *synchronous.*

In these low-volume indeterminate-demand processes, as the work appears, each unit of work should be processed as far through the value stream as possible before setting it down. When work flow must end for the unit of work, create a way to manage the work until the next step can be run. The use of supermarkets and FIFO lanes, as shown in Figure 17.3, can be used even in these low-volume settings to manage the work.

Whatever the team decides, make sure that the work is visible and that the idea of how to keep that work visible is included in a kaizen burst on the Future State Map.

Focus on Showing Positive Changes

As you and the project team develop the map, you may begin to recognize the fact that there are too many employees involved in the value stream being mapped. There may be a natural tendency among managers and employees alike to begin the discussion of "eliminating" jobs. It is your responsibility to keep this discussion positive.

For Value Stream Mapping to work as it was originally created and presented to the business world, all employees must be involved. Each and every person working within the value stream must not only understand what a map set says, but must be given the opportunity to provide input into the map-development process. Therefore, when discussion of job elimination occurs, you must steer the discussion in a positive direction. You must make sure that everyone involved knows that there are ways to eliminate jobs without firing or laying off employees. Attrition is the simple solution, but reassignment of duties to work on project teams is another. You must not let this negative talk leave the mapping room. Overall, as your processes become more efficient, costs will decrease, customer satisfaction will increase, and all of that will cause sales to increase. This will create new jobs in other areas. Use your employees to fill these new positions.

Other negative discussion that occurs include certain employees' abilities to do tasks. Take this opportunity to lead the conversation toward a discussion of skills matching. Use the knowledge of the team to align employees within the value stream with the new tasks and duties created through the Future State Mapping exercise.

Emphasize Reduction of Bureaucracy

One powerful discussion for you to lead while creating the Future State Map concerns the bureaucratic burdens (such as excess paperwork, waiting on approvals, etc.) that many transactional employees face every day. Have employees state which approvals, audits, checks, meetings, and other activities that they believe are non-value-added activities that they currently must endure to complete their duties. Look for any and every waste associated with these burdens, and develop solutions that can be incorporated into the future state. Eliminating as many of these NVA activities as possible can quickly result in big cost savings and more satisfied employees.

Show How Jobs Can Be Simplified

Perhaps this is a given in the manufacturing world of Value Stream Mapping (VSM), but the concept of simplifying job duties and tasks can also be a big winner for the transactional value stream. An extremely powerful question to ask team members and employees within the value stream is, "What can we stop doing right now that will have zero negative impact on the process and customer?"

For example, it is amazing how many unnecessary signatures can be eliminated. Reducing the number of signatures not only eliminates unnecessary processing, but also can eliminate very large blocks of time wasted while waiting for those signatures. Another great example is eliminating 100% audits of clerical staff work. Instead, use the best methods from numerous other sectors to reduce audits to a meaningful level, and generate a real return on the time and effort invested.

Mapping teams should leave no stone unturned in their quest to simplify transactional employees' jobs. It does not take much in the way of eliminating tasks that employees view as a waste of time and effort to create strong advocates of the methods used in Value Stream Mapping and the projects that come out of these maps.

Emphasize Work Flow and Reduced Handling of Work

Much of this book focuses on identifying where work stops and how to get it flowing. For transactional employees, the need for creating flow is not always readily visible. However, there is another way to get the message across. Instead of focusing on how to create flow, push the concept of eliminating unnecessary handling of work.

You can show the effects of excess handling by reviewing the Current State Map and looking for changeover time and unnecessary processing. Total up these times and create a single number that represents the annual time requirement. It may even be useful to calculate the dollar value of this wasted effort.

Spend the time necessary to find where multiple handlings of work exist and look for ways to combine process steps, just as is done in manufacturing processes. Sorting and resorting, filing and refiling, as well as creating batches of paperwork for copying are perfect examples of these situations. Work as a team to find ways, such as those shown in Figure 17.3, to simplify the work of employees and eliminate this unnecessary handling and processing.

The goal in all of this has already been discussed in this chapter. Move transactional work as far as possible through the value stream before setting it down. By creating synchronous flow whenever possible, and moving it step by step in order without stopping the flow, more work can be completed, and employees can be much more efficient without working harder … just smarter.

Using the Ideal State as a Tool

One final point to address in aiding the transactional Value Stream Mapper to create a Future State Map includes a discussion of the ideal state. This ideal state, or long-term vision, can come into play much quicker, and become much more problematic, in transactional settings than in production value streams.

In manufacturing environments, the Ideal State Map often includes new equipment and/or the introduction of new technologies. For the operator working in this setting, it is much easier to understand the concept of "use what you have now." Because much of this equipment and new technology requires substantial capitalization, these employees recognize and understand the idea of long-term plans and phased implementation.

However, in transactional environments, the employees do not always see it this way. With the exception of enterprise-wide software applications and systems, much of the change employees are accustomed to seeing does not require large amounts of capital, or the employees have little or no knowledge of the change until the day it is implemented. Therefore, these employees may struggle some with the idea of "what can we do right now?"

To combat this situation, it may be necessary to create the Ideal State Map first. The sky is the limit. Use everyone on the team to create this long-term vision. No idea is too big or too small. Use the exact same methodology as we have talked about in this chapter and in Chapter 16 to get to a point where you have a clean Ideal State Map, with all the kaizen bursts required to make it a reality.

Then work backwards. Start eliminating ideas that the team (or management) says cannot be completed in the next 6–12 months. Make sure everyone understands why items removed cannot be accomplished. Discuss the cost, legal issues, and/or corporate policy that require stockholder or board approval, as well as any other relevant factors.

Production versus Transactional: The Path Is the Same

Overall, the path to creating a Future State Map is the same for both production and transactional environments. The tools and concepts used in improving the value stream are no different in transactional settings than those used for manufacturing value streams. And because many "transactional" value streams are actually production processes anyway, it is possible to quickly apply these concepts.

The bigger challenge with creating Future State Maps in a transactional world is the people. You must address *quickly* any fears, concerns, and misconceptions that people may have. Addressing these issues upfront while developing the future state can provide not only a faster process, but also a much more enjoyable experience for both you and the employees in the value stream.

Case Studies in Transactional Environments

Future State Map 1
Case Study: American Fidelity Assurance Company
Insurance company—claims processing

Figure 17.5 is a Future State Map from American Fidelity Assurance Company. It shows a claims-processing value stream that, for the most part, functions exactly as a production process does. However, due to the push at the front of the process, where the customer is also the supplier, the employees within the value stream must react quickly when demand on the service increases.

This fluctuation in demand and the minor differences between claims received from various parts of the country became the focus of the project team as a future state was being envisioned.

Through kaizen, the Lean initiative team was able to significantly reduce claim turnaround time. One year prior to this improvement event, average department turnaround was 4 days, but different processing teams serving various areas of the country were averaging 3 days, 4+ days, and 5+ days, respectively. Within one month of implementation, turnaround was consistent across teams at 2 days. The initiative team accomplished this through balancing the workload (smaller teams pull fewer claims than larger teams), eliminating motion (no more sorting and resorting), and reducing excess processing (replacing a 100% audit process with simpler, more meaningful controls). By implementing these changes and standardizing procedures, the project team estimated that up to 15 defects identified in the current state would be eliminated or greatly reduced.

In addition to the very visible results presented here, American Fidelity was able to ensure that employees were provided uninterrupted time each day to process claims by dedicating staff to this task on a rotating basis. Teamwork has become a very visible part of the department since the Lean changes have been made, and two of the employees have had enough time made available that they are now assigned part-time as Lean facilitators working on Lean improvements throughout the organization.

Future State Map 2
Case Study: Path Links Pathology Services
Health care organization—histology laboratory

Figure 17.6 is a Future State Map from Path Links Pathology Services in the United Kingdom. The Path Links Lean team attacked the histology laboratory

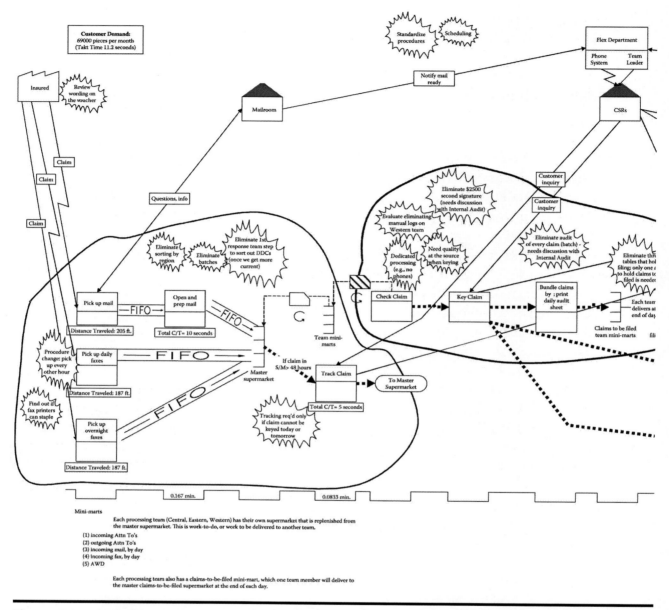

Figure 17.5 *Actual* **Future State Map from American Fidelity Assurance Company (insurance company—claims processing).**

at Lincoln County Hospital in Lincolnshire, England, as their first Lean project. The focus of the mapping exercise and Lean project work addressed the basics of Lean: identifying and eliminating waste. As a result of the work, a number of immediate gains were identified, and a model for histology modernization was developed. Initial significant gains identified included:

■ A reduction in the number of processing steps from 15 to 8 (47%)
■ Labor savings of 1.0 full-time employee (6%)
■ Productivity gains (40%)
■ Efficiency gains; reduction in turnaround times (50%)

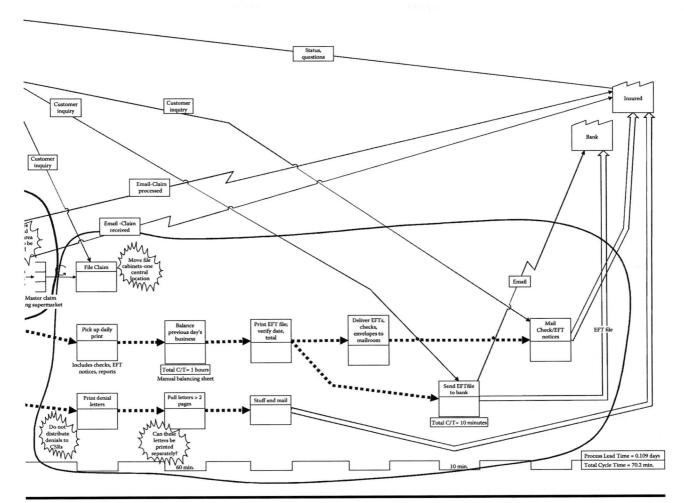

Figure 17.5 (Continued).

According to Path Links Assistant General Manager Mick Chomyn, in addition to the very visible results presented above, Path Links was able to target key areas for investment in facilities, equipment, and IT (information technology) solutions to achieve maximum realization of benefits identified from the VSM exercise, thereby unlocking further potential gains toward achieving optimum process efficiency.

Overall, Path Links has seen the potential for achieving rapid, significant, and sustained benefits from Lean applications in its histopathology laboratory processes and is anticipating equivalent gains by extending Lean to all other laboratory disciplines and nonlaboratory activities.

Once the FSM has been created, Chapter 18 will show you how to create an action plan for moving from current state to future state.

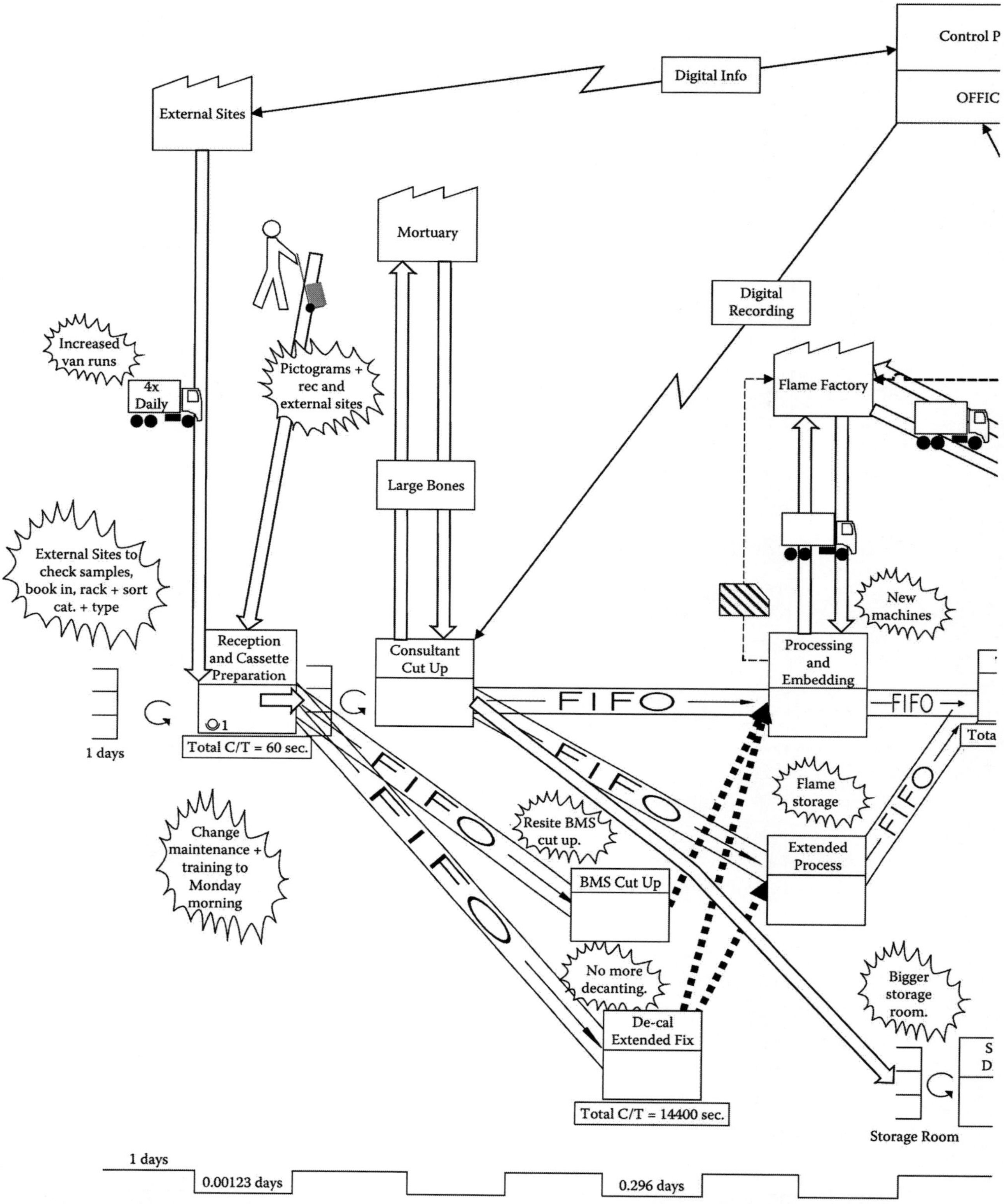

Figure 17.6 *Actual* **Future State Map, from Path Links Pathology Service (health care organization—histology laboratory).**

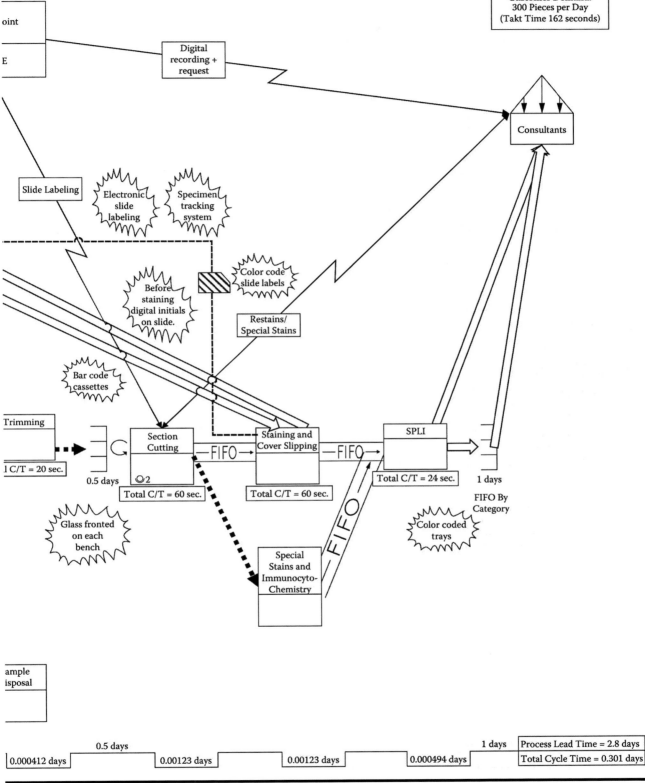

Figure 17.6   (Continued).

IMPROVEMENT STATE: CREATING THE STRUCTURE FOR USING YOUR INSIGHTS AND KNOWLEDGE TO IMPROVE THE PROCESS

Chapter 18

Creating the Action Plan

A good plan, violently executed now,
is better than a perfect plan next week.

General George S. Patton Jr.

Introduction

Value Stream Mapping, as a tool to continuous improvement, provides some of the most powerful and important information a project team can capture during the planning stages for a project. Regardless of the improvement methodology—whether it's Lean, Six Sigma, reengineering, or total quality management—the data and ideas that come from these maps can, and should, quickly jump-start a project.

The tool itself relies on observation and speed. Observing what is actually happening, documenting what you see, and presenting the results is powerful all on its own. Yet, when you or the project team can perform this exercise at a near breakneck speed, the momentum that is gained is priceless. Seeing the current state transformed on paper into a future-state vision in less than two days will almost always capture people's attention and generate excitement from those seeking positive change to the process they live in.

Even though there may be agreement on how to create the Value Stream Map set, many mappers and project teams struggle when it comes to connecting the actual mapping work to an action plan. Nevertheless, developing the *action plan*, or a project outline that includes all process improvement tasks, is equally important—*and* it should be completed at the same fast-paced speed used when capturing the current state and creating the vision for the future. All actions added to the plan should be focused on improving the process by eliminating waste. This chapter describes how to select tasks for the action plan, as well as how to structure the plan.

The secret lies in how you and the project team use the Future State Map to develop this action plan. Remembering that the Future State Map is the blueprint for change is the single focal point for developing a good plan for improvement. The team must not get bogged down by trying to create the perfect plan. As General George S. Patton so bluntly stated, "A good plan today is better than a perfect plan next week." The logic behind this statement was simple: It really doesn't matter what you plan, or how perfect you may think the plan is; when the plan is put into action, things will change. Therefore, get a good plan in place and move forward to implementation.

Value Stream Mapping provides a methodology of its own for creating the action plan. It is centered on the Future State Map. The concept moves at the same speed as the mapping exercise. The power of this plan development lies within your ability to stick to the rules and move forward to implementation.

Identify the Process Loops

The initial step in creating an action plan from a Future State Map set is to identify your *process loops*. These are subsets of the process flow portion of your map and associated communication.

To identify the process loops on a Future State Map, start at the beginning of the process flow. Move through the process steps until the flow stops. This is easily seen by the existence of a push arrow, a supermarket, or a FIFO (first in, first out) lane. This first process loop is commonly called the *supplier loop*. To document this loop, draw a line around the control point, the supplier, the first supermarket, or the FIFO lane, and any process steps that may occur prior to the supermarket or FIFO lane. Figure 18.1 provides an example of how to draw this loop. Be sure and label the loop by giving it a name that is descriptive of the process steps in the loop. Typically the supplier loop is labeled "supplier loop."

Next, look at the end of the process flow on the map. The last process loop, commonly referred to as the *customer loop*, is identified by finding the last point where flow stops prior to being shipped (or provided to) the customer. Once again, look for the last occurrence of a supermarket or FIFO lane. Similar to the supplier loop, the customer loop is documented by drawing a line around the control point, the customer, and the last supermarket or FIFO lane, as well as any process steps that may exist after the supermarket or FIFO lane, as shown in Figure 18.2.

When reviewing the Future State Map, as shown in Figure 18.3, the project team will see that both ends of the process flow have been captured in loops and that all remaining process steps may or may not continually flow. If the remaining flow is broken by occasional supermarkets or FIFO lanes, the team should break this into multiple process loops. Otherwise, the remaining steps in the process can be captured as a single process loop, as shown in Figure 18.4.

When you're documenting these additional process loops, draw the lines to include the supermarket or FIFO lane on either end of the loop. As you can see in Figures 18.4 and 18.5, the loops overlap each other. However, whereas Figure 18.4 demonstrates the impact of continuous flow through the middle of the value stream, Figure 18.5 shows the effects of additional supermarkets and

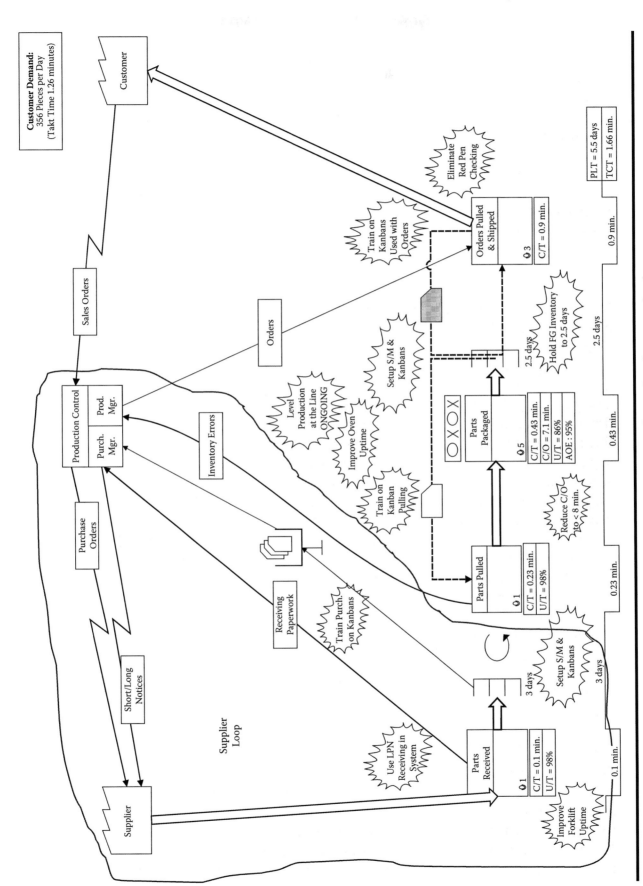

Figure 18.1 Drawing the supplier loop to show all supplier process steps and associated communication.

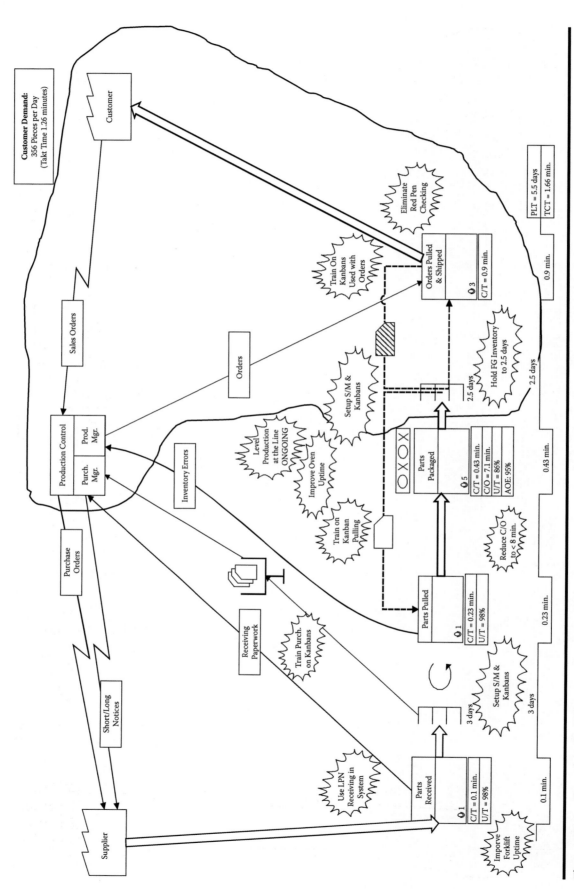

Figure 18.2   Drawing the customer loop to show all customer process steps and associated communication.

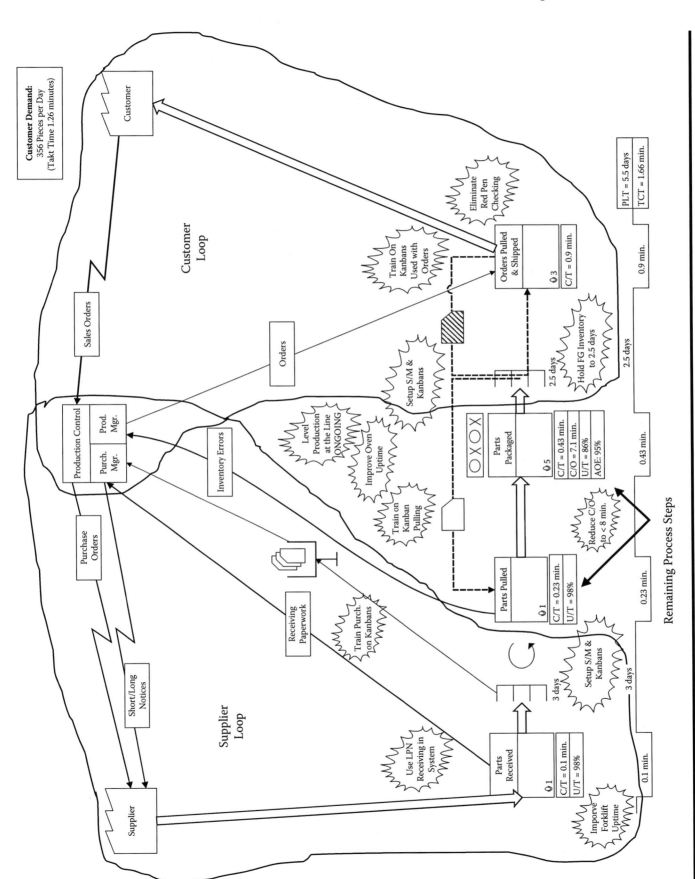

Figure 18.3 Reviewing the remaining process steps after the customer and supplier loops have been identified.

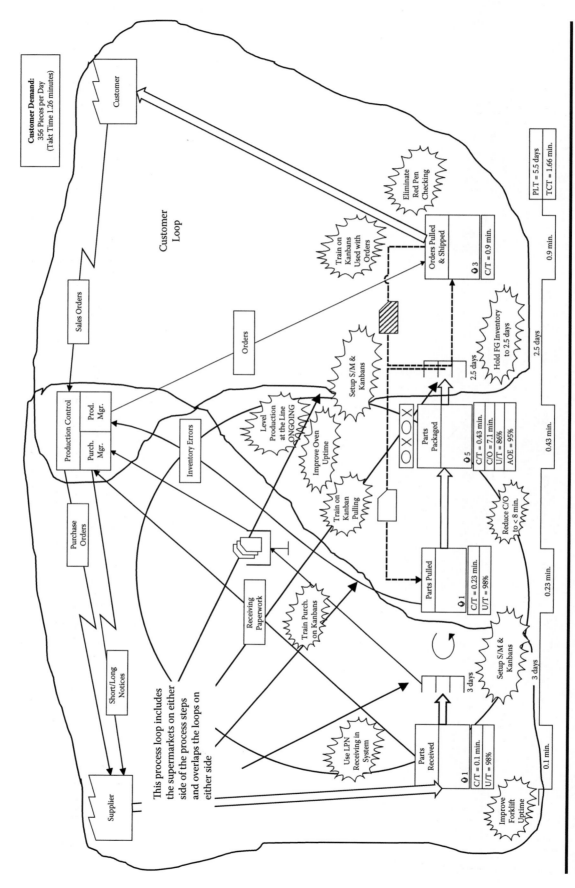

Figure 18.4 When creating the remaining process loops, extend each loop to and overlap supermarkets and the adjacent process loops.

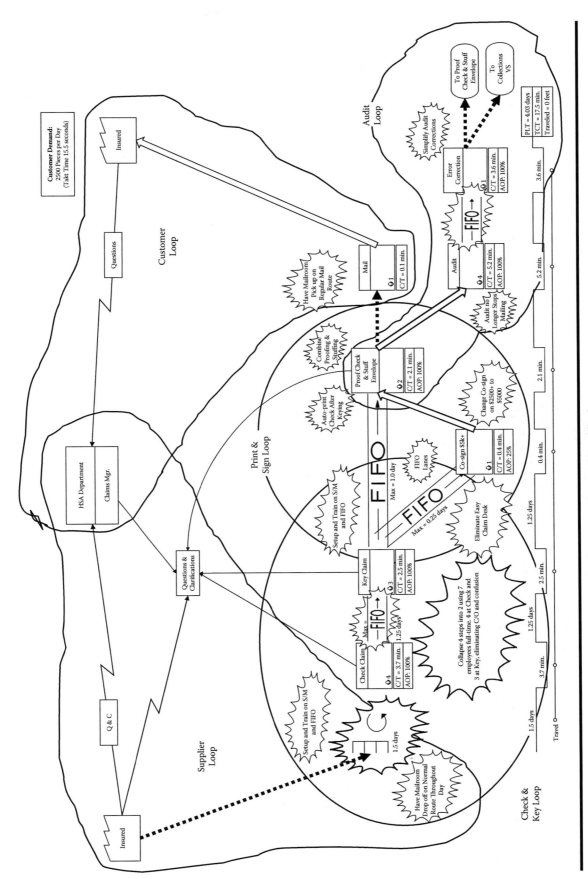

Figure 18.5 *Actual* **Future State Map that has had all process loops identified.**

FIFO lanes. More supermarkets and FIFO lanes have a tendency to lead to more process loops.

In the event that there are numerous FIFO lanes or supermarkets established in the middle of the process flow with only one process step in between two FIFO symbols, the team might elect to group several process steps and associated FIFO lanes together to form a process loop, as shown in Figure 18.5. Other times, it may be easier to attack the value stream one process step and a FIFO lane, or supermarket, at a time.

The project team can make a determination as to what is included in a loop during the identification exercise. As you can see in Figure 18.5, the additional steps were broken into three distinct, yet overlapping, loops. Each one was given a name to simplify action plan development. What a loop is named is entirely up to the team.

Prioritize the Process Loops

Once the process loops have been identified, the team must prioritize the loops, ranking them from most important to least important. Although this may sound relatively harmless and easy, as the team progresses through this work, it can quickly become complex. Each member of the project team may have his or her own thoughts about what is important. In addition, management may have stated certain goals and objectives prior to the mapping exercise that influence team members' decisions. Do not let these subjective thoughts interfere with the process.

List each process loop on a flipchart or whiteboard. Underneath each process loop name, list all kaizen bursts that are contained within the loop drawn on the Future State Map. Ensure that all kaizen bursts on the map are listed underneath a process loop, even if you have left a burst outside of all loops. Using the Future State Map in Figure 18.5, this list would appear as shown in Figure 18.6.

You may notice that some kaizen bursts that were contained within more than one process loop are listed multiple times on the chart in Figure 18.6. This is to be expected. In this manner, whichever loop is attacked first will complete those tasks. They can then be marked off the other process loop's list of tasks.

Brainstorm with the team to see if any additional ideas come out that need to be added to the Future State Map. If any ideas do emerge, add them to the map and the list. Once this is done, the team is ready to prioritize.

Tie Priority to Key Performance Indicators

The fastest and easiest way to establish the priority of the list is to use your organization's key performance indicators (KPIs) as your guiding force. Review the KPIs, and then number the process loops from highest to lowest priority, with "1" being the highest priority.

Supplier Loop:
- Setup and train on supermarkets and FIFO lanes
- Have mailroom drop off on normal route throughout day
- Set supermarket size at 1.5 days

Customer Loop:
- Have mailroom pick up on regular mail route

Check & Key Loop:
- Setup and train on supermarkets and FIFO lanes
- Have mailroom drop off on normal route throughout day
- Set supermarket size at 1.5 days
- Establish FIFO lane after "Check Claim" with max of 1.25 days
- Collapse 4 steps into 2 using 7 employees full-time: 4 at Check and 3 at Key, eliminating C/O and confusion
- Establish FIFO lane after "Key Claim" to "Proof Check" with max of 1.0 days
- Establish FIFO lane after "Key Claim" to "Co-sign $5k+" with max of 0.25 days
- Eliminate easy claim desk

Print & Sign Loop:
- Establish FIFO lane after "Key Claim" to "Proof Check" with max of 1.0 days
- Establish FIFO lane after "Key Claim" to "Co-sign $5k+" with max of 0.25 days
- Eliminate easy claim desk
- Setup and train on supermarkets and FIFO lanes
- Auto-print checks after keying
- Combine proofing and stuffing
- Change co-sign on $2,500+ to $5,000+

Audit Loop:
- Audit no longer stops mailing
- Establish FIFO lane after "Audit" to "Error Correction"
- Simplify audit corrections

Figure 18.6   A complete list of all kaizen activities (process improvement tasks) listed beneath their respective process loops.

Using this approach may require you to meet with upper-level management or the Continuous Improvement Council, or it may require you to review documentation of the organization's strategic plan. Regardless of where this information comes from, using it as a guideline for improvement will preclude many struggles and debates that may occur in the absence of such goals and objectives.

Establish Your Criteria for Prioritization

If your organization has no KPIs, or if the Continuous Improvement Council decides that an alternative set of criteria is necessary to achieve the desired project results, then you must develop a criteria list. This list may include anything important to the organization (or team). However, you must remember that the goal in continuous improvement (whether it is Lean, Six Sigma, or some other discipline) is to *achieve positive change in the process while eliminating waste*.

Some typical criteria used to establish priority include (but are not limited to) the following changes:

- Are fast and easy to complete
- Are most visible to the workforce (to demonstrate the power of continuous improvement)
- Address the biggest problem to the customer
- Address the biggest problem to the supplier
- Address the biggest problem to employees within the value stream

---

Flipchart Based List of Prioritized Process Loops

(5) Supplier Loop
- Setup and train on supermarkets and FIFO lanes
- Have mailroom drop off on normal route throughout day
- Set supermarket size at 1.5 days

(1) Customer Loop
- Have mailroom pick up on regular mail route

(4) Check & Key Loop
- Setup and train on supermarkets and FIFO lanes
- Have mailroom drop off on normal route throughout day
- Set supermarket size at 1.5 days
- Establish FIFO lane after "Check Claim" with max of 1.25 days
- Collapse 4 steps into 2 using 7 employees full-time; 4 at check and 3 at key, eliminating C/O and confusion
- Establish FIFO lane after "Key Claim" to "Proof Check" with max of 1.0 days
- Establish FIFO lane after "Key Claim" to "Co-sign $5k+" with max of 0.25 days
- Eliminate easy claim desk

(2) Print & Sign Loop
- Establish FIFO lane after "Key Claim" to "Proof Check" with max of 1.0 days
- Establish FIFO lane after "Key Claim" to "Co-sign $5k+" with max of 0.25 days
- Eliminate easy claim desk
- Setup and train on supermarkets and FIFO lanes
- Auto-print checks after keying
- Combine proofing and stuffing
- Change co-sign on $2,500+ to $5,000+

(3) Audit Loop
- Audit no longer stops mailing
- Establish FIFO lane after "Audit" to "Error Correction+"
- Simplify audit corrections

Figure 18.7   The prioritized list of process loops from the Future State Map in Figure 18.5. Note that the action items, or process improvement tasks, are not prioritized at this point in time.

- Address customer satisfaction issues
- Effect biggest ROI
- Effect fastest ROI
- Facilitate employees' acceptance of change (fastest buy-in)
- Pertain to the toughest employees to convince

Once these criteria are established, the project team can review each process loop and determine the priority order of the loops. If you are keeping the list on a whiteboard or flipchart, as opposed to in an electronic file, the list may look something like the chart shown in Figure 18.7.

Prioritize the Work within Each Loop

Once you and the project team have prioritized the process loops, you must then prioritize each action item contained within each loop. As mentioned, the action items are those kaizen bursts and other ideas that must be accomplished in order

---

Flipchart List of Prioritized Process Loops & Action Items

(5) Supplier Loop
      (2) Setup and train on supermarkets and FIFO lanes
      (1) Have mailroom drop off on normal route throughout day
      (3) Set supermarket size at 1.5 days
(1) Customer Loop
      (1) Have mailroom pick up on regular mail route
(4) Check & Key Loop
      (2) Setup and train on supermarkets and FIFO lanes
      (1) Have mailroom drop off on normal route throughout day
      (3) Set supermarket size at 1.5 days
      (5) Establish FIFO lane after "Check Claim" with max of 1.25 days
      (4) Collapse 4 steps into 2 using 7 employees full-time; 4 at check and 3 at key,
            eliminating C/O and confusion
      (6) Establish FIFO lane after "Key Claim" to "Proof Check" with max of 1.0 days
      (8) Establish FIFO lane after "Key Claim" to "Co-sign $5k+" with max of 0.25 days
      (7) Eliminate easy claim desk
(2) Print & Sign Loop
      (7) Establish FIFO lane after "Key Claim" to "Proof Check" with max of 1.0 days
      (6) Establish FIFO lane after "Key Claim" to "Co-sign $5k+" with max of 0.25 days
      (5) Eliminate easy claim desk
      (4) Setup and train on supermarkets and FIFO lanes
      (3) Auto-print checks after keying
      (2) Combine proofing and stuffing
      (1) Change co-sign on $2,500+ to $5,000+
(3) Audit Loop
      (1) Audit no longer stops mailing
      (2) Establish FIFO lane after "Audit" to "Error Correction"
      (3) Simplify audit corrections

Figure 18.8   A flipchart-based prioritized list of process loops, with the action items prioritized as well. When using flipcharts, it may not be to the team's advantage to rewrite the entire list. Instead, simply write the priority number next to each item.

to effect positive change in the value stream. To prioritize these action items, use the same criteria and methodology that you used to prioritize the process loops. Once this is completed, the list may look something like the example shown in Figure 18.8.

Many continuous improvement practitioners take this list, key it into a spreadsheet, project management software, word processing file, etc., and then manage the project from this document. Other practitioners prefer to leave the list exactly as shown in Figures 18.7 and 18.8, i.e., on the whiteboard or flipchart. The team then works directly off of this list throughout the project. The mindset for this approach is that the team can quickly move from the planning stage to implementation.

Regardless of the approach, the results are the same once change begins to occur. As you complete action items, you should review the results against your prioritized list. It may be necessary to change the priority, depending on the results. You need to ensure that every member of the team, as well as any management personnel who are involved, understands that as tasks are finished, the results will dictate what happens next. This is what General Patton was referring to in his now-famous quote.

There are many ways to monitor the progress of the action plan, from Gantt charts and project plans (like those presented in *Learning to See*) to software applications specifically designed for project management. Regardless of the tools used to monitor and manage the work, remember that the most important part of implementation is *reviewing the priority of remaining tasks once an action item has been completed.*

Present Your Maps to the Workforce

Once an action plan has been established, the project team should present the entire map set, i.e., both the Current State and Future State Maps, to the employees working within the value stream. This session should be conducted in similar fashion to the presentation of the Current State Map (described in Chapter 15).

The team needs to explain what the new symbols on the map are, why decisions were made to make changes to the value stream, and how the changes will be accomplished. The team should show the completed action plan to the audience and ask for feedback. There may be some resistance to change, and the project team needs to know where this resistance exists as they start implementing.

The team should acknowledge all input in a positive manner and take note of any ideas that are worth studying, as well as whether they can be included in the project about to be initiated, or may be viable in a future project. If an idea offered from the workforce does not get implemented during the project, a team member needs to discuss the reason(s) with the employee who made the suggestion. Once again, positive and continual feedback creates employee buy-in, even when an idea is not used.

In the event that a new idea comes out during this meeting, it will require the team to reconvene and adjust the Future State Map and action plan. Do not wait until the team is back at the discussion table. Mark up the Future State Map during the workforce meeting, and then redraw the map later. Write directly on the action plan any changes that are accepted.

Present Your Maps to the Council

The final phase prior to project implementation involves reviewing the map set with the Continuous Improvement Council. To gain the support from the top of the organization, the project team needs to ensure that not only does its champion understand what the future state and action plan entail, but also that the council is supportive of the proposed changes.

This review should be conducted simultaneously with the presentation to the workforce. By conducting this review at the same time, the council is able to see the attitude of the employees within the value stream. The council members can listen to the project team interact with employees, address any concerns and new ideas, and monitor the attitudes of employees that may be roadblocks to change. This provides greater buy-in on the part of the council as well as demonstrating additional backing and support for the project team.

Council members have the ability to speak up just as the employees within the value stream do, get their ideas heard in an open forum, and help the champion and project team set the last piece of the puzzle in place prior to project implementation. This concept of combined meetings is aligned with the overall concept of Value Stream Mapping due to the speed at which it all occurs, eliminating repetitive meetings to simply explain the same thing to multiple audiences.

With all the planning work now complete, the team is ready to implement change. Chapter 19 will lay out the details of how this change should occur.

Chapter 19

Implementing Change

We progress because we are willing to change.

Thomas J. Watson

Introduction

The time for strategy is over. Now the process of change can begin. But this does not mean that Value Stream Mapping is complete. Just like all other aspects of continuous improvement, Value Stream Mapping is never finished. As the project work progresses, the team may find that it is necessary to return to the map set and to update and modify both the Future State Map and the action plan.

To implement successfully, the project team should follow a standardized approach to implementation of the action plan. Lean implementation provides a great number of the tools and concepts required to make change a reality, and it implements change at the same speed as mapping the process. This is not intended to detract from the power of other process improvement methodologies but, rather, to align Value Stream Mapping with the methodology with which it is most closely associated, Lean.

Lean brings a continuous improvement methodology to the project team that fits perfectly with the concepts of Value Stream Mapping. Even though many other methodologies and disciplines have begun to utilize Value Stream Mapping as the process mapping tool of choice, these practitioners are finding that starting their projects out using Lean tools and concepts can produce fast results. Quick victories, fast return on investments, and early employee buy-in make it much easier to complete successful projects. To be successful, though, project teams must be disciplined. They must understand how Lean concepts are used, and how improvements are reported and monitored.

Assign a Value Stream Manager

Early in the Lean journey (or any other continuous improvement journey that is just adopting the concept of Value Stream Mapping), it is important that a Value Stream Manager be assigned to each value stream. This manager is responsible for monitoring the value stream—in other words, looking for changes in the process and/or communication flow.

The Value Stream Manager does not have to be a manager in the organization. For that matter, this position does not even need to be filled by a supervisor. Equally important, this assignment should never be anything remotely resembling a full-time position, because it typically takes less than 5% of the employee's time each week. The job of Value Stream Manager can be performed by any employee who is respected by both his or her peers and management and who has a working knowledge of both Value Stream Mapping and the changes that have been implemented. Using the Value Stream Maps and having metrics in place to monitor the activity of the process, the Value Stream Manager can use these existing control mechanisms to look for adverse changes in the process. Because the role is to monitor the value stream for adverse changes and to bring the correct people into a meeting, it does not require a member of the management team to fulfill this role.

The Value Stream Manager must be respected by *employees within the value stream* and must understand the flow as it is documented or changed to date. The Value Stream Manager *must* have direct access to a member of the management team who can call a meeting of the right personnel to discuss changes in the process. This requires an open-door policy that allows employees in such a position to bypass any formal chain-of-command policy and talk directly to the decision maker who can call a meeting. The Value Stream Manager does not need to have the power to *run* a meeting, only the responsibility and accountability to *ask* for a meeting when necessary. Figure 19.1 summarizes the role and responsibilities of the Value Stream Manager.

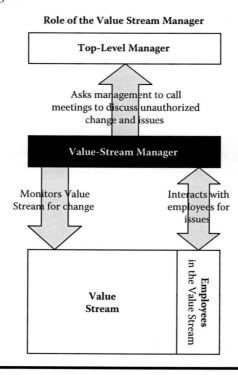

Role of the Value Stream Manager

Top-Level Manager

Asks management to call meetings to discuss unauthorized change and issues

Value-Stream Manager

Monitors Value Stream for change

Interacts with employees for issues

Value Stream

Employees in the Value Stream

Figure 19.1   A visual representation of the role of the Value Stream Manager.

The common practice is to assign a Value Stream Manager once positive changes have been implemented through project work. However, some of the ways that Value Stream Mapping is being used to assist with project prioritization and project acceptance decisions at the level of the Continuous Improvement Council may suggest that Value Stream Managers should be introduced when the Current State Map is completed.

It is strongly recommended that Value Stream Managers have the knowledge and skills not only to interpret a Value Stream Map, but also to be capable of mapping the value stream. Having this mapping ability not only makes it easier for the Value Stream Manager to compare what is observed in the process, but it also provides more credibility with coworkers and management alike.

The Value Stream Manager must be given time throughout the day or week to monitor the process. Comparing what is actually occurring against the Current State Map, when no change has been initiated, gives great insight into what is happening on a day-to-day basis. If there is visible change in the tasks, volumes produced, or even the number of employees assigned, the Value Stream Manager needs to report this information to the decision maker, the Lean champion, the Lean manager, or even the Executive Council to call a meeting. This information alone may escalate the value stream's priority to (or near) the top of the project list.

For value streams where change has been implemented, this role becomes even more critical. The Value Stream Manager must be diligent in monitoring the changes. If the process begins to revert to the "old ways," or if employees within the process begin to make changes without proper guidance and input from project teams or management, it is possible that the improvements made during a project will produce no positive impact.

Additionally, assigning someone as Value Stream Manager gives a voice to the value stream. This individual can speak for the value stream and its employees, informing champions and the council when the project work is not complete or is ineffective.

The Value Stream Manager must be held accountable for drift in the process—not for the drift occurring, but for discussing the changes in the process with employees, for attempting to self-correct these issues, and for reporting the process change to the Lean manager and/or council. As previously mentioned, the Value Stream Manager should use posted Value Stream Maps as visual indicators and provide adverse changes in metrics to identify this drift in the process.

Another duty essential to successful monitoring and continuous improvement of the value stream is to hold the Value Stream Manager responsible for periodic remapping of the current state. This proactive approach to mapping provides excellent proactive data to the Lean manager and council in search of successes and opportunities within the organization.

Attacking the Action Plan

Regardless of the continuous improvement methodology employed by the organization, Value Stream Mapping lends itself well to the concept of kaizen. Although *kaizen* is literally translated from Japanese as "good change," it is more appropriately defined as "rapid, good, continual change." This concept, which is used in a cultural fashion with many Japanese companies, empowers the work force to immediately stop a functioning value stream at any time when a problem is encountered. All persons required to identify the root cause and a solution are gathered, and the issue is resolved as quickly as possible.

Applying this concept culturally in the United States and many other countries is extremely difficult. For many organizations, the focus is, and always has been, on producing product or results. This focus overrides the need to immediately fix what is broken. Instead, work orders and requests are submitted, and the problem, unless it is fatal in nature, is corrected whenever the right employees are available. In the meantime, extra effort and possibly even rework is required to produce acceptable results through a temporary fix.

To make the concept of kaizen more palatable to these organizations, Lean practitioners have adapted kaizen to the culture. Because many of these same organizations view process improvement as very structured, using project management tools with time frames and deadlines attached, the concept of kaizen is introduced to fit this format. Kaizen has been broken into three categories to make it more acceptable and understandable to the workforce:

Point kaizen: Although this is not kaizen in the truest sense of the word, point kaizen has become an excellent way to introduce the concept and gain acceptance. Point kaizen consists of those improvement activities that happen instantaneously when a problem is encountered, and they generally last one day or less.

Focused kaizen: this is a slightly more intense effort than point kaizen, lasting two to three days.

Kaizen events or kaizen blitzes: This is the most common form of "kaizen" found in these cultural settings. For those organizations wishing to avoid the Japanese terminology altogether, these are often called *rapid improvement projects* or *rapid improvement events*. These events are typically five days in duration, with very definite starting and ending dates, to fit a culture of "projects must have a specific time frame."

Many times, kaizen events comprise a planning event where the mapping is completed and utility and other structural changes are initiated. Once these structural changes have been completed, the team reconvenes and spends an additional five days attacking the action plan. Figure 19.2 summarizes the three types of "kaizen" used in the United States; the rest of this discussion focuses on kaizen events, as this is how the majority of U.S. companies have come to apply the Japanese concept of kaizen.

The Concept of Kaizen *As Introduced to the United States*	
Kaizen Event or Kaizen Blitz A.K.A. Rapid Improvement Project (RIP) or Rapid Improvement Event (RIE)	Five days of concentrated effort focused on implementing as many action plan items as possible
Focused Kaizen	Two to three days of focused effort creating as much positive change as possible
Point Kaizen	Immediate efforts to produce positive change lasting less than one day

Figure 19.2   Kaizen as it has generally been applied in the United States.

As the concepts of Lean have been introduced into some sectors, such as higher education, these extended kaizen events might include the presentation of the maps and action plan to interested parties to gain agreement prior to change being initiated. Although not really even close to the true meaning of kaizen, this has proven effective in introducing the concept and proving the power of the discipline in a variety of sectors and industries.

Using the kaizen approach, project team leaders (often called facilitators) can assign multiple action or task items from within the highest-priority process loop to project team members and immediately begin the process of change. If there are more team members than tasks, additional loops may be attacked at the same time.

The secret to success is to ensure that all team members meet regularly throughout the kaizen event to review task progress and success. This continual realignment of tasks and reprioritization of effort is vital to the success of the event. Unlike more traditional process improvement methodologies and project management concepts, kaizen requires a certain amount of fluidity to change as necessary, to overcome the realities of working with people and live processes.

Using Action Plans for a Structured and Goal-Oriented Approach to Improvement

As discussed throughout this chapter, implementing change to achieve the future state can be conducted by using the action plan as the guiding document. Keeping the team focused on the results generated through multiple kaizen events or improvement projects can easily center on the action plan. Team members not only see the prioritized plan in a structured manner, but they also can easily review this plan against the Future State Map on an ongoing basis.

Because it is not the norm to complete all aspects of change associated with a Future State Map in a single week, the need to manage and refocus efforts over a period of time is crucial to successful implementation. Keeping the action plan visible and updated throughout the life of the kaizen efforts must be maintained. To this end, the Value Stream Maps and action plan may be displayed within the value stream itself, alongside other pertinent information to show the workforce what is happening.

For those organizations that have a more formalized and structured culture, the use of a project plan may be essential to gain the acceptance of employees and management alike. Rother and Shook introduced this concept in their book, *Learning to See*. The tool (which is not new by any means to the process improvement world) consists of a Gantt chart with action items listed and target implementation dates shown. Figure 19.3 provides an example of a Gantt chart-based project plan.

Using Lean Progress Charts

For organizations focusing on Lean methodologies and working on creating a Lean culture, the Value Stream Maps and action plan are often used in conjunction with a Lean progress chart. This chart focuses on how successful the organization, facility, or employees within the value stream are in their learning, using, and maintaining the concepts of Lean as positive change is implemented. This approach provides Value Stream Mappers within Lean organizations the opportunity to rapidly revisit each of the listed Lean concepts in search of additional opportunities for improvement throughout the journey to create the future state.

This concept of combining the Value Stream Map set and action plan with Lean concepts places great emphasis on searching for best methods in all tasks contained within the value stream. As each action plan task is addressed, the team can interactively review how well the team and the employees in the process have implemented Lean concepts. The level of training provided, along with the employees' ability to sustain the changes, can be measured and in turn utilized to determine how much more effort is required to create the Lean culture desired.

A *Lean progress chart* lists each Lean concept that the project team wants to introduce and sustain within the value stream. Each concept is shown with a section devoted to training, implementation, and sustainability. The overall success, as well as that of each component, is measured as "percent complete" on the chart, allowing for the team and the employees in the area to see their progress. Figure 19.4 shows a sample Lean progress chart.

By using this approach after each action item has been implemented, the team can review the changes made, monitor the results, and assess how much additional effort may be required to create an environment where best methods are in place and a Lean culture exists. This requires the team members to not only look at who was trained and how training was conducted; it also requires them to conduct an evaluation of the implemented change. This review compares the change with similar tasks and duties throughout the organization in a search for best methods within the organization. Finally, as the value stream is repeatedly

PROCESS LOOP NAME:	ACTION ITEM/TASK	WEEKLY SCHEDULE												TASK OWNER	DUE DATE	COMPLETE
		1	2	3	4	5	6	7	8	9	10	11	12			
Customer Loop	Mailroom pickup on regular route	■												Chris	11 May 07	X
	Change co-sign from $2500 to $5000	■												Bob	11 May 07	X
	Combine proofing & stuffing													Karen	11 May 07	X
	Auto-print checks													Bob	25 May 07	
Print & Sign Loop	Setup and train on supermarkets/FIFO			■										Chris	25 May 07	X
	Eliminate easy claim desk			■										Sarah	25 May 07	X
	Establish FIFO Lane for co-sign			■										Bob	25 May 07	
	Establish FIFO Lane after Key Claim													Bob	25 May 07	
Audit Loop	Audits no longer stop mailouts	■												Karen	11 May 07	X
	Establish FIFO lane after Audit					■								Karen	8 Jun 07	
	Simplify audit Corrections step													Karen	8 Jun 07	
	Have mailroom drop off on normal route	■												Chris	11 May 07	X
	Setup and train on supermarkets/FIFO					■								Chris	8 Jun 07	
	Set supermarket size at 1.5 days													Chris	8 Jun 07	
Check & Key Loop	Collapse 4 steps into 2 with only 7 employees								■					Bob/Chris	29 Jun 07	
	Establish FIFO Lane after Key Claim			■										Bob	25 May 07	X
	Eliminate easy claim desk			■										Sarah	25 May 07	
	Establish FIFO Lane for co-sign													Sarah	25 May 07	
	Establish FIFO Lane after Key Claim													Bob	25 May 07	
Supplier Loop	Have mailroom drop off on normal route	■				■								Chris	11 May 07	X
	Setup and train on supermarkets/FIFO													Bob	8 Jun 07	
	Set supermarket size at 1.5 days													Bob	8 Jun 07	

VALUE STREAM: HSA Processing
VALUE STREAM MANAGER: Bob Taylor
DATE: 7 May 07

VALUE STREAM PLAN

Figure 19.3 Example of a Gantt chart-based project plan.

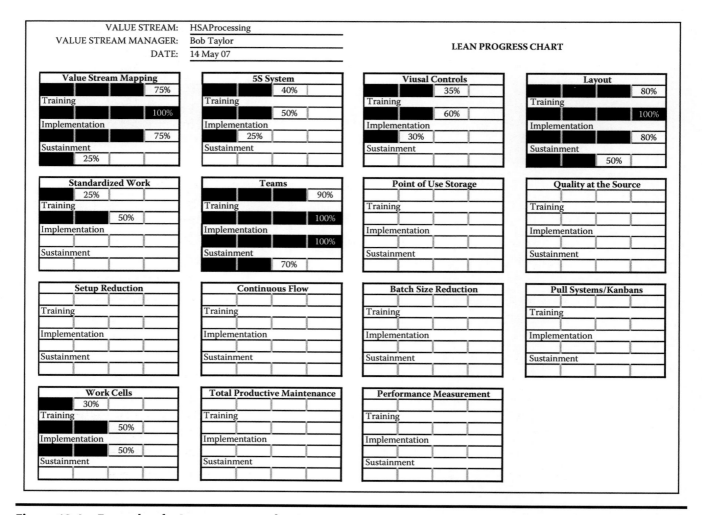

Figure 19.4 Example of a Lean progress chart.

worked on by both the team and the employees working within the process, an assessment of how capable the employees are of sustaining the changes must be made. The results can be posted to the progress chart and displayed in a visible location where all employees can see the chart.

Speed and Accountability Are Critical to Success

Regardless of how you set goals and keep them visible to the workforce, taking advantage of Value Stream Mapping means moving through the planning stage to implementation as quickly as possible. The speed at which change can be made using this technique provides evidence to employees that this approach is not just a "flavor of the month." As employees see action items implemented, their acceptance, involvement, and ownership will increase significantly.

When implementing change at such a rapid pace, there must be accountability in place to ensure that the methodology selected for change is being followed.

The project manager or facilitator must hold each team member accountable for completing his or her assignments on time. Management must support the facilitator and not only provide adequate time to complete tasks, but also take corrective action with employees who repeatedly fail to fulfill their project duties.

Sticking to the methodology is critical to success. When change is being made with speed, missing or skipping a step can mean disaster. Facilitators must be aware of this and use the concepts and techniques necessary to complete a project or Lean event.

By using the action plan and Lean progress documents as discussed earlier, the facilitator can stay focused on the goals and objectives of the project. However, because speed can make or break a project in many instances, the team may choose to use the flipchart method discussed in Chapter 18, where the action plan is simply listed and prioritized on the flip chart or whiteboard.

Bringing the team together multiple times throughout the day to review progress will help keep the team focused on the plan. These meetings do not need to take much time at all, and they can generally be accomplished in 10–15 minutes. Management can and should be invited to these meetings to provide updates and to solicit support and assistance when required.

Facilitators need to be capable of self-managing their work over time. Management's role is to support and assist when asked, not to interject opinion and desire. The facilitator should be accountable to the executive council, not to a single manager. This accountability includes regular updates to the executive council.

These updates should be focused and effectively communicate progress—or the lack thereof. Council members can use these meetings not only to understand the amount of progress being made, but also to learn about roadblocks and other issues with the value stream. Working with the facilitator, the Lean champion, and the Lean manager, the council can provide any and all necessary support to continue moving toward the goals of the project.

Focus on Your Specific Goals

As the project progresses, metrics should be maintained in a visible manner. Creating a display board with metrics provides a way for the project team as well as all employees in the value stream to see the progress. Metrics should reflect the organization's strategic goals and objectives. Aligning these project measurements with the key performance indicators (KPIs) of the organization enables the continuous improvement work to stay focused on achieving the goals of the company.

Additional metrics may be included that have meaning to the employees in the value stream. When listening to employees voice their concerns about issues and opportunities during brainstorming sessions, you may identify possible metrics that demonstrate success faster and in an easier to understand format than some KPIs. Figure 19.5 provides a sample set of metrics for a value stream.

Metric	Baseline	Previous	% Improvement	Most Recent	% Improvement from Most Recent	% Improvement from Baseline
# of Pieces of Paper Generated	19	9	52.6%	3	66.7%	84.2%
Travel Path of Work Order in-house (in feet)	1265	723	42.8%	253	65.0%	80.0%
# of Employee "Touches"	28	11	60.7%	5	54.5%	82.1%
Avg. Age of Work Orders Waiting Assignment	24.1	7.2	70.1%	1.3	81.9%	94.6%
% of Work Orders Submitted by Email	26.8%	63.4%	136.6%	91.1%	43.7%	239.9%

Figure 19.5   A sample set of metrics showing the baseline, previous measurement, and most recent measurement, along with the percentage of change throughout the Lean journey.

Finally, as progress is observed, the results should be conveyed to management in a format that allows for financial impact to be understood. Because any change that is implemented should ultimately result in improvement to the bottom line, it is critical that metrics provide data to support and substantiate the change, as shown in Figure 19.5.

However, when dealing with the financial impact, it may be necessary for accountants and financial analysts to rethink the traditional ways of financial reporting. Implementing change at a fast pace may create a situation where traditional financial reports are misleading. The executive council must understand these potential situations and be prepared to have the financial staff of the organization retrained to think differently and also to strongly support the mapping and project team.

Once the change has been implemented, your job is done … right? But what about continuous improvement? Chapter 20 will discuss how to move your process beyond today's needs in preparation for tomorrow's.

Chapter 20

Remember
It's Continuous Improvement

Success is never ending: failure is never final.

Rev. Robert H. Schuller

Creating a Value Stream Map set and implementing change is just the beginning. Truly subscribing to the concept of continuous improvement means that you have embarked on a never-ending journey—one that will have successes and setbacks, celebrations and frustrations. As you head down the path to success, understand one thing: Value Stream Mapping never ends.

This concept we call Value Stream Mapping is intended to be an integral part of the journey. Understanding that this is a repetitive tool and promoting the concept to all employees is essential to creating a culture that embraces the technique. With it, you can see the flow, understand the issues, and create a vision of the future. Without it, it is easily possible to muddle along without goals or a destination. Success relies on staying focused. Value Stream Mapping provides the tools to start down the path to success.

Failure comes from a culture that resists change. This resistance to change is what holds organizations back. Customers' demands and expectations change on a daily basis. If we are not able to quickly change to meet or exceed those demands and expectations, the customers will find someone who will meet their expectations. When this occurs, the organization loses. Over time, if this unwillingness to change is not turned around, the organization will cease to exist.

Failure also comes from complacency. Many organizations generate substantial savings and have powerful success stories of change. But many of these same organizations rest on their laurels once the financial results are reported. Making *some* change is not enough. Thinking that your organization is good enough is not good enough. Or worse: "We aren't broke. So why fix it?" This mindset is

245

just as dangerous as those who are resistant to change. The competition will pass you by—and so will the customers.

The major problem with these attitudes is that the employees do not see the big picture. The failure is in their inability to see long term and to understand that success means continually changing to meet customer expectations. Without the vision, without seeing the big picture, many organizations are doomed to repeat the failure experienced by so many others.

Success, on the other hand, comes from accepting change. Winning comes from a culture that *embraces change* and *pursues perfection.* Setting lofty goals, empowering employees to do the things necessary to accomplish those goals, and accepting the rough spots along the road are the things that set great organizations apart.

Success comes from understanding that the road to perfection is a journey of continuous improvement. Making change in small pieces, at a pace in the beginning that is acceptable to both employees and management, is how change starts. As the culture comes to accept change, the speed and amount of change will grow as well. By starting with those things that are easy to change, and by working with the employees accepting or wanting change, success will come.

But with all continuous improvement initiatives, there must be a way to guide this change:

- Through *Current State Maps*, Value Stream Mapping provides the methodology necessary to capture the opportunity for change.
- The *Future State Map* produces the vision for perfection.
- From the Future State Map, an *action plan* provides the implementation structure necessary to succeed.

Knowing that you can attack the value stream over and over again is quite comforting to many people. Having a picture of the future gives employees a way to "see" the future. And when change happens in small bites, the workforce has time to absorb and understand the change prior to more changes being forced on them.

As you start this journey by mapping a value stream, you will face many challenges. To succeed, you must be able to convince the employees of the need to change. You must be able to show the workforce what the current state looks like. Employees must be able to see and understand the current world in which they live.

The future state provides the vision for what the process can and should look like. It provides the blueprint for change. And if a longer-term vision is necessary, you can create an *Ideal State Map.* This ideal state is the ultimate, no-limits vision of the future.

But you must remember: this is only the beginning. Value Stream Mapping is not a "one and done" tool used at the beginning of the journey, never to be repeated. Value Stream Mapping, just like so many other continuous improvement tools, is to be used from now on. If you quit, it's not *continuous* improvement.

Do not believe those who say: "We've achieved the future state. We're done." You are never done. When the team, management, or employees within the value stream begin to realize they are close to the Future State Map, it is time to remap. This is the time to remap the Current State Map and create a new vision of the future.

It's not about how good you are today; it's about how good you are at getting better for the future.

The journey has just begun.

Bibliography

Keyte, Beau, and Drew Locher. *The Complete Lean Enterprise*. New York, NY: Productivity Press, 2004.

Nash, Mark, Sheila Poling and Sophronia Ward. *Using Lean for Faster Six Sigma Results*. New York, NY: Productivity Press, 2006.

Principles of Live Manufacturing with Live Simulation, NIST/MEP (National Institutes of Standards and Technology/Manufacturing Extension Partnership): Gaithersburg, Maryland.

Rother, Mike, and John Shook. *Learning to See*. Cambridge, MA: Lean Enterprise Institute, 1999.

Shingo, Shigeo. *Revolution in Manufacturing: Single-minute Exchange of Die System*. New York, NY: Productivity Press, 1985.

Shingo, Shigeo. *Quick Changeover for Operators: SMED System (Shop floor)*. New York, NY: Productivity Press, 1996.

Tapping, Don, and Tom Shuker. *Value Stream Management for the Lean Office*. New York, NY: Productivity Press, 2003.

Womack, James and Daniel T. Jones. *Lean Thinking*. New York, NY: Simon & Schuster, 1996.

Quality Glossary

The following glossary contains general terminology used in production and transactional industries concerning improvement methodologies. All words defined in this glossary are not contained in this book. It is designed to help the user understand a broader scope of terms, necessary within continual improvement initiatives.

Business Excellence, Lean, and Six Sigma Terminology

5S system: The Japanese concept for organization and housekeeping:

1. Sort (Seiri): determine what is needed and what is not
2. Straighten, or Set in order (Seiton): a place for everything and everything in its place
3. Shine (Seiso): clean everything
4. Standardize (Seiketsu): create the rules to monitor the first three Ss
5. Sustain (Shitsuke): create culture through training and communication

5 whys: Refers to the practice of asking, five times, why the failure has occurred in order to get to the root cause/causes of the problem.

Andon: A tool of visual management originating from the Japanese word for "lamp." A light that provides a signal or has meaning. Andon at many manufacturing facilities is an electronic device: audio and/or color-coded visual display. Lights placed on machines or on production lines to indicate operation status.

Availability of equipment: The percentage of time that a piece of equipment is available to be utilized by the *value stream.*

Availability of personnel: The percentage of time that employees are available to work in the *value stream.*

Balanced scorecard: The scorecard balances traditional performance measures with more forward-looking indicators in four key dimensions:

1. Financial
2. Integration/operational excellence
3. Employees
4. Customers

Batch-and-queue: Processing more than one item and then moving those items forward to the next operation before they are all actually needed there—thus items need to wait in a queue. Also called "batch-and-push." Contrast with *continuous flow processing.*

Batch-size reduction: Lean concept or tool that strives to reduce batch size to the optimal level to meet the customer demand at the next step of the process. The goal is one-piece flow. However, when one-piece flow is not possible, the goal should be to reduce the batch size as far as possible and still be able to respond to customer demands and expectations.

Benchmarking: The concept of discovering what is the best performance (in a particular area or process) being achieved, whether in your company, by a competitor, or by an entirely different industry. Once this is determined, use this information to improve your own processes.

Best practice: A way or method of accomplishing a business function or process that is considered to be superior to all other known methods.

Black Belt: *Six Sigma* team leaders responsible for implementing process improvement projects (*DMAIC* or *DFSS*) within the business to increase customer satisfaction levels and business productivity (top-line growth and bottom-line results). Black Belts are knowledgeable and skilled in the use of the Six Sigma methodology and tools. Black Belts run the Six Sigma projects.

Business excellence: A level of performance in which a company achieves and sustains "best in industry (world-class) results" for critical factors deemed to be vital to business success, as defined by the key *stakeholders* of the business.

Business process quality management: The concept of defining macro and micro processes, assigning ownership, and creating responsibilities of the owners.

Business value added: A step or change made to the product that is necessary for future or subsequent steps but is not noticed by the final customer.

Capability: The capability of a product, process, practicing person, or organization is the ability to perform its specified purpose—based on tested, qualified, or historical performance—to achieve measurable results that satisfy established requirements or specifications.

Cause: A factor (X) that has an impact on a response variable (Y); a source of *variation* in a process or a product or a system. Anything that adversely affects the nature, timing, or magnitude of an adverse effect.

Cell: Operating a true continuous flow on workstations placed close together in the order of processing, sometimes in a "U" shape. Cell staff may handle multiple processes, and the number of employees is changed when the customer demand rate changes. The "U" shaped equipment layout is used to allow more alternatives for distributing work elements among staff, and to quite often permit the leadoff and final operations to be performed by the same employee.

Cellular processing and decision: Linking of operations into the most efficient combination to maximize value-added content while minimizing waste.

Champion: Business leaders and senior managers who ensure that resources are available for training and projects, and who are involved in project tollgate reviews. There are different levels of champions. Two types are organizational champions and project champions. Project champions own the Six Sigma or Lean projects.

Change agent: A person who leads a change project or business-wide initiative by defining, researching, planning, building business support, and carefully selecting volunteers to be part of a change team. Change agents must have the conviction to state the facts based on data, even if the consequences are associated with unpleasantness.

Change management: The process responsible for controlling and managing requests to effect changes to the business infrastructure or any aspect of business services to promote business benefits and results. Change management also controls and manages the implementation of the changes.

Changeover: When a piece of software, a machine, or a staff member has to stop processing in order to change and process a different item. For example, an accounting clerk is processing accounts payable (A/P) and must stop, file A/P claims, pull accounts receivable (A/R) records, change software screens, and then process A/R items.

Charter (project): A document or sheet that clearly scopes and identifies the purpose of a *quality improvement* project. Items specified include background case, purpose, team members, scope, timeline, expected results and benefits, etc.

Content time: See *work content time.*

Continuous flow processing: Items are processed and moved from one processing step to the next step one piece at a time. Each step processes only the one piece that the next step needs, and the transfer batch size is one unit. Sometimes called "single-piece flow" or "one-piece flow." Contrast with *batch-and-queue.*

Continuous improvement: Adopting new activities and eliminating those that are found to add little or no value. The goal is to increase effectiveness by reducing inefficiencies, frustrations, and waste (rework, time, effort, material, etc.). The Japanese Lean term is *kaizen.*

Control chart (process-behavior chart): A graphical tool for monitoring changes that occur within a process, by distinguishing *variation* that is inherent in the process (common-cause or routine variation—predictable process) from variation that yields a change to the process (special-cause or exceptional variation—unpredictable process).

Control plan: The intent of a process control plan is to control the product characteristics and the associated process variables to ensure capability (around the identified target or nominal) and stability of the product over time.

Cost of quality: Cost of quality is the amount of money a business loses because its product or service was not done right in the first place or was not produced as close to target as possible.

Critical to quality (CTQ): CTQs are the key measurable characteristics of a product or process whose performance standards or specification limits must be met in order to satisfy the customer. They align improvement or design efforts with customer requirements.

Customer: A person who purchases the end product or service that a business produces.

Customer demand: Amount of product needed based upon the amount a customer requires at any given time.

Customer focus: The concept that the customer is the only person qualified to specify what *quality* means. This leads to detailed analyses of the customer: Who are the customers? What are their needs? What features are required of our products/services? How do customers rate our products/services versus our competitors and why? How can we keep our customers satisfied?

Customer requirements: The wants and needs of the customer (*Voice of the Customer*) in stated or implied terms.

Cycle time: Cycle time is the elapsed time required to process one unit of good work through a process step. Often defined as the elapsed time from good piece to good piece at a single step in the process.

Dashboard: A dashboard is a tool used for collecting and reporting information about vital customer requirements and/or your business's performance for key customers. Dashboards provide a quick summary of process and/or product performance.

Data: Data are factual information or measures used as a basis for reasoning, discussion, or calculation. The "right" data and its analysis are critical to achieve *quality improvement.*

Defect: Any type of undesired result is a defect—a failure to meet one of the acceptance criteria of your customers. A defective unit may have one or more defects.

Defects per million (DPMO): The average number of defects per unit observed during an average production run divided by the number of opportunities to make a defect on the product under study during that run normalized to one million.

Demand: Amount needed, as defined by the customer.

Deming Cycle (PDSA): (Also known as PDCA) A continuous *quality improvement* model consisting of a logical sequence of four repetitive, fluid steps for *continuous improvement* and learning: plan, do, study (check), and act.

Design of experiment (DOE): A design of experiment (DOE) is a structured, organized method for determining the relationship between factors (Xs) affecting a process and the output of that process (Y). Used in the Improve phase of *Six Sigma* to determine best improvement strategy.

DFSS (Design for Six Sigma): An integral part of a *Six Sigma* quality initiative structure for designing or redesigning products and processes. Uses a DMADV framework, which consists of five interconnected phases: define, measure, analyze, design, verify (DMADV). Design for Six Sigma is used for new product/service introduction.

DMAIC: An acronym for five interconnected phases: define, measure, analyze, improve, and control. Incremental process improvement using *Six Sigma* methodology. DMAIC (pronounced duh-may-ick) refers to a data-driven quality strategy for improving processes, and is an integral part of the Six Sigma quality initiative.

Drift: As components age and equipment undergoes changes in temperature or sustains mechanical stress, critical performance gradually degrades. This is called drift. When this happens, your test results become unreliable and both design and production quality suffer. While drift cannot be eliminated, it can be detected and contained through the process of calibration.

Effect: An effect is that which is produced by a *cause*; the impact a factor (X) has on a response variable (Y).

Eight wastes of Lean: The eight wastes are at the root of all non-value-added activity within your organization. The eight wastes consist of:

1. **D**efects
2. **O**verproduction
3. **W**aiting
4. **N**ot utilizing people
5. **T**ransportation
6. **I**nventory
7. **M**otion
8. **E**xcess processing

Any or all of these create "downtime."

EPE: Refers to the "every-part-every" interval, which is a measure of process size and length. For example, if a computer system is able to change over and produce all required checks, regardless of type (accounts payable, payroll, etc.), during a three-week cycle, then the batch size for each individual check type is three weeks. Thus this process is covering every part every (EPE) three weeks.

Excess inventory: Any product supply in excess of the absolute minimum requirement to meet customer demand.

FIFO: Stands for "first in, first out," which means that items processed by one step are used up in the same order by the next step. FIFO is one way to regulate a queue between two decoupled processes when a *supermarket* or continuous flow are impractical. A FIFO queue is filled by the supplying process and emptied by the customer process. When a FIFO queue gets full, the supplying process must stop producing until the customer process has used up some of the inventory.

Financial metrics: Used to measure the gains of a project. Financial metrics convert the process improvements (measured through the primary process metric) into hard or soft dollars.

Flow: A main objective of the entire Lean processing effort, and one of the key concepts that passed directly from Henry Ford to Taiichi Ohno (Toyota's production manager after WWII) in the manufacturing world. Ford recognized that, ideally, production should flow (or move) continuously all the way from raw material to the customer and envisioned realizing that ideal through a production system that acted as one long conveyor.

Flowchart: A graphical representation (picture) of a process, depicting inputs, outputs, and units of activity. It represents the entire process at a high or detailed (depending on your use) level of observation, allowing analysis and optimization of *workflow.* Current-state flowcharts show a picture of the process as it currently operates. Future-state flowcharts can be drawn to show desired process flow.

Focused kaizen: Improvements made within a *value stream* using *kaizen* techniques; the events usually last two to three days.

Goal: A goal is a targeted value by a design team while building a quality process/product. A goal can also be defined as a customer voice—what the customer is asking for or specifying.

Green Belt: An employee of an organization who has been trained on the improvement methodology of *Six Sigma* and will lead a process improvement or *quality improvement* team as part of their full-time job. Their degree of knowledge and skills associated with Six Sigma is less than that of a *Black Belt* or *Master Black Belt.* Extensive product knowledge in their company is a must in their task of process improvement. The Green Belt usually serves as a Six Sigma team member or leads smaller, less complex projects requiring less advanced tools and analysis.

Group products/services: Products/services with similar process tasks can be grouped into a product family.

Hard savings: *Six Sigma-* or Lean-project benefits that provide you with bottom-line profitability results that can be measured.

Heijunka: The act of leveling the variety and/or volume of items processed at a task step over a period of time. Used to avoid excessive batching of product types and/or volume fluctuations, especially at a *pacemaker* process.

In-control process: An in-control process is one that is free of special causes of *variation.* Stable and in-control, with random variation only, both mean the same thing, i.e., the process behaves equally over time. Such a condition is most often evidenced by a control chart that displays an absence of exceptional variation. "In control" refers to a process unaffected by special causes. A process that is "in control" is affected only by common causes or routine variation (predictable process). A process that is out of control is affected by special causes in addition to the common causes affecting the mean and/or variance (unpredictable process).

Inventory: Product supply on hand.

Inventory (excess): Any product supply in excess of the absolute minimum requirement to meet customer demand.

JIT (just-in-time manufacturing): A planning system for manufacturing processes that optimizes availability of material inventories at the manufacturing site to only what, when, and how much is necessary.

Kaizen: Japanese term that means *continuous improvement*. Continuously improving in incremental steps. The word translated from Japanese and embracing the cultural use in Japan is: rapid, continuous, good change.

Kanban: The actual term means "signal." It is one of the primary tools of a *JIT* system. It signals a cycle of replenishment for production and materials. It maintains an orderly and efficient flow of materials throughout the entire manufacturing process. It is usually a printed card that contains specific information such as part name, description, quantity, etc., that gives instruction for production or conveyance of items in a *pull system*. Can also be used to perform *kaizen* by reducing the number of kanban in circulation, which highlights line problems.

Lead time: The time required for one piece to move all the way through a process or *value stream*, from start to finish. Envision timing a marked item as it moves from beginning to end.

Lean enterprise: Initiative focused on eliminating all waste in all processes.

Lean manufacturing: Initiative focused on eliminating all waste in manufacturing processes.

Lean Six Sigma: An integrated methodology and infrastructure using the tools, techniques, and skills from *Lean enterprise principles* and *Six Sigma* necessary to optimize your processes. Lean focuses on process speed, and Six Sigma focuses on process quality.

Lean thinking: A way of thinking that specifies value, lining up all value-creating activities along a *value stream* to make value flow smoothly at the pull of the customer in pursuit of perfection. Lean focuses on elimination of non-value-added activity (waste) and on process speed (speed, efficiency, process flow).

Lean toolbox: A set of tools, techniques, and activities used to accomplish *Lean thinking*. Some of these include *pull systems*, work cells, total productive maintenance (TPM), performance measurement, setup reduction, quality at the source, *continuous flow, batch-size reduction, standardized work*, teams, POUS (point of use storage), *visual controls, Value Stream Mapping, 5S system*, layout, SMED (single minute exchange of dies), CEDAC (cause and effect diagram with addition of cards), *poka-yoke*, etc.

Low-hanging fruit: Those improvements and innovations that can be suggested and implemented immediately when they become apparent.

Malcolm Baldrige National Quality Award: The annual self-evaluation covers the following seven categories of criteria:

1. Leadership
2. Strategic planning
3. Customer and market focus
4. Information and analysis

5. Human resource focus
6. Process management
7. Business results

The National Institute of Standards and Technology (NIST), a federal agency within the Department of Commerce, is responsible for managing the Malcolm Baldrige National Quality Award. The American Society for Quality (ASQ) administers the Malcolm Baldrige National Quality Award under a contract with NIST.

Master Black Belt: Master Black Belts are *Six Sigma* quality experts. A Master Black Belt's main responsibilities may include training and mentoring of *Black Belts* and *Green Belts*; helping to prioritize, select, and charter high-impact projects; maintaining the integrity of the Six Sigma measurements, improvements, and tollgates; and developing, maintaining, and revising Six Sigma training materials. The Master Black Belt should be a resource for utilizing *statistical process control* and advanced *design of experiment* tools (skills that are typically just outside the Black Belt's knowledge base) within processes.

Milk run: Routing a delivery vehicle in a way that allows it to make pickups and drop-offs at multiple locations on a single travel loop, as opposed to making separate trips to each.

Motion (Excess): Any movement of product or machine, or employee movement, that does not add value to the product or service.

Muda: See *waste*.

Noise: Process input that consistently causes *variation* in the output measurement that is random, common, and expected and, therefore, not controlled, is called noise. Noise also is referred to as routine variation or common-cause variation.

Non-value-added activity: Any activity within a process that the customer is not willing to pay for.

Non-value-added time: The time for those work elements that add no value to the product or service from the customer's point of view.

Not utilizing people: Not using your employees' mental, creative, and physical abilities.

Operational definitions: Definitions that ensure measurements are made consistently. There are three parts:

1. The criterion: what you are measuring
2. The method: how you are measuring (i.e., measuring device)
3. The specific instructions: rounding of final answer, etc.

Output: The result of a process. The deliverables of the process, such as products, services, processes, plans, and resources.

Overproduction: Making or producing more, sooner, or faster than is required by the next step in the process.

Paced withdrawal: A timed sequence of withdrawal of finished product from the *pacemaker* process. Paced withdrawal is a tool for pacing a process to ensure flow.

Pacemaker: A process step, frequently at the downstream (customer) end of the value stream, that sets the pace and speed of the process to respond to orders from external customers. The pacemaker is the most important step in a process because how you operate or "set the pace" here determines how well you can serve the customer.

Point kaizen: Improvements made at an individual process step. Usually completed in less than one day. (See also *kaizen*.)

Poka-yoke: Japanese term that means mistake proofing. A simple device used to prevent errors in the process. A poka-yoke device is one that prevents incorrect parts from being made or assembled, or easily identifies a flaw or error.

Procedures: Procedures are the largest volume of instructional content representing practical knowledge; they include all types of human decision making, such as guides, help text, methods, instructions, policies, regulations, standards, and technical practices. A procedure is a set of conditional instructions that affect the human interactions involving customers, information workers, and service suppliers.

Process: A series of steps or actions that lead to a desired result or output. A set of common tasks that creates a product, service, process, or plan that will satisfy a customer or group of customers. A sequential series of steps leading to a desired outcome. Processes are largely affected by one or more of the following factors:

Personnel who operate the processes
Materials that are used as inputs (including information)
Machines or equipment being used in the process (in process execution or monitoring/measurement
Methods (including criteria and various documentations used along the process)
Work environment

Understanding how these factors interact and affect processes is a key consideration in process studies.

Process behavior charts: See *control chart*.

Process control: The features or mechanisms that control the execution of a process, including process initiation, selection of process steps, selection of alternative steps, iteration of steps within a loop, and process termination.

Process control plan: The process control plan ensures that the improvements established by your project will not deteriorate once the improved process is returned to the process owners.

Process kaizen: Improvements made at an individual process or in a specific area. (See also *kaizen*.)

Process lead time: Door-to-door time for the process, including all inventory within the process, usually measured in days or weeks.

Process loops: Also known as *value stream loops*. Segments of a *value stream* whose boundaries are typically marked by *supermarkets*. Breaking a value stream into loops is a way to divide future state implementations into manageable pieces.

Process management: The concept of defining macro and micro processes, assigning ownership, and creating responsibilities of the owners.

Process map: A hierarchical method for displaying processes that illustrates how a product or transaction is processed. It is a visual representation of the *workflow* either within a process, or an image of the whole operation. Process mapping comprises a stream of activities that transforms a well-defined input or set of inputs into a predefined set of outputs.

Process owner: The individual(s) responsible for process design and performance. The process owner is accountable for sustaining the gain and identifying future improvement opportunities on the process.

Processing (excess): Any effort that adds no value to the product or service from the customer's point of view.

Processing time: The time a product is actually being worked on in a machine or work area.

Product: A product is an outcome of a process or activity; it could be a defined object or service.

Project scope: Defined and specific project beginning and end points; sets the boundaries of the project. The more specific the details (what's in scope and what's out of scope), the less a project may experience "scope creep."

Project selection: Means by which projects are selected in an organization. Selection criteria should be defined and tied directly to achieving the organization's strategic goals and objectives.

Pull system: An alternative to scheduling individual processes, where the customer process withdraws the items it needs from a *supermarket*, and the supplying process produces to replenish what was withdrawn. Used to avoid push. A method of controlling the flow of resources by replacing only the amount that has been consumed. (See also *kanban, push system*.)

Push system: Resources are provided to the customer based on your businesses forecasts or schedules.

Quality: Continuous and dynamic adaptation of products and services to fulfill or exceed the requirements or expectations of all parties in the organization, the customer, and the community as a whole.

Quality control: Also called statistical quality control. The managerial process during which actual process performance is evaluated and actions are taken on unusual performance. It is a process to ensure whether a product meets predefined standards and that requisite action is taken if the standards are not met.

Quality function deployment (QFD): A structured methodology and mathematical tool used to identify and quantify customers' requirements and translate them into key critical parameters. In *Six Sigma*, QFD helps you to prioritize actions to improve your process or product to meet customers' expectations.

Quality improvement: A systematic and continuous activity to improve all processes and systems in the organization to achieve an optimal level of performance. The organized creation of beneficial changes in process performance levels.

Quality management: A systematic set of activities to ensure that processes create products with maximum *quality* at minimum *cost of quality*.

Queue time: The time a product spends waiting in line for the next processing step.

Reengineering: Reengineering is focused on achieving dramatic, breakthrough improvements, often by the application of new technologies.

Rework: Work done to correct defects.

Root cause: An identified reason for the presence of a defect or problem. The most basic reason that, if eliminated, would prevent recurrence. The source or origin of an event.

Root-cause analysis: Study of original reason for nonconformance within a process. When the *root cause* is removed or corrected, the nonconformance is eliminated.

Scope: Generally, the extent to which a process or procedure applies. Project scope defines the boundaries of a project.

Scorecard: An evaluation device, usually used to evaluate how well your business is performing. Can also be in the form of a questionnaire that specifies the criteria your customers will use to rate your business's performance in satisfying their requirements.

Sigma: The Greek letter "s" (σ, sigma) refers to the standard deviation of a population.

Sigma level: Determining sigma levels of processes (one sigma, six sigma, etc.) allows process performance to be compared throughout an entire organization, because it is independent of the process. It is merely a determination of opportunities and defects, although the terms are appropriately defined for that specific process. Sigma is a statistical term that measures how much a process varies from perfection, based on the number of *defects per million* units.

One Sigma = 690,000 defects per million units
Two Sigma = 308,000 defects per million units
Three Sigma = 66,807 defects per million units
Four Sigma = 6,210 defects per million units
Five Sigma = 233 defects per million units
Six Sigma = 3.4 defects per million units

Signal: Process input that sometimes causes *variation* in the output measurement that is specific and unexpected and, therefore, is called a signal. Signals also are referred to as exceptional variation or special-cause variation.

SIPOC: Stands for suppliers, inputs, process, output, and customers. You obtain inputs from suppliers, add value through your process, and provide an output that meets or exceeds your customer's requirements. Visually depicted, it includes product and information flow.

Six Sigma: A strategy-driven, process-focused, project-enabled, organizational-improvement initiative. The goal of Six Sigma is to increase profits by reducing variability and defects and eliminating waste that undermines customer loyalty, leading ultimately to bottom-line profitability and top-line growth. Six Sigma is a methodology that provides businesses with the tools to improve the capability of their business processes. This increase in performance and decrease in process *variation* leads to defect reduction and vast improvement in profits, employee morale, and quality of product. Six Sigma focuses on process quality.

Soft savings: *Six Sigma* and Lean project benefits such as reduced time to market, cost avoidance, lost-profit avoidance, improved employee morale, enhanced image for the organization, and other intangibles may result in additional savings and benefits to your organization, but are harder to quantify or measure.

Spaghetti diagrams: Visual layout and flow of the process as you would walk through it, following it from beginning to end.

Stakeholder: People who will be affected by the project or can influence it but who are not directly involved with doing the project work.

Stakeholder analysis: A tool used to identify and enlist support from *stakeholders*. It provides a visual means of identifying stakeholder support so that you can develop an action plan for your project.

Standard operating procedures (SOP): Documents that capture best practices for meeting standard work.

Standardized work: Doing the same thing, the same way, each and every time, with as little non-value-added time/task as possible.

Statistical process control (SPC): The application of statistical methods to identify and "control" the special-cause or exceptional *variation* in a process.

Statistical thinking: The process of using wide-ranging and interacting data to understand processes and problems and to determine best solutions.

Statistics: The mathematics of the collection, organization, and interpretation of numerical data.

Strategic planning: A disciplined effort to produce fundamental decisions and actions that shape and guide what an organization is, what it does, and why it does it, with a focus on the future. Determines the strategic goals and objectives of the organization, short and long term.

Supermarket: A controlled inventory that is used to supply a process with the next unit of work or with parts for the next unit of work. Supermarkets usually have *kanbans* associated with them to signal automatic replenishment.

Supply-chain management: Managing the movement of goods from raw materials to the finished product delivered to customers. Supply-chain management aims to reduce operating costs, lead times, and inventory and to increase the speed of delivery, product availability, and customer satisfaction.

Synchronous flow: The concept of flowing an item through a process in time with the steps downstream to avoid bottlenecks. Acting differently than *continuous flow*, which relies upon *kanbans* and one-piece flow, synchronous flow regulates the process through balanced work, minimal handling of the item, and timing of tasks and deadlines.

System kaizen: Improvement aimed at an entire value stream. (See also *kaizen*.)

System of Profound Knowledge: Deming advanced the System of Profound Knowledge (SoPK), which he said consisted of four main subheadings:

Knowledge of *variation*: a knowledge of common-cause (routine) and special-cause (exceptional) variation

Knowledge of systems: understanding that all the parts of a business are related in such a way that if you focus on optimizing one part, other parts may suffer

Knowledge of psychology: what motivates people

Theory of knowledge: how we learn things

Systems thinking: Seeing interrelationships rather than linear cause–effect chains, and seeing processes of change rather than snapshots at a single point in time (Peter Senge's book, *The Fifth Discipline*).

Takt time: Lean production uses Takt time as the rate or time that a completed product must be finished to meet customer demand. Takt time is established by the rate at which the customer buys your product. Takt time is used to design *pacemaker* processes, to assess process conditions, to develop material-handling containerization, to direct process routing, to determine problem–response requirements, and so on. Takt is the heartbeat of a Lean system. Takt time is calculated by dividing the available production time by the quantity the customer requires in that same amount of time.

Team leader: The person who leads or directs a team of people to complete a task or project.

Throughput: Output or production over a period of time.

Total content time: The cumulative labor time used to complete production of one unit through each step of the process. Does not include wait time, travel times, or other non-value-added activities.

Total cycle time: Cycle time is the total time from the beginning to the end of your process, as defined by your business and your customer. It is the total elapsed time to move a unit of work from the beginning to the end of a physical process. Also explained as the observed cycle times at each step in a process added together—the cumulative time of all process steps and cycle times throughout the process.

Total quality management (TQM): A conceptual and a philosophical context that requires management and human resources commitment to adopt a perpetual improvement philosophy, through succinct management of all processes, practices, and systems throughout the organization to achieve effectiveness in the organizational performance.

Total work content time: The observed work content or labor times at each step in a process added together.

Travel/transportation: The unnecessary or excess travel of people, product, forms, or parts around a facility or organization.

Uptime reliability: The percentage of time that a piece of equipment, computer, or network operates properly at the exact moment when it is needed.

Value: Value is the exchange for which a customer pays. It is a product or service's capability that is provided to a customer at the right time and at an appropriate price, as defined in each case by the customer.

Value-added activity: To be a value-added action, the action must meet all three of the following criteria:

1. The customer is willing to pay for this activity.
2. It must be done right the first time.
3. The action must somehow change the product or service in some manner.

Value-added time: The time for those work elements that adds value to the product or service from the customer's point of view.

Value chain: A graphical representation of an organization's structure. The chain depicts those processes that actually produce the product or service— these are at the heart or center of the picture. Every other process (including management) is shown as a support process or function. The key is to optimize the value chain by aligning the *Voice of the Process* to the *Voice of the Customer.*

Value proposition: The proposition that states that:

Businesses have a right to produce and offer products and services that yield the highest possible profits.
Customers have a right to expect the highest quality products and services at the lowest possible cost.

The value proposition establishes this strategic alignment as critical to all improvement efforts.

Value stream: All the steps (both value-added and non-value-added) in a process that bring a product or service through the flows essential to producing that product or service. All activities, both value-added and non-value-added, that are required to bring a product from raw material into the hands of the customer, to fulfill a customer requirement from order to delivery, and to complete a design from concept to launch. Value stream improvement usually begins at the door-to-door level within a facility, and then expands outward to eventually encompass the full value stream.

Value stream loops: Also known as *process loops*. Segments of a *value stream* whose boundaries are typically marked by *supermarkets*. Breaking a value stream into loops is a way to divide future state implementations into manageable pieces.

Value Stream Manager: Person responsible for creating a Future State Map and leading door-to-door implementation of the future state for a particular product family. Makes change happen across departmental and functional boundaries.

Value Stream Mapping: A paper-and-pencil tool that helps you to see and understand the flow of material and information as a product or service makes its way through the *value stream*. Value Stream Mapping is typically used in Lean, and it differs from typical process mapping in *Six Sigma* in three ways:

1. It gathers and displays a far broader range of information than a typical process map.
2. It tends to be used at a broader level, i.e., from receiving of raw material to delivery of finished goods.
3. It tends to be used to identify where to focus future projects, subprojects, and/or *kaizen* events.

It involves two stages:

The Current State Map follows a process's path from beginning to end and draws a visual representation of every process step in the material/service and information flows.

Then draw a Future State Map of how value should flow. The most critical map is the Future State Map which shows proposed, improved process design.

Variation: The fluctuation or movement over time in process output. Can be seen visually by using process behavior (control) charts. (See also *control chart*.)

Visual controls: Simple signals that provide an immediate understanding of a situation or condition.

Voice of the Customer (VOC): Describes the stated and unstated needs or requirements of the customer. The voice of the customer can be captured in a variety of ways: direct discussion or interviews, surveys, focus groups, customer specifications, observation, warranty data, field reports, complaint logs, etc.

Voice of the Process (VOP): Term used to describe what the process is telling you—what it is capable of achieving, whether it is predictable or unpredictable, and what significance to attach to individual measurements. The key is to align the Voice of the Process to the *Voice of the Customer*.

Waiting, or Wait time: Any amount of time spent waiting for anything when the process cannot flow.

Waste: Any activity that consumes resources but creates no value for the customer.

WIP: Work in process: any inventory between raw material and finished goods.

Work content time: The actual amount of labor time an item or product requires to be completed by a process step, as timed by direct observation.

Workflow: Steps in the process.

Index

5S scores, 89
5S system, defined, 251
5 whys, defined, 251

A

Accountability critical to success, 242–243
Accuracy level necessary, 121
Action plan development, 221ff, 239–240
Alternate paths in process stream mapping, 45–47
Andon, defined, 251
AOE, see Availability of equipment (AOE)
AOP, see Availability of personnel (AOP)
At rest product, 42
Availability of equipment (AOE), 85–87
    defined, 251
    in map, 80
    NVA time, 87
    in transactional process, 101–102
Availability of personnel (AOP), 103–105
    defined, 251
    problems of, 206–207

B

Balanced scorecard, defined, 251
Batch-and-queue, defined, 252
Batch-size reduction, defined, 252
Benchmarking, defined, 252
Best practice, defined, 252
Big picture shown in map, 121
Black Belt, defined, 252
Blanket purchase orders, 35
Blueprint for change, 175
Bottlenecks shown in map, 122
Bureaucratic burdens, 210
Business excellence, defined, 252
Business process quality management, defined, 252
Business value added, defined, 252
Buy-in, 154–155, 203
    of employees, 159ff

C

Capability, defined, 252
Case study
    manufacturing, 77–78, 197
    transactional, 109–110, 155–157, 213–217
Cause, defined, 252
Cell, defined, 252
Cellular processing and decision, defined, 252
Champion, defined, 252–253
Change
    embracing, 246
    implementation of, 235ff
Change agent, defined, 253
Change management, defined, 253
Changeover, defined, 253
Changeover time, 82–83
    in map, 80
    in transactional process, 100–101
Charter, defined, 253
Close enough concept, 72, 121
Communication
    formal, 139–140
    informal
        documenting, 143–144
        icon, 143
    in process and transactional systems, 148–151
Communication control point, 137–139
Communication flow
    in production systems, 133ff
        types, 133–134
    in transactional systems, 148
    in value stream map, 6
Communication levels, 145–146
Component count, 89
Connectivity (network), 101–102
Content time, defined, 266
Continuous flow processing, 207, 222, 228
    defined, 253
Continuous improvement, 207, 245–247
    defined, 253
    VSM as tool for, 221